Generic and Innovator Drugs:
A Guide to FDA Approval Requirements
Fifth Edition

by Donald O. Beers

2003 Supplement Highlights

Originally written to provide a readily usable reference concerning the Drug Price Competition and Patent Term Restoration Act of 1984 (the Waxman-Hatch Act), *Generic and Innovator Drugs* has been expanded in subsequent editions to address the Generic Drug Enforcement Act of 1992, the Generic Animal Drug and Patent Term Restoration Act of 1988, the Export Reform and Enhancement Act of 1996, and the FDA's rules applicable to the approval process for breakthrough drugs for serious diseases. The fifth edition includes a chapter on the user fee provisions of the Food and Drug Administration Modernization Act of 1997 and substantial discussion of generic drug approval that is not dependent on the 1984 statute.

The 2003 Supplement includes the following highlights:
- A new chapter on FDA regulation of biologic drugs
- An updated explanation of the interpretation by FDA and the courts of the market exclusivity provisions FDA administers
- An explanation of the new user fee legislation and FDA commitments in response to that legislation
- An updated chapter reflecting new FDA requirements on drug export requirements

This supplement also has a table of cases, table of statutes, and index, which reflect its contents.

12/02

For questions concerning this shipment, billing, or other customer service matters, call our Customer Service Department at 1-800-234-1660.

For toll-free ordering, please call 1-800-638-8437.

© 2003 Aspen Publishers

GENERIC AND INNOVATOR DRUGS

A Guide to FDA Approval Requirements

2003 Supplement

Donald O. Beers

PUBLISHERS

1185 Avenue of the Americas, New York, NY 10036
www.aspenpublishers.com

This publication is designed to provide accurate and authoritative information in regard to the subject matter covered. It is sold with the understanding that the publisher is not engaged in rendering legal, accounting, or other professional services. If legal advice or other professional assistance is required, the services of a competent professional person should be sought.

—From a *Declaration of Principles* jointly adopted by a Committee of the American Bar Association and a Committee of Publishers and Associations

© 2003 Aspen Publishers, Inc.
www.aspenpublishers.com

All rights reserved. No part of this publication may be reproduced or transmitted in any form or by any means, electronic or mechanical, including photocopy, recording, or any information storage and retrieval system, without permission in writing from the publisher. Request for permission to make copies of any part of this publication should be mailed to:

Permissions
Aspen Publishers
1185 Avenue of the Americas
New York, NY 10036

Printed in the United States of America

Library of Congress Cataloging in Publication Data

Beers, Donald O.
    Generic and innovator drugs : a guide to FDA approval requirements / Donald O. Beers. — 5th ed.
    p.   cm.
    Includes index.
    ISBN 0-7355-0281-1 (hardcover)
    ISBN 0-7355-3732-1 (supplement)
    1. Drugs—Generic substitution—Law and legislation—United States.   2. Drugs—United States—Generic substitution—Patents.   3. Patent extensions—United States.   I. Title.
KF3894.G45B443   1999
344.73′04233—dc21   97-37519
   CIP

About Aspen Publishers

Aspen Publishers is a leading publisher of authoritative treatises, practice manuals, services, and journals for attorneys, corporate and bank directors, accountants, auditors, environmental compliance professionals, financial and tax advisors, and other business professionals. Our mission is to provide practical solution-based how-to information keyed to the latest original pronouncements, as well as the latest legislative, judicial, and regulatory developments.

We offer publications in the areas of accounting and auditing; antitrust; banking and finance; bankruptcy; business and commercial law; construction law; corporate law; criminal law; environmental compliance; government and administrative law; health law; insurance law; intellectual property; international law; legal practice and litigation; matrimonial and family law; pensions, benefits, and labor; real estate law; securities; and taxation.

Other Aspen Publishers products treating intellectual property and licensing issues include:

Art Law Handbook
Business Method Patents
The Commercial Law of Intellectual Property
Copyright
Domain Name Disputes
Drafting Internet Agreements
Drafting License Agreements
Drafting Print and Online Publishing Agreements
Drafting Technology Patent License Agreements
E-Business Legal Handbook
E-Copyright Law Handbook
Epstein on Intellectual Property
Guide to Registering Trademarks
Handbook of Intellectual Property Claims and Remedies
Intellectual Property for the Internet
Intellectual Property Law Update
Intellectual Property Litigation: Pretrial Practice
Kohn on Music Licensing
The Law of Chemical and Pharmaceutical Invention
The Law of Internet Disputes

License Agreements: Forms and Checklists
Licensing Desk Book
Licensing Royalty Rates
Licensing Update
Patent Claim Construction
Patent Interference Practice Handbook
Patent Practice Handbook
Patent Technology Intelligence Report
Perle and Williams on Publishing Law
Protecting Trade Secrets, Patents, Copyrights, and Trademarks
Software Patents
Technology Transfer Guide
Trademark Law

ASPEN PUBLISHERS
www.aspenpublishers.com

SUBSCRIPTION NOTICE

This Aspen Publishers product is updated on a periodic basis with supplements to reflect important changes in the subject matter. If you purchased this product directly from Aspen Publishers, we have already recorded your subscription for the update service.

If, however, you purchased this product from a bookstore and wish to receive future updates and revised or related volumes billed separately with a 30-day examination review, please contact our Customer Service Department at 1-800-234-1660, or send your name, company name (if applicable), address, and the title of the product to:

**ASPEN PUBLISHERS
7201 McKinney Circle
Frederick, MD 21704**

CONTENTS

Sections listed below appear only in the supplement and not in the main volume.

Foreword	xi
Chapter 1 FDA Approval Requirement	1
Chapter 2 Full New Drug Applications	3
Chapter 3 Abbreviated New Drug Applications and "Paper NDAs"	11
Chapter 4 Delaying Approval of Competitive Products	19
Chapter 5 Public Availability of NDA Data	43
Chapter 6 Potential for Government Compensation of Innovators	45
Chapter 7 The Orphan Drug Amendments	47
Chapter 8 Debarment	49
Chapter 9 FDA Fraud Policy	53

Chapter 10
Accelerated Approvals 55

Chapter 11
Export and Import Requirements 57

Chapter 12
Prescription Drug User Fees 63

Chapter 13
FDA Regulation of Biologic Drugs 71

        § 13.01   What Is a Biologic? 71
        § 13.02   Biologic Approval Requirements 72
        § 13.03   Generic Biologics? 74

Appendices

85. Guidance for Industry—Applications Covered by Section 505(b)(2) 77

86. March 7, 2002 Memorandum to Jay Siegel, Office of Therapeutics Research and Review (CBER), from Marlene E. Haffner, Office of Orphan Products Development, Food and Drug Administration, re: Analysis of Exclusivity Issues in the Serono BLA for Rebif 93

87. Guidance for Industry—Fast Track Drug Development Programs—Designation, Development, and Application Review 99

88. June 4, 2002 letter from Tommy Thompson, Food and Drug Administration, transmitting goals and procedures of the Prescription Drug User Fee Act of 1992 125

89. Prescription Drug User Fee Act of 1992, Reauthorization, performance goals and procedures (June 19, 2002) 127

90. Section 262, Public Health Service Act (biologics license), 42 U.S.C. 262 145

CONTENTS

91. Guidance for Industry—Court Decisions, ANDA Approvals, and 180-Day Exclusivity Under the Hatch-Waxman Amendments to the Federal Food, Drug, and Cosmetic Act (March 2000) 147

92. Food and Drug Administration, Proposed Rule on Patent Listing Requirements and 30-Month Stays on ANDAs, 67 Fed. Reg. 65448 (October 23, 2002) 155

Table of Cases 175

Table of Statutes 181

Table of Authorities 185

Subject Index 189

FOREWORD

Not surprisingly, there have been developments in nearly all of the areas covered by this volume since the fifth edition appeared in late 1998. An update at this point is therefore appropriate. The reader should be aware, however, of the potential for significant legislative changes in the Waxman-Hatch Act. A bill that would have made important changes in that statute passed the Senate in Summer 2002 but ultimately was not enacted. Nevertheless, legislative changes may well be made in the near future. If significant amendments are made, we will update the book once again.

In addition, in October 2002 FDA issued proposed changes to its regulations governing the submission of patent information in NDAs and the sending of notices of patent challenges. It is unclear at this writing whether and in what form those proposed amendments will be finalized. The proposal is described in this update and included in the Appendix.

This update reflects the work of a number of law clerks and attorneys at Arnold & Porter, to whom I extend my thanks. As always, I welcome comments or questions from readers. My phone number is (202) 942-5012 and my e-mail address is *donald_beers@aporter.com*.

September 2002   Donald O. Beers

CHAPTER 1
FDA APPROVAL REQUIREMENT

§ 1.01 MARKETING NEW DRUGS; GENERAL REQUIREMENTS

Page 1-2. Change the last sentence of footnote 1 to read:

This chapter will focus on FDA regulation of drugs whose approval status is determined under the FDCA. *See* Chapter 13 in this supplement for a description of the approval requirement applicable to biologic drugs.

Page 1-2. Add to footnote 5:

See Chapter 13 *infra*.

§ 1.05 DETERMINATION OF "NEW DRUG" STATUS

[C] Declaratory Orders Under DESI II

Page 1-41. Replace the two paragraphs under this subsection and footnotes 185-187 with the following:

The long DESI evaluation of drugs approved prior to 1962 is essentially if not totally complete. The FDA had expressed an intention to begin a review of other unapproved prescription drugs that have been marketed under the theory that they are covered by the 1938 "grandfather clause"[185] or that they did not fit the "new drug" definition. There was, at one point, discussion of FDA plans to approach these various products on a class basis in a new DESI-type program (commonly known, though not by FDA, as DESI II). Such a program would presumably result in orders declaring drugs to be "new drugs" that could not be marketed without FDA approval.

In one interesting matter, FDA sought to declare levrothyroxine to be a "new drug."[186] The principal manufacturer of this drug resisted and filed a citizen petition seeking a determination that the drug was in fact not a "new drug."[187] On April 26, 2001, FDA denied that petition.[187.1] FDA took the position that it was appropriate for it to consider its belief that no levrothyroxine product had been shown to demonstrate consistent potency and stability as a basis for a conclusion that no such product had been generally recognized by experts as safe and effective. While the petitioner argued that the "new drug" definition did not address issues covered by FDA's authority to regulate "good manufacturing practices," FDA disagreed. FDA also pointed to reformulations of the product over time as undercutting any argument that this drug was not a "new drug."

While the principal manufacturer of this product was arguing its new drug status, other manufacturers were submitting NDAs and obtaining FDA approval. Ultimately, the petitioner acquiesced in FDA's decision and itself submitted an NDA.

[185] *See* Section 1.04[E], *supra*.
[186] 62 Fed. Reg. 43535 (Aug. 14, 1997).
[187] Petition of Knoll Pharmaceutical Co., Docket No. 97N-0314/CP2 (Sept. 25, 1998).
[187.1] Letter from Dennis E. Baker to Knoll Pharmaceutical Co., Docket No. 97N-0314/CP2 (Apr. 26, 2001).

§ 1.06 FDA ENFORCEMENT POLICY

[A] Prescription Drug Enforcement Policy

Page 1-50. Add to footnote 225:

This policy was upheld in *United States v. Sage Pharmaceuticals, Inc.*, 210 F.3d 475 (4th Cir. 2000). The court rejected an equal protection argument that to enforce the new drug provisions against defendant, which had also been sued for good manufacturing practice violations, was unfair when new drug charges were not being brought against competitors. 210 F.3d at 480.

Chapter 2
FULL NEW DRUG APPLICATIONS

§ 2.01 GENERALLY

Page 2-2. Change the last reference in footnote 2 to read:

See Section 2.02[C], *infra.*

§ 2.02 NEW DRUG APPLICATIONS—CONTENT

[A] Safety and Effectiveness Data

Page 2-3. Add to footnote 12:

There is one limited but potentially important exception to the requirement of clinical studies to show effectiveness. Pursuant to legislation passed in 2002, Pub. L. 107-188, 116 Stat. 594, Section 123, FDA finalized regulations, proposed before enactment of the statute, that describe situations in which animal studies could be used to prove effectiveness for drugs intended for use against lethal or permanently disabling toxic substances for which efficacy studies in humans would be ethically impermissible. *See* 67 Fed. Reg. 37988 (May 13, 2002), adding 21 C.F.R. 314.600-314.650 (NDA regulations) and 21 C.F.R. 601.90-601.95 (biological products regulations).

Page 2-4. Add to footnote 13:

62 Fed. Reg. 13650 (Mar. 21, 1997). *See also* final guidance, released after enactment of the 1997 legislation, 63 Fed. Reg. 27093 (May 15, 1998).

Page 2-5. Change the last sentence of footnote 22 to read:

FDA issued a guidance on submission of abbreviated study reports in 1999, 64 Fed. Reg. 49496 (Sept. 13, 1999). The guidance was, at the time of this writing, available on the FDA Web site: ⟨www.fda.gov/cber/gdlns/abbrev.htm⟩.

[C] Patent Information

Page 2-7. Change the third sentence to read:

Patents claiming the drug include both active ingredient (*i.e.*, drug substance) patents and composition or formulation (*i.e.*, product) patents.[37]

Page 2-7. Add at the end of the first full paragraph:

On October 24, 2002, FDA issued a proposed regulation that would clarify which types of patents are appropriately submitted in new drug applications. The proposed regulation would make it clear that NDA applicants should not submit process patents, patents claiming packaging, patents claiming metabolites, and patents claiming intermediates.[38.1] FDA stated, on the other hand, that product by process patents should be submitted. In addition, FDA clarified its position that patents that claim a physical form of a drug substance different from the physical form approved in the NDA are appropriately submitted if that physical form should be considered the "same" active ingredient as the active ingredient in the approved NDA.[38.2]

[38.1] Proposed 21 C.F.R. 314.53(b), 67 Fed. Reg. 65448, 65464 (Oct. 24, 2002) (Appendix 92 to this supplement).

[38.2] *Id.* Note that the proposed regulations would require the NDA applicant to state specifically that the physical form covered by the patent would in fact be the same active ingredient as the ingredient in the approved NDA for purposes of approval of an ANDA or 505(b)(2) application. Proposed 21 C.F.R. 314.53(c)(2)(Patent Decl. C.3).

Page 2-7. Change the citation at the end of footnote 37 to read:

Ben Venue Labs., Inc. v. Novartis Pharmaceutical Corp., 10 F. Supp. 2d 446, 456-58 (D.N.J. 1998).

Page 2-7. Add at the beginning of footnote 38:

21 C.F.R. 314.53(b) ("Process patents are not covered by this section and information on process patents may not be submitted to FDA.").

FULL NEW DRUG APPLICATIONS § 2.02[C]

Page 2-7 to 2-8. Change the carryover sentence to the following:

If the patent issues after the application is submitted[39] or even after it is approved,[40] the patent information must be submitted within 30 days of issuance of the patent.

Page 2-8. Change the last cite in footnote 41 to read:

21 U.S.C. 360b(d)(1)(G) (NADA).

Page 2-8. Add at the end of footnote 42:

The court in *aaiPharma Inc. v. Thompson*, 296 F.3d 227, (4th Cir. 2002), considered the meaning of this provision, having found that FDA's listing of patent information was ministerial and that FDA's proper role was simply to rely on the NDA applicant to decide what patent information should be submitted. The court concluded that FDA need only determine before approval whether the applicant included in the NDA either patent information or a statement that there were no applicable patents, and that the statute's reference to withdrawal of approval for lack of appropriate patent information was intended to enforce the requirement that such information be submitted with respect to NDAs already approved at the time of enactment of the Waxman-Hatch Act. 296 F.3d at 239-41.

Page 2-8. Change the first two sentences of the first full paragraph to the following:

Previous editions of this book have noted that there was no particular incentive for an applicant not to submit patent information to the NDA. The situation has, however, become more complex. Both the Federal Trade Commission and private antitrust plaintiffs have begun to focus on patent listing as a potential violation of antitrust laws.[42.1] Thus, if the question is a close one, the NDA applicant may prefer not to submit the information and thus avoid the risk that the submission will be attacked. In addition, new drug applicants are sometimes faced with situations in which the patents proposed to be listed do not belong to them.[42.2] Note that, if the innovator company concludes that a third party patent does not meet the standard for listing because it does not cover the approved product, there does not appear to be any avenue for the third party to obtain judicial review of that decision.[42.3]

§ 2.02[C]   GENERIC AND INNOVATOR DRUGS

FDA, in its regulations, did add a penalty for a failure to submit required patent information in a timely manner (*i.e.*, either with the original NDA or within 30 days of the date a patent issues after submission of the NDA or after its approval).

[42.1] *See, e.g., Prepared Statement of the Federal Trade Commission: Hearing Before the Committee on Commerce, Science and Transportation*, United States Senate (Apr. 23, 2002) (statement of Timothy J. Muris, Chairman of the Federal Trade Commission), *available at* ⟨www.ftc.gov/os/2002/04/pharmtestimony.htm⟩; *In re Buspirone Patent Litigation*, 185 F. Supp. 2d. 363 (S.D.N.Y. 2002).

[42.2] *See, e.g., aaiPharma Inc. v. Thompson*, 296 F.3d 227 (4th Cir. 2002); *American Bioscience, Inc. v. Thompson*, 269 F.3d 1077 (D.C. Cir. 2001).

[42.3] *See aaiPharma Inc. v. Thompson*, 296 F.3d 227 (4th Cir. 2002), in which the court agreed with FDA that FDA's listing of patent information is a ministerial act and that, therefore, FDA's only obligation was to list information provided by the manufacturer. The court in that case concluded, in *dicta*, that because the Federal Circuit had held that a generic company could not seek injunctive relief against an NDA holder to require a delisting of a patent, *Andrx Pharm., Inc. v. Biovail Corp.*, 276 F.3d 1368, 1373-74 (Fed. Cir. 2002), "it follows that a third-party patentee could not sue an NDA holder to compel listing of a patent." *aaiPharma*, slip op. at 11. *Accord, American Bioscience, Inc. v. Bristol-Myers Squibb Co.*, 2000 WL 1278348 (Sept. 7, 2000) (dissolving temporary restraining order and denying preliminary injunction sought by third-party patent holder against NDA holder to require listing of patent on grounds that there is no private right of action to enforce FDCA). *Compare American Bioscience v. Thompson*, 269 F.3d 1077 (D.C. Cir. 2001), in which the court found FDA had acted arbitrarily by misinterpreting the innovator company's communication concerning patent listing and removing the patent listing. In that case, the court ordered the approval of the abbreviated new drug application in question to be vacated.

Page 2-9. Replace "Id." at the end of footnote 43 with the following:

54 Fed. Reg. 28910. *See American Bioscience, Inc. v. Thompson*, 269 F.3d 1077 (D.C. Cir. 2001).

Page 2-9. Change the fifth sentence in the first full paragraph, and its accompanying footnote, to read:

A generic manufacturer objecting to the listing of a patent in the Orange Book may not have any effective remedy.[47]

[47] There does not appear to be, under existing law, any realistic avenue to judicial relief. In *Ben Venue Labs., Inc. v. Novartis Pharmaceutical Corp.*, 10 F. Supp. 2d 446 (D.N.J. 1998), the court accepted that such a suit for injunction was appropriate, but did not find the listing to be improper. However, in *Mylan Pharmaceuticals, Inc. v. Thompson*, 268 F.3d 1323 (Fed. Cir. 2001), the Court of Appeals for the Federal Circuit held that a generic applicant could not seek declaratory judgment that a patent should not be listed,

FULL NEW DRUG APPLICATIONS § 2.02[C]

concluding that improper listing of the patent was not a defense to a patent infringement case. *Accord, Andrx Pharm., Inc. v. Biovail Corp.*, 276 F.3d 1368, 1373-74 (Fed. Cir. 2002) (neither declaratory judgment nor injunction available under either FDCA or patent laws in suit against patent holder to "delist" a patent). Other challengers to listings have unsuccessfully sought relief against FDA under the Administrative Procedures Act. *See, e.g., Watson Pharmaceuticals, Inc. v. Henney,* 194 F. Supp. 2d 442 (D. Md. 2001) (upholding FDA's position that FDA should not address the merits of patent listing because FDA had no patent expertise). Although one district court ruled that a 30-month period could be shortened (or eliminated) because a late listing of a patent effectively delayed litigation, that decision was later overturned by the Court of Appeals for the Federal Circuit. *Andrx Pharmaceuticals, Inc. v. Biovail Corp.,* 276 F.3d 1368 (Fed. Cir. 2002). *See also aaiPharma Inc. v. Thompson,* 296 F.3d 227 (4th Cir. 2002) (rejecting challenge to decision not to list). *But see American Bioscience Inc. v. Thompson,* 269 F.3d 1077 (D.C. Cir. 2001) (requiring listing when the court concluded that the NDA applicant had submitted and not withdrawn patent information). At the time of this writing, there is not yet a decision holding that a suit for injunction premised directly on the antitrust laws would not be an option to a company seeking delisting.

Page 2-9 to 2-10. Change the carryover sentence to read:

The FDA does ask that applicants submit declarations signed by the applicant or patent holder that formulation, composition, and/or method of use patents claiming a drug cover drugs either submitted for approval or currently approved by the FDA under Section 505.[48]

Page 2-10. Change footnote 48 to read:

21 C.F.R. 314.53(c)(2)(i)(2002). Note that, in FDA's proposed new regulations, the declaration required would be more detailed. It would require specific identification of the claim numbers in the patents that claim each approved product or substance and would, for the first time, require a declaration that a particular use covered by a use patent had been approved by FDA. Proposed 21 C.F.R. 314.53(c)(2)(i)(67 Fed. Reg. 65448, 65464 (Oct. 24, 2002)).

Page 2-10. Change footnote 49 to read:

21 C.F.R. 314.53(c)(2)(ii)(2002). The FDA proposal would require that the post-approval declaration identify the patent claims that claim the drug substance, drug product, or method of use that is approved. Proposed 21 C.F.R. 314.53(c)(2)(ii), 67 Fed. Reg. 65465.

§ 2.02[C]   **GENERIC AND INNOVATOR DRUGS**

Page 2-10. Add at the end of footnote 50:

Cf. Ben Venue Laboratories, Inc. v. Novartis Pharmaceutical Corp., 10 F. Supp. 2d 446, 455 (D.N.J. 1998) (Suggesting that the *Pfizer* decision is no longer reliable precedent for the proposition that only drug product patents may be listed because it predated FDA's final regulations.)

Page 2-10. Insert after the first sentence of footnote 53:

It is now most often used in its electronic form on the FDA Internet Web site, ⟨www.fda.gov/cder/ob/default.htm⟩. The patent information is keyed to the drug listings on FDA's Web site, and is also published by FDA in a separate docket listing that is also available on FDA's Web site.

Page 2-11. Change the first sentence of footnote 54 to read:

See Approved Drug Products with Therapeutic Equivalents Evaluations, 22d ed. (2002), pages vii to xxi.

Page 2-11. Change the first sentence after the citation in footnote 55 to read:

The regulation is explicit on the information that must be submitted, including a literature search to support a three-year exclusivity claim.

Page 2-11. Change footnote 56 to read:

FDCA Sections 505(c)(3)(D)(iii), (iv); 505(j)(5)(D)(iii), (iv); 21 U.S.C. 355(c)(3)(D)(iii), (iv); 355(j)(5)(D)(iii), (iv). *See* Section 4.02[G], *infra*.

Page 2-11. Change the last sentence of the first full paragraph, and its accompanying footnote, to read:

Five years of exclusivity against submission of an ANDA or 505(b)(2) NDA may be claimed for the first approval of a new chemical entity.[57]

   [57] FDCA Sections 505(c)(3)(D)(ii); 505(j)(5)(D)(ii); 21 U.S.C. 355(c)(3)(D)(ii); 355(j)(5)(D)(ii). *See* Section 4.02[F], *infra*.

FULL NEW DRUG APPLICATIONS § 2.04

§ 2.03 NEW DRUG APPLICATIONS—PROCEDURE

[B] Approval Process

Page 2-14. Change the citation at the end of footnote 73 to read:

21 C.F.R. 314.50(l) (2002).

Page 2-16. Change the second full paragraph of this page and footnotes 86 and 87 to read:

In its performance goals in connection with passage of the 1997 user fee provisions, FDA stated its intention to change its regulations to substitute a "complete response" letter for approvable and non-approval letters.[86] FDA never did, however, change its regulations.[87]

[86] *See* Appendix 75 to the main volume, Enclosure, VIII.A. This renaming was to follow the lead of the Biologics Center, which in turn was responding to the biotechnology industry's concern about the company's negative connotations of approvable and non-approval letters to investors.
[87] *See* 21 C.F.R. 314.110, 314.120 (2002).

[C] Refusal to Approve

[1] Opportunity for a Hearing

Page 2-17. Change footnote 89 to read:

FDCA Section 505(c)(1)(B), 21 U.S.C. 355(c)(1)(B).

§ 2.04 SUPPLEMENTAL NEW DRUG APPLICATIONS

Page 2-20. Change the first full sentence on this page to read:

FDA, by regulation, purports to require manufacturers to submit supplements with studies supporting labeling for pediatric use of approved drugs in situations where FDA identifies a need for such studies.[109]

[109] 21 C.F.R. 201.23(d), 63 Fed. Reg. 66632 (Dec. 2, 1998). It is not clear that FDA has the authority to require such pediatric testing, and the regulation was invalidated by the decision of the court in *Association of American Physicians and Surgeons, Inc. v. USFDA*, 2002 WL 31323411 (D. D.C. Oct. 17, 2002).

CHAPTER 3

ABBREVIATED NEW DRUG APPLICATIONS AND "PAPER NDAs"

Note: In the next edition of this book, the title of this chapter will be changed to refer to "505(b)(2) NDAs" instead of "Paper NDAs," as FDA has now clearly adopted the former term.

§ 3.02 ABBREVIATED NEW DRUG APPLICATIONS UNDER 505(j); QUALIFYING DRUGS

[B] Termination of Listed Drug Status

[2] Voluntary Withdrawal from the Market

Page 3-12. Add to footnote 39:

FDA now includes in a so-called "Discontinued Section" of the Orange Book drugs that have been discontinued and designates on that list those that have been determined to have been withdrawn for safety or effectiveness reasons in response to citizen petition received by FDA since 1995. The list is, unfortunately, not available on the FDA Internet Web site. Note that FDA has also been required, *see* FDCA Section 503A(b)(1)(C), 21 U.S.C. 353a(b)(1)(C), to publish a list of drug products withdrawn or removed from the market because of lack of safety or effectiveness so that those drugs may not be compounded by pharmacists. *See* 21 C.F.R. 216.24 for that list. That list focuses on active ingredients as opposed to particular products but, for example, chlorhexidine gluconate topical propriations, whose withdrawal was determined to be for safety reasons in response to an ANDA petition, appears on this list. *Id.*

§ 3.02[C] GENERIC AND INNOVATOR DRUGS

Page 3-13. Add after the first full paragraph:

One difficult issue was determining whether a generic applicant could obtain approval of an ANDA containing the old labeling of a listed drug when the new labeling was protected by exclusivity. FDA addressed this issue in a draft guidance document.[43.1] FDA decided that ANDA applicants could reference the prior labeling of the innovator product, but only if FDA determined, after review of a petition submitted by the prospective ANDA applicant, that the innovator labeling had not been changed for reasons of safety or effectiveness.[43.2] Once the exclusivity or patent protection for the innovator labeling changes has expired, FDA expects the ANDA applicant to submit a supplement to change its labeling to match that of the innovator.[43.3]

[43.1] CDER, Guidance for Industry Referencing Discontinued Labeling for Listed Drugs in Abbreviated New Drug Applications, Draft Guidance (Oct. 2000), *available at* ⟨www.fda.gov/cder/guidance/3660dft.htm⟩. Note, however, that the trade press reports that the FDA's Office of Chief Counsel has raised concerns about whether there is legal authority to support this draft guidance. FDC Reports, Vol. 64, No. 14, p. 24 (Apr. 8, 2002).
[43.2] *Id.*, Section IV.B.
[43.3] *Id.*, Section V.F.

[3] Change in Terms of Approval

Page 3-13. Change the cross-reference at the end of footnote 42 to read:

See note 8 *supra.*

[C] Suitability Petitions

Page 3-14. Add footnote 47.1 callout at the end of the paragraph:

... Waxman-Hatch Act.[47.1]

[47.1] Note, however, that FDA's pediatric study rule, 21 C.F.R. 314.55(a) has been interpreted to apply to any petition asking for a change in dosage form, active ingredient, or route of administration. *See* Guidance for Industry: Recommendations for Complying with the Pediatric Rule (Draft Guidance Nov. 2000), Section II.B., *available at* ⟨www.fda.gov/cder/guidance/3578dft.htm⟩. *See also* letter from Gary Buehler to Kala Patel, 99P-2252 (Apr. 24, 2002). Under those rules, if a waiver is not available, clinical studies in the appropriate pediatric population must be completed. If such studies are required, then the suitability petition must be denied. Since the effective date of the pediatric rules, the number of suitability petitions that have been granted has fallen dramatically. If the invalidation of the pediatric study rule, *Association of American Physicians*

ANDAs AND "PAPER NDAs" § 3.03[A]

and *Surgeons v. USFDA*, 2002 WL 31323411 (D. D.C. Oct. 17, 2002) is not overturned on appeal or in Congress, this may of course change.

[1] Permitted Deviations

Page 3-15. Change the citation and last sentence in footnote 48 to read:

The District Court upheld FDA's decision, but the Court of Appeals determined that there was no reason to reach the merits of the dispute because the issue was not ripe. *Pfizer, Inc. v. Shalala*, 1 F. Supp. 2d 38 (D.D.C. 1998), *aff'd in part, rev. in part, Pfizer, Inc. v. Shalala*, 182 F.3d 975 (D.C. Cir. 1999).

[2] Procedures for Filing

Page 3-19. Change the textual sentence in footnote 68 to the following:

For human drugs it may be advisable to send a fifth "desk copy" to the Office of Generic Drugs of the FDA's Center for Drug Evaluation and Research.

§ 3.03 ABBREVIATED NEW DRUG APPLICATIONS UNDER 505(j); CONTENTS

[A] Equivalence or Similarity to Listed Drug

[1] Labeling

Page 3-27. Change the citation at the end of carryover footnote 101 to read:

See FDCA Section 505(j)(8)(B)(ii), 21 U.S.C. 355(j)(8)(B)(ii).

[2] Active Ingredient

Page 3-27. Change the second citation in footnote 103, lines 3-7, to read:

Cf. 49 Fed. Reg. 50878 (Dec. 31, 1984) (new approvals required for animal drug products of rDNA technologies even if active substance is identical in molecular structure to a previously approved product); 51 Fed. Reg. 23309, 23312 (June 26, 1986) (less categorical statement of same point).

[4] Bioequivalence

Page 3-31. Change the citation at the end of footnote 116 to read:

FDCA Section 505(j)(7)(A)(i)(III), 21 U.S.C. 355(j)(7)(A)(i)(III).

[B] Patent Certification

Page 3-41. Change the first sentence of footnote 156 to read:

The FDA asks for the following certification: "In the opinion and to the best knowledge of (name of applicant), there are no patents that claim the listed drug referred to in this application or that claim a use of the listed drug." 21 C.F.R. 314.94(a)(12)(ii) (2002).

[3] Invalid, Unenforceable, or Non-Infringed Patent

Pages 3-43 to 3-44. Change the second textual sentence in footnote 163 and its accompanying citation to read:

FDA regulations, however, allow a claim of unenforceability to satisfy the statutory language, requiring a certification that the "patent is invalid, unenforceable, or will not be infringed." 21 C.F.R. 314.94(a)(12)(i)(A)(4) (2002).

Page 3-45. Change footnote 173 to read:

21 C.F.R. 314.95(e) (2002). FDA at one time proposed to amend its regulations on patent notice to allow the notice to be sent by a variety of means, including fax and electronic mail, with evidence of delivery but not of receipt. *See* 63 Fed. Reg. 11174 (Mar. 6, 1998). FDA withdrew that proposed rule, however, based on comments from patent holders that large corporations are unable to track receipts of delivery by means other than certified mail, return receipt requested. 65 Fed. Reg. 12154 (Mar. 8, 2000).

Page 3-46. Change the first phrase of the first full paragraph to read:

FDA's regulations require

ANDAs AND "PAPER NDAs" § 3.03[C]

Page 3-47. Add footnote 181.1 callout after the third sentence of the second paragraph:

... non-compliance or incomplete compliance.[181.1]

[181.1] In *AstraZeneca AB v. Mutual Pharmaceutical Co.*, 2002 WL 393119 (E.D. Pa. Mar. 12, 2002) the court found that the notice at issue served its purpose of alerting the patentee to the possibility of infringement and thus did not grant the requested relief of ordering withdrawal of an allegedly deficient notice. In two cases, however, courts held that deficient or baseless notices could support a finding that the generic company should be held liable for attorneys' fees. *See Yamanouchi Pharmaceutical Co., Ltd. v. Danbury Pharmacal, Inc.*, 231 F.3d 1339, 1347-48 (Fed. Cir. 2000); *Eli Lilly and Co. v. Zenith Goldline Pharm., Inc.*, No. IP 99-38-C H/K, 2001 WL 1397304 at *25-26 (S.D. Ind. Oct. 29, 2001).

Page 3-48. Add after the first full paragraph:

The statute also requires the ANDA or 505(b)(2) NDA applicant to provide notice when it amends its application to include a Paragraph IV certification.[185.1] Such an amendment may occur when the generic applicant initially makes a "Paragraph III" certification not challenging the patent and later amends its application to include a "Paragraph IV" challenge. Another time when an amendment would occur is when a patent is issued after the submission of the ANDA or § 505(b)(2) NDA but prior to approval of that application. FDA's regulations, current at the time of this writing, would require the sending of a notice in each of those circumstances. In its proposed regulations, however, FDA would not require the sending of a notice when the application was amended to include a Paragraph IV certification to a patent if there had previously been a Paragraph IV certification to another patent in that application.[185.2] This change in FDA position is based on a strained reading of the word "include" in the statute as not requiring such a notice when the generic application already includes a Paragraph IV certification. This proposed reading is likely to draw significant comments and may, if challenged, be invalidated by a reviewing court.

[185.1] FFDCA §505(j)(2)(B)(iii), 21 U.S.C. 355(j)(2)(B)(iii) (ANDA); FDCA § 505(b)(3)(C); 21 U.S.C. 355(b)(3)(C) (505(b)(2) NDA). The FDA regulations in place as of this writing reflect that requirement 21 C.F.R. 314.95(d). As discussed in the text, however, in its proposed regulations, FDA would not require a notice to be sent in a situation in which a Paragraph IV certification had previously been made with respect to another patent in the same ANDA or 505(b)(2) NDA. *See* proposed 21 C.F.R. 314.95(a)(3), 67 Fed. Reg. 65448, 65465 (Oct. 24, 2002) (Appendix 92 to this supplement).

[185.2] *Id.*

[D] Other Requirements

Page 3-50. Change the first sentence of the last paragraph on this page to read:

FDA has interpreted the statutory language to permit it to refuse approval of ANDAs in circumstances in which "there is a reasonable basis to conclude that one or more of the inactive ingredients of the proposed drug or its composition raises serious questions of safety."

Page 3-51. Change the first textual sentence of footnote 199 to read:

The question of what constitutes an inactive ingredient, which must be the same as in the listed drug for parenteral products, as opposed to a non-ingredient "impurity," which arguably need not be the same, was litigated in *Serono Laboratories, Inc. v. Shalala*, 974 F. Supp. 29, 34-35 (D.D.C. 1997), *rev'd* 158 F.3d 1313, 1326 (D.C. Cir. 1998) (concluding it was unnecessary to address FDA's argument that the substances in question were not "inactive ingredients" but rather were "impurities").

§ 3.04 ABBREVIATED NEW DRUG APPLICATIONS UNDER 505(j); PROCEDURE

[A] Time Constraints

Page 3-52. Change the first citation in footnote 206 to read:

FDCA Section 505(j)(5)(A), 21 U.S.C. 355(j)(5)(A) (ANDA)

[C] Withdrawal of Approval

[3] Withdrawal Pursuant to Section 308

Page 3-62. Change footnote 255 to read:

FDCA Section 308(a)(1), 21 U.S.C. 335c(a)(1)

Page 3-63. Change footnote 257 to read:

FDCA Section 308(a)(2), 21 U.S.C. 335c(a)(2)

ANDAs AND "PAPER NDAs" § 3.05

Page 3-63. Change footnote 258 to read:

FDCA Section 308(c), 21 U.S.C. 335c(c)

Page 3-63. Change the citation in footnote 259 to read:

FDCA Section 308(b), 21 U.S.C. 355c(b)

Page 3-63. Change footnote 260 to read:

FDCA Section 308(d), 21 U.S.C. 335c(d)

§ 3.05 505(b)(2) APPLICATIONS ("PAPER" NDAs)

Page 3-63. Add before subsection [A]:

The FDA has interpreted the provisions of the statute imposing restrictions on so-called "505(b)(2) NDAs" as affirmatively authorizing a type of NDA in which the applicant would in effect rely on the safety and effectiveness data in another applicant's NDA. Specifically, FDA says that a 505(b)(2) NDA can rely on the FDA's "finding of safety and/or effectiveness for an approved drug product."[260.1] This expansive reading is contained in a draft guidance,[260.2] and has been challenged by the innovator industry.[260.3]

FDA's interpretation of its statute is traditionally accorded weight and its position may be upheld. A close look at the statutory language, however, shows that the provisions in question do not authorize anything. Instead, they place restrictions. An explanation of the history of this provision and FDA's regulation implementing it follows.

[260.1] CDER, Guidance for Industry: Applications Covered by Section 505(b)(2), pg. 2 (Draft, October 1999) (copy in Appendix 85 to this supplement). *See* Section 3.05[A][1] of the main volume for a discussion of the importance of "findings" in the approval of pre-1984 ANDAs.

[260.2] *Id.*

[260.3] Petition of Pfizer Inc. and Pharmacia Corp., Docket No. OIP-0323, July 27, 2001 (seeking amendment of guidance so as not to permit a 505(b)(2) applicant to rely on another applicant's non-public data and not to permit findings of therapeutic equivalence between a 505(b)(2) NDA drug and the innovator drug it copies).

[A] Applications Covered

[1] Abbreviated New Drug Applications Submitted Under Section 505(b)

Page 3-66. Change the first citation in footnote 272 to read:

21 C.F.R. 314.55(b)(2) (1987) (now withdrawn)

[2] Literature-Based NDAs

Page 3-69. Add callout for footnote 286.1 at the end of the first sentence of the second full paragraph:

... "relied upon" by the applicant.[286.1]

[286.1] FDA's Draft Guidance, note 260.1 *supra*, requires the applicant to identify the listed drug for which FDA made a finding on which the applicant relies, or which was the subject of studies on which the applicant relies, or that is a pharmaceutical equivalent of the 505(b)(2) NDA drug. (Appendix 85 at 7-8.)

[3] Variants of Listed Drugs

Page 3-72. Add to footnote 300:

The issue was raised again in the Pfizer/Pharmacia petition referred to in note 260.3, *supra*.

CHAPTER 4
DELAYING APPROVAL OF COMPETITIVE PRODUCTS

§ 4.01 TWO KINDS OF DELAY

Page 4-3. Change the first sentence, and its accompanying footnote, to read:

Certain provision of the Waxman-Hatch Act delay the date on which approvals of ANDAs and "505(b)(2) NDAs"[1] can be made effective.

[1] In previous editions of this book, the term "paper NDA" has been used to refer to NDAs described in FDCA Section 505(b)(2), 21 U.S.C. 355(b)(2). FDA has, however, referred to such applications as "505(b)(2) applications," both in regulations and guidances, and in this update, for clarity, we adopt that FDA usage. What might fairly be called "paper NDAs" (applications that contain safety and effectiveness data taken from the published literature) are, in fact, only a subset of applications believed, by FDA at least, to meet the criteria for a 505(b)(2) application. For a discussion of the genesis of the term "paper NDA," *see* Section 3.05[A][2] of the main volume.

Page 4-3. Add to footnote 3:

The statute was further amended in relatively minor ways in 1997, Pub. L. 105-115, § 124(b), 1998, Pub. L. 105-277, § 101(a), and 1999, Pub. L. 106-113, § 4732(b)(11).

§ 4.02 EXCLUSIVITY

[A] The "Exclusivity" Provisions

Page 4-4. Change footnote 6 to read:

FDCA Sections 505(j)(5)(D)(v) and 505(c)(3)(D)(v), 21 U.S.C. 355(j)(5)(D)(v), 355(c)(3)(D)(v). Exclusivity under this provision expired in 1986.

§ 4.02[C]   GENERIC AND INNOVATOR DRUGS

[C]   **Blocked Versions of the Drug**

Page 4-10. Change the first sentence of the first full paragraph to:

    Title II of the Waxman-Hatch Act defines "drug product" to mean "the active ingredient of a new drug . . . including any salt or ester of the active ingredient, as a single entity or in combination with another active ingredient."

[F]   **New Chemical Entities Approved After Enactment**

Page 4-15. Add to footnote 54:

This section has now been repealed, Pub. L. 105-115, Nov. 21, 1997. *See* Section 4.02[I] of the main volume.

Page 4-19. Change the first sentence of the first full paragraph to read:

    In its regulations, FDA requires that the patent litigation be commenced not only within the year after submission of the ANDA or 505(b)(2) NDA could be made (*i.e.*, between the date four years after submission of the original NDA and five years after that submission) *but also* within 45 days of receipt of notice that the submitting applicant has certified that the patent is invalid or not infringed.

Page 4-21. Delete the last sentence of footnote 85.

[G]   **New Clinical Investigations Essential to Approval**

Page 4-22. Change the third sentence to read:

In each case, effective approval of an ANDA or 505(b)(2) NDA may be delayed for three years after the approval, after the September 24, 1984 date of the enactment of the amendments, of a new drug application or supplement which "contains reports of new clinical investigations (other than bioavailability studies) essential to approval of the application [supplement] and conducted or sponsored by the applicant [person submitting the supplement]."

Page 4-22. Change the first textual sentence of footnote 88 to read:

Nearly identical language appears in each of the provisions discussed in this section.

DELAYING APPROVAL OF COMPETITIVE PRODUCTS § 4.02[H]

[2] New Investigation

Page 4-24. Change the parenthetical at the end of footnote 92 to read:

(copy in Appendix 59 to the main volume)

Page 4-24. Change the first full sentence of the carryover paragraph to the following:

Under FDA regulations, a study, to be "new," must not have been submitted to the FDA and relied upon to demonstrate effectiveness of a drug for any indication or "safety for a new patient population" in the context of a previous application, and the results of the study must not duplicate the results of another study that had been relied on for those purposes in a previous application.

[3] "Conducted or Sponsored By"

Page 4-26. Insert before the final citation in footnote 103:

Id. See also

[4] "Essential Investigations"

Page 4-28. Change footnote 111 to read:

Upjohn Co. v. Kessler, 938 F. Supp. 439 (W.D. Mich. 1996).

[H] Challenge to Patent Status

Page 4-34. Change the third sentence of the first paragraph to read:

If such a certification (commonly referred to as a "paragraph IV certification") has been made in an ANDA or an ANADA, the statute states that any subsequent ANDA or ANADA for the same drug that contains such a certification may not be approved until 180 days after the earlier of either (1) the date the FDA receives notice from the first applicant "of the first commercial marketing of the drug under the previous application" or (2) the date of the decision of a court holding the patent(s) subject to certification to be invalid or not infringed.

§ 4.02[H] GENERIC AND INNOVATOR DRUGS

Page 4-34. Change the third textual sentence of footnote 131 to read:

Thereafter, FDA considers the ANDA not to contain a paragraph IV certification.

Pages 4-35 through 4-42. Delete the text from the first full paragraph on page 4-35 to the bottom of page 4-42 and replace with the following:

FDA's attempt to implement the 180-day exclusivity provision has led to repeated litigation, much of which FDA has lost. FDA, in 1999, proposed a rule to resolve the various issues relating to this provision.[133] The proposal was not finalized, some of the positions were overturned by courts, and the proposal has now been withdrawn.[134] Because each new court decision seems to bring a change to the interpretation of the 180-day provision, understanding this provision has become a challenge. As of this writing, the following appears to be the situation:

An applicant can gain exclusivity without successfully defending a patent suit. FDA's regulation initially stated that 180-day exclusivity would be awarded only to a company that had successfully defended a patent litigation brought as a result of its submission of a paragraph IV certification.[135] That position was inconsistent with a decision interpreting this provision that predated the regulations.[136] FDA's regulation was generally accepted for several years. Thereafter, however, its position that there had to be a successful defense of a patent litigation in order to qualify for exclusivity was overturned in the courts.[137] FDA then published a guidance document saying that it would no longer enforce the successful defense requirement.[138] FDA subsequently published an interim rule removing the successful defense requirement from the regulation.[139]

The first applicant need not be sued to earn exclusivity. After changing its position about the need for a successful defense of patent litigation, FDA was sustained in its position that a generic applicant, in order to earn 180-day exclusivity, need not even be sued in response to its paragraph IV certification.[140]

Separate periods for different dosage strengths. FDA has concluded that separate 180-day exclusivity periods will apply to different dosage strengths of drugs. Thus, if Company *A* is the first to file an ANDA challenging a patent for a 5 mg dosage strength of a drug and Company *B* is the first to file with respect to a 10 mg dosage, each will be granted exclusivity with respect to its respective dosage strength. This position was challenged and upheld in court.[141]

DELAYING APPROVAL OF COMPETITIVE PRODUCTS § 4.02[H]

Separate periods for each patent. The 180-day exclusivity provisions apply to particular patents as opposed to particular products. Thus, if Company A is the first to challenge one patent on a product and Company B is the first to challenge a second patent on the same product, both companies are entitled to 180-day exclusivity. This presents an obvious problem in some circumstances. If there is no court decision because the patent holder does not sue or the cases are settled without decision, the generic companies could find themselves effectively blocking each other indefinitely. FDA resolved that situation with respect to omeprazole delayed-release capsule products by deciding that the two generic companies entitled to exclusivity for different patents should share that exclusivity. Under the FDA's formulation, neither of the two companies was blocked by the other's 180-day exclusivity. The 180-day exclusivity vis-à-vis all other applicants started with the marketing by either company.[142] It is not clear that FDA's solution to this problem is supported by the statute, but neither claimant to exclusivity challenged the decision.

At the time of this writing, however, another FDA decision involving 180-day exclusivity for a separate strength of omeprazole is being challenged. In that case, the generic applicant argues that exclusivity should not be awarded for individual patents.[143]

First paragraph IV applicant is only applicant that can obtain exclusivity. One area that has been less than clear is what happens if the first ANDA applicant to challenge a patent either loses or settles its patent litigation before that litigation reaches a decision or if it simply does not pursue approval of the ANDA. FDA's regulation requires an applicant that has had final judgment entered against it finding the patent to be infringed to amend its paragraph IV certification to a "paragraph III" certification stating the expiration date of the patent. The regulation then states that, upon receipt of such an amendment, "the application will no longer be considered to be one containing a [paragraph IV] certification."[144] A fair reading of this regulation would suggest that, in that circumstance, since the first application is no longer considered to contain a paragraph IV certification, the next application containing such a certification would be considered the first for purposes of 180-day exclusivity. FDA argued in the *Mova* case, on the other hand, that this was simply a "housekeeping" provision.[145]

The issue was revisited in a subsequent case in which the first generic applicant had apparently changed its certification to a paragraph III certification after a settlement but FDA continued to take the position that

that applicant retained its exclusivity. The court announced itself to be "baffled" by FDA's position.[146]

In another case, the first ANDA applicant to make a paragraph IV certification settled patent litigation but did not change its certification from paragraph IV to paragraph III. In response to a citizen petition, FDA decided that FDA could "effectively" change the certification for the applicant and thus remove eligibility for exclusivity. The court overturned that part of FDA's decision.[147]

In the now-withdrawn proposed regulation on this subject, FDA had proposed that only the first applicant could be eligible for exclusivity and that the first applicant could lose its eligibility if it lost its case or otherwise changed its certification from paragraph IV to paragraph III.[148] With the withdrawal of that proposed regulation, the proper interpretation of the 180-day exclusivity period on this point is uncertain. FDA seems most likely, however, to adhere to the position that only the first ANDA applicant to make a paragraph IV certification will be entitled to exclusivity. If that applicant loses the patent suit, then either it retains its exclusivity or no one has exclusivity. If there is a settlement but the first applicant declines to withdraw its ANDA or amend its certification, FDA and the courts may stretch to find a way to remove any exclusivity that would apply.[149]

FDA believes exclusivity can be transferred. The statute does not provide that an applicant that has earned 180-day exclusivity can sell that exclusivity to another generic applicant. Nevertheless, FDA has taken the position that the applicant can waive exclusivity vis-à-vis another applicant. An attempt to invalidate that position, in the context of a request for a temporary restraining order, was unsuccessful.[150]

"Court" means District Court, with exceptions. As noted, the 180-day exclusivity period may begin on "the date of a decision of a court . . . holding the patent which is the subject of the certification to be invalid or not infringed." FDA had, by regulation, taken the position that the court whose decision would begin the 180-day period would be either the Court of Appeals or, only if there were no appeal, the District Court (*i.e.*, the trial court).[151] A roughly parallel provision appears in the section of the statute that provides a 30-month period during which an ANDA application may not be approved if patent litigation is commenced in response to a paragraph IV notice.[152] FDA had adopted the same interpretation of "court" with respect to the latter provision, but that position was overturned by the decision of a district court, later vacated on mootness

grounds, that thought that the 30-month period must end with the decision of the trial court, whether or not there was an appeal.[153]

In a subsequent case involving the 180-day provision itself, the court again found that the "decision of a court" reference applied to the decision of a trial court even if there was an appeal.[154] In that case, however, the court, having found FDA's position incorrect, nevertheless did not require FDA to start the 180-day period with the trial court decision, because it thought that would be inequitable to the company that had relied on the FDA interpretation.

FDA thereafter issued a guidance in March 2000 in which it essentially accepted the court's position. Thus, it said that, for any NDA for which the first paragraph IV certification was made after issuance of the guidance, the decision of the court would be considered to be the decision of the trial court, whether or not there was an appeal. For any drug for which there had been an ANDA with a paragraph IV certification before issuance of the guidance, on the other hand, the old rule would be applied.[155] Subsequently, FDA issued an interim rule formalizing this position and revoking its prior regulation to the contrary.[156]

In another case, the court addressed a situation in which a trial court had found a patent invalid or not infringed and the matter was subsequently settled. The court thought that that trial court decision started the 180-day period.[157] This raises the question whether, should there be a challenge to FDA's position with respect to what might be considered "grandfathered" situations when the first paragraph IV certification of the ANDA in question was before March 2000, FDA's reliance on its old interpretation would be sustained.

Court decision triggering exclusivity need not involve the first paragraph IV applicant. While it may appear at first reading of the statute that the court decision that would begin 180-day exclusivity should be the decision in a case involving that applicant, FDA has taken a different view. FDA believes that the 180-day exclusivity should start with any decision in any case involving the patent covered by the certification. That position, when challenged, was upheld by the Fourth Circuit.[157.1] This means, of course, that a company's 180-day exclusivity can be running out during a time in which that applicant does not have approval to market its product.

Declaratory judgment actions can trigger exclusivity. A court has concluded that a decision in a declaratory judgment action brought by a subsequent applicant, even a decision dismissing that action for lack of case or controversy because the patent holder has no intention of enforcing its patent with respect to the generic, can start the 180-day period.[157.2]

§ 4.02[H]   GENERIC AND INNOVATOR DRUGS

This reading of the statute to encourage the filing of declaratory judgment suits where there is no case of controversy is a strange one. It apparently reflected the court's frustration with the statute that would otherwise have kept a second applicant off the market indefinitely while the first applicant was delayed in obtaining approval, in a situation in which no one had been sued for infringement for the patent at issue.

Marketing under the innovator's NDA triggers the start of exclusivity. The second trigger to begin the 180-day exclusivity period is the commercial marketing of the ANDA product. This recognizes that a generic applicant may, in some circumstances, be willing to market prior to a court decision if it is sued for patent infringement (after the 30-month period expires). It also provides a usable trigger when there has been no patent suit at all. What happens when the first applicant settles its patent dispute and agrees to market under the patent holder's NDA? The FDA, upheld by one court, has concluded that the marketing under the NDA should be considered commercial marketing under the ANDA, an obvious fiction that was presumably accepted by the court because of its perceived equity.[157.3]

Exclusivity is extended to avoid overlap with pediatric exclusivity. One issue involving interpretation of the 180-day exclusivity provision has been resolved by legislation. An ANDA applicant had challenged one patent with a paragraph IV certification but had submitted a paragraph III certification with respect to a second patent on the same drug, indicating a willingness to wait until that patent had expired. That patent holder then obtained pediatric exclusivity, extending for six months the time in which FDA could not approve the ANDA after expiration of the latter patent.[157.4] This raised a possibility that the ANDA applicant, if successful in its patent challenge, could find its 180-day exclusivity running during the time that the pediatric exclusivity had extended the FDA's inability to approve the application because of the second patent. In 2001, Congress amended the pediatric exclusivity provision to extend the 180-day period to make up for time lost because of pediatric exclusivity on a separate patent.[157.5] This legislative change appears to be the result of effective special pleading. It would not address the situation in which the 180-day exclusivity was effectively useless because a second patent, as to which a paragraph III certification had been made, had not yet expired when the 180-day exclusivity began to run.

[133] 64 Fed. Reg. 42873 (Aug. 6, 1999).
[134] 67 Fed. Reg. 66593 (Nov. 1, 2002). *See also* 67 Fed. Reg. 33040, 33045 (May 13, 2002).

DELAYING APPROVAL OF COMPETITIVE PRODUCTS § 4.02[H]

[135] 21 C.F.R. 314.107(c)(1) (1997) (now revoked). This provision of the regulation was officially revoked in 63 Fed. Reg. 59712 (Nov. 5, 1998). The prior provision is explained at 59 Fed. Reg. 50352-53 (Oct. 3, 1994).

[136] *Inwood Laboratories, Inc. v. Young*, 723 F. Supp. 1523 (D.D.C. 1989), *appeal dismissed*, 43 F.3d 712 (D.C. Cir. 1989). *See* 59 Fed. Reg. 50353 (Oct. 3, 1994). Dicta in a subsequent case, however, broadly approved FDA's policy of requiring defense of a lawsuit as a prerequisite for the 180-day exclusivity. *See Mylan Pharmaceuticals, Inc. v. Sullivan*, No. 89-0036-C (K) (N.D. W. Va. May 5, 1989).

[137] *Mova Pharmaceutical Corp. v. Shalala*, 955 F. Supp. 128 (D.D.C. 1997), *aff'd*, 140 F.3d 1060 (D.C. Cir. 1998); *Granutec, Inc. v. Shalala*, Nos. 97-1873, 97-1874, 1998 WL 153410 (4th Cir. 1998) (unpublished disposition noted at 139 F.3d 889 (Table)). *See also Andrx Pharmaceuticals, Inc. v. Friedman*, Civ. No. 98-0099 (D.D.C. Mar. 30, 1998) (also rejecting FDA's position and ordering the second ANDA applicant to cease marketing until the 180-day period had expired).

[138] FDA, "Guidance for Industry: 180-day Generic Drug Exclusivity under the Hatch-Waxman Amendments to Federal Food, Drug, and Cosmetic Act" (Appendix 76 to main volume), availability announced in 63 Fed. Reg. 37890 (July 14, 1998).

[139] 63 Fed. Reg. 59710 (Nov. 5, 1998).

[140] *Purepac Pharmaceutical Co. v. Friedman*, 162 F.3d 1201 (D.D.C. Cir. 1998). This author represented Hoffmann La-Roche and Syntex (U.S.A.) Inc., the patent holder, as intervenors supporting FDA's position in that case.

[141] *Apotex, Inc. v. Shalala*, 53 F. Supp. 2d 454 (D.D.C. 1999), *aff'd*, 1999 WL 956686 (D.C. Cir. Oct. 8, 1999).

[142] Letter from Gary Buehler to Andrx Pharmaceuticals Inc., Nov. 16, 2001, accessible on FDA's Web site at ⟨www.fda.gov/cder/ogd/shared_exclusivity.htm⟩. Thereafter, both holders of shared exclusivity lost their patent challenges in the district court, while another ANDA applicant prevailed. *See In re Omeprazole Patent Litigation*, _____ F. Supp. _____, 2002 WL 31319475 (S.D.N.Y. Oct. 16, 2002).

[143] *Dr. Reddy's Laboratories v. Thompson*, No. 02-CV-452 (D.N.J. filed Jan. 31, 2002). That case also raised the question whether a certification for another patent, which Dr. Reddy's was the first to challenge, expired when that patent expired. FDA has taken the position in the past that 180-day exclusivity expires at patent expiration. *See* 64 Fed. Reg. 42873, 42877.

[144] 21 C.F.R. 314.94(a)(12)(viii)(A) (2002).

[145] 140 F.3d at 1071 n.13. The court expressed skepticism of this reading. *Id.*

[146] *Mylan Pharmaceuticals, Inc. v. Henney*, 94 F. Supp. 2d 36, 57 (D.D.C. 2000), *vacated as moot sub nom. Pharmachemie B.V. v. Barr Laboratories, Inc.*, 276 F.3d 627 (D.C. Cir. 2002). While that court found FDA's position on the regulation arbitrary and capricious, its holding appears to have been that the applicant had exclusivity that had expired.

[147] *Mylan Pharmaceuticals, Inc. v. Thompson*, 207 F. Supp. 2d 476 (N.D. W. Va. 2001).

[148] 64 Fed. Reg. at 42876.

[149] *Mylan Pharmaceuticals, Inc. v. Thompson*, 207 F. Supp. 2d 476, 487 (N.D. W. Va. 2001) is an example of a case in which FDA tried to strip a settling ANDA applicant of exclusivity on two grounds. The court rejected the first, discussed above, *i.e.*, FDA's attempt to deem a certification changed. The court, however, concluded that the exclusivity

§ 4.02[J] GENERIC AND INNOVATOR DRUGS

had begun to run based on the marketing by the generic applicant of the innovator's product under the innovator's NDA. That holding is flatly inconsistent with the statutory requirement that 180-day exclusivity starts with first marketing under the ANDA. *See* discussion in text *infra*.

[150] *Boehringer Ingelheim Corp. v. Shalala*, 993 F. Supp. 1 (D.D.C. 1997). In the now-abandoned proposed regulation, FDA said that it would permit waivers in favor of a particular applicant or applicants only after the 180-day period had begun to run and that, prior to the beginning of the period, an applicant with exclusivity could only choose to relinquish it altogether. 64 Fed. Reg. 42881. FDA's explanation was that, prior to exclusivity being triggered, it is always possible that the first applicant could lose its eligibility for the exclusivity.

[151] *See* 21 C.F.R. 314.107(e)(1) (1999) (now revoked).

[152] FDCA Sections 505(j)(5)(B)(iii)(I), (505)(c)(3)(C)(i), 21 U.S.C. 355(j)(5)(B)(iii)(I), 355(c)(3)(C)(i). *See* discussion in Section 4.03[A] of the main volume and this supplement.

[153] FDA's position was set out in 21 C.F.R. 314.107(e)(1) (1999) (now revoked). That court decision may be found in *TorPharm Inc. v. Shalala*, Civ. No. 97-1925(JR), 1997 U.S. Dist. LEXIS 21983 (D.D.C. Sept. 15, 1997), *remanded*, 1998 U.S. App. LEXIS 4681 (D.D.C. Cir. Feb. 5, 1998), *vacated on remand* (D.D.C. Apr. 9, 1998). This author was counsel for intervenor GlaxoWellcome Inc. in that case.

[154] *Mylan Pharmaceuticals, Inc. v. Shalala*, 81 F. Supp. 2d 30 (D.D.C. 2000).

[155] Guidance for Industry, "Court Decisions, ANDA Approvals, and 180-day Exclusivity under the Hatch-Waxman Amendments to the Federal Food, Drug, and Cosmetic Act" (March 2000), published at 65 Fed. Reg. 16922 (Mar. 30, 2000).

[156] 65 Fed. Reg. 43233 (July 13, 2000).

[157] *Mylan Pharmaceuticals, Inc. v. Henney*, 94 F. Supp. 2d 36, 54 (D.D.C. 2000), *vacated as moot sub nom. Pharmachemie B.V. v. Barr Laboratories, Inc.*, 276 F.3d 627 (D.C. Cir. 2002).

[157.1] *Granutec, Inc. v. Shalala*, 1998 WL 153410 (4th Cir. Apr. 3, 1998) (unpublished opinion noted at 139 F.3d 889 (Table)).

[157.2] *Teva Pharmaceuticals, USA, Inc. v. FDA*, 182 F.3d 1003 (D.C. Cir. 1999), *on remand*, 1999 WL 1042743 (D.D.C. Aug. 19, 1999), *aff'd*, 254 F.3d 316 (D.C. Cir. 2000). This author was counsel for intervenors Hoffmann-LaRoche Inc. and Syntex (U.S.A.) Inc. in the first appeal in this matter.

[157.3] *Mylan Pharmaceuticals, Inc. v. Thompson*, 2001 WL 1654781 (N.D. W. Va. Apr. 18, 2001).

[157.4] *See* Section 4.02[j] of the main volume and this supplement.

[157.5] FDCA Section 505A(k), 21 U.S.C. 355a(k), added by Pub. L. 107-109 (2002).

[J] Pediatric Study Exclusivity

Page 4-43. Add after the first sentence:

The pediatric exclusivity provision was extended, and modified somewhat, in 2002.[163.1]

[163.1] Pub. L. 107-109 (2002).

DELAYING APPROVAL OF COMPETITIVE PRODUCTS § 4.02[J]

Page 4-44. Replace the last two sentences of the carryover paragraph, and accompanying footnotes, with the following:

This provision, as amended, applies to drugs for which NDAs have been submitted prior to October 1, 2007.[166] Congress will presumably consider extending the statute further as that date approaches.[167]

[166] FDCA Section 505A(n), 21 U.S.C. 355a(n).

[167] The FDA had effectively supported the 2002 reenactment of this provision in a report it filed with Congress, pursuant to FDCA Section 505A(n), 21 U.S.C. 355a(m), on the effect of the statute. That report and other information concerning the implementation of the pediatric provision may be found at ⟨www.fda.gov/cder/pediatric/⟩.

Page 4-44. Change footnote 168 as follows:

FDCA Section 505A(b), 21 U.S.C. 355a(b).

Pages 4-44 to 4-45. Replace the carryover paragraph with the following:

The original statute required FDA to develop a list of approved drugs for which it believed development of pediatric information would produce health benefits.[169] FDA produced a list that included almost all pharmaceuticals.[170] In the 2002 amendment of the statute, Congress wisely did away with the requirement of a list. Now, exclusivity for an already approved drug is available if FDA makes a written request for pediatric studies, the request identifies a timeframe for completion of the studies, the NDA holder agrees to the request, the studies are completed within the timeframe, and acceptable reports of the studies are submitted to FDA.[171]

[169] *See* former FDCA Section 505A(b), 21 U.S.C. 355a(b) (2000) (now repealed).

[170] *See* 63 Fed. Reg. 27733 (May 20, 1998).

[171] FDCA Section 505A(c), 21 U.S.C. 355a(c). Note that, if a written request for pediatric studies had been made prior to approval of a drug but that request had not been accepted, the statute permits FDA to make a second request after approval under subsection (c). *See* FDCA Section 505A(d)(4)(F), 21 U.S.C. 355a(d)(4)(F). The sponsor must notify FDA whether it accepts a post-approval written request within 180 days of its receipt. FDCA Section 505A(d)(4)(A), 21 U.S.C. 355a(d)(4)(A). If it does not accept the request, FDA may refer the request to the Foundation for the National Institutes of Health (established under 42 U.S.C. 290b), which may then conduct the studies. FDCA Section 505A(d)(4)(B), 21 U.S.C. 355a(d)(4)(B).

§ 4.02[J] **GENERIC AND INNOVATOR DRUGS**

Page 4-45. Delete the first full paragraph and its accompanying footnotes.

Page 4-46. Insert footnote 175.1 callout in the second line of the carryover paragraph:

... fairly respond to the written request,[175.1]

[175.1] In one situation in which pediatric exclusivity was denied, the applicant challenged the decision in court on the grounds that FDA had failed to consider whether the reports fairly responded to the request. The court agreed that FDA had not addressed that standard and ordered FDA to grant exclusivity during the pendency of a temporary restraining order. *Merck and Co., Inc. v. FDA*, 148 F. Supp. 2d 27 (D.D.C. 2001). FDA subsequently agreed that it had employed an improper standard, and the matter was remanded to FDA, which granted the exclusivity.

Page 4-47. Change the first three sentences of the first full paragraph to read:

FDA has been pushing hard for studies in pediatric patients, even promulgating regulations that would permit it to require that such studies be performed.[183] It is by no means clear that FDA has the legal authority to require that such studies be performed and they have been invalidated by a district court decision.[183.1] As no additional exclusivity is available for any drug that is off-patent and for which market exclusivity has run out, there will certainly be drugs for which the sponsor will have little economic incentive to perform pediatric studies.[183.2]

[183] *See* 63 Fed. Reg. 66632 (Dec. 2, 1998), adding 21 C.F.R. § 201.23, 314.55, and 601.27 and amending several other related regulations to impose such a potential requirement.

[183.1] *Association of American Physicians and Surgeons v. USFDA*, 2002 WL 31323411 (D. D.C. Oct. 17, 2002). FDA had, prior to that decision, initially announced that it was suspending the regulation and then reversed itself. *See* "U.S. Backs Pediatric Tests In Reversal on Drug Safety," Washington Post, page A3 (Apr. 20, 2002). The 2002 statute does provide mechanisms for government funding for pediatric investigations of drugs for which exclusivity is not available or not considered a sufficient inducement to pharmaceutical companies to perform requested studies. *See* Public Health Service Act Section 409I and FDCA Section 505A(d)(4), 21 U.S.C. 355a(d)(4).

[183.2] The 2002 legislation attempts to deal with this problem by providing a mechanism for government funding of studies for which no exclusivity benefit is available. Public Health Service Act 409I(c), 42 U.S.C. 284m(c). The opportunity to propose a contract to perform a government-funded study is first offered to any manufacturer of the drug, and then, if none steps forward, to all other parties. *Id.*, Section 409I(c)(1), (2), 42 U.S.C. 284m(c)(1), (2).

DELAYING APPROVAL OF COMPETITIVE PRODUCTS § 4.02[K]

Page 4-47. Add to the last full paragraph:

A court challenge to FDA's position was rejected, at least at the preliminary injunction stage.[185.1]

[185.1] *National Pharmaceutical Alliance v. Henney*, 47 F. Supp. 2d 37 (D.D.C. 1999).

Page 4-48. Change footnote 186 to read:

FDCA Section 505A(g), 21 U.S.C. 355a(g).

Page 4-48. Change footnote 188 to read:

FDCA Section 505A(g), 21 U.S.C. 355a(g).

Page 4-48. Change the first sentence of footnote 189 to read:

FDA, Pediatric Exclusivity Guidance (Appendix 77-5).

Page 4-48. Change footnote 191 to read:

FDA, Pediatric Exclusivity Guidance (Appendix 77-8).

Page 4-48. Delete the second sentence of the third (carryover) paragraph and footnote 192.

Page 4-49. Change footnote 193 to read:

FDA notes that "[a]greements to perform Phase 4 studies or other communications concerning pediatric studies" will not be considered official requests qualifying for exclusivity. *Id.* (Appendix 77-9).

[K] Procedures for Resolving Disputes

[1] Initial Agency Decision

Page 4-49. Add to footnote 196:

The Green Book is, at the time of this writing, available in electronic form at ⟨www.fda.gov/cvm/greenbook/greenbook/html⟩.

§ 4.02[K] GENERIC AND INNOVATOR DRUGS

[2] Citizen Petition Procedure

Page 4-50. Add to footnote 199:

Observers have noted that FDA seems now more likely to issue a response to a citizen petition before approving the generic product addressed in that petition than it had in the past. One explanation for this posture is that FDA was severely criticized for its failure to put together a comprehensive administrative record on an issue in dispute in *Upjohn Co. v. Kessler*, 938 F. Supp. 439, 442-43 (W.D. Mich. 1996). A response to a citizen petition is one way for FDA to create an organized administrative record and a comprehensible explanation of its position in advance of litigation.

[4] Seeking Judicial Resolution

Page 4-52. Add to footnote 205:

But see Baker Norton Pharmaceuticals, Inc. v. United States Food and Drug Administration, 132 F. Supp. 2d 30, 34 (D.D.C. 2001) (failure to raise arguments in citizen petition is not waiver that prevents judicial review). For an example of a case in which the court found a failure to exhaust remedies because the intervenor had not raised an argument in the context of its comments on a citizen petition to the agency, *see Mylan Pharmaceuticals, Inc. v. Henney*, 94 F. Supp. 2d 36, 45 (D.D.C. 2000), *vacated as moot sub nom. Pharmachemie B.V. v. Barr Laboratories, Inc.*, 276 F.3d 627 (D.C. Cir. 2002). *But see Mylan Pharmaceuticals, Inc. v. Thompson*, 207 F. Supp. 2d 476, 488-89 (N.D. W. Va. 2001), in which the court found that there was no requirement that plaintiff have filed comments on a citizen petition leading to the challenged FDA action as a prerequisite for that plaintiff seeking judicial review.

Page 4-53. Add to footnote 210:

Note that, in at least one case, the failure of a party to raise an issue in commenting on a citizen petition was found by the court to be a failure to exhaust administrative remedies preventing that party from raising that issue in judicial review. *See* note 205, *supra* (this supplement).

DELAYING APPROVAL OF COMPETITIVE PRODUCTS   § 4.03[A]

§ 4.03   PATENT CONSIDERATIONS

[A]   Date of Approval

Page 4-56. Add callout for footnote 218.1 in the second line of the first full paragraph:

... date of receipt,[218.1]

[218.1] Thus, there is a strong incentive for the patent holder to bring suit within 45 days of the receipt of notice if suit is appropriate. For a case suggesting that delay in bringing the lawsuit to the end of the 45 days could be considered failure to expedite the patent litigation, thus endangering the 30-month stay (*see* Section 4.03[B] of the main volume), *see Andrx Pharmaceuticals, Inc. v. Biovail Corp.*, 276 F.3d 1368, 1376 (Fed. Cir. 2002).

Page 4-57. Add to footnote 221:

Interestingly, the parallel provision concerning so-called "505(b)(2) NDAs," FDCA Section 505(c)(3)(C)(i), 21 U.S.C. 355(c)(3)(C)(i), like the regulation, uses the word "may" instead of the word "shall" found in the ANDA provision.

Page 4-57. Replace the last sentence on this page and the corresponding footnote with the following:

In its original regulations, FDA stated that it would make the generic approval effective on the date of the final judgment from which no appeal could be taken or had been taken.[222] This position was deleted from FDA's regulation, and FDA now relies upon a guidance document that states that that original position applies only when the ANDA is for a drug for which some ANDA contained a paragraph IV certification challenging a patent before the guidance was issued in March 2000, with the 30-month period being terminated by a district court decision finding the patent invalid or not infringed for all other ANDAs.[222.1]

[222] 21 C.F.R 314.107(e)(1) (2000) (since amended, *see* discussion in this supplement). Note that petitions for certiorari to the Supreme Court were not considered appeals under the regulation.

[222.1] Guidance for Industry, "Court Decisions, ANDA Approvals, and 180-Day Exclusivity under the Hatch-Waxman Amendments to the Federal Food, Drug, and Cosmetic Act," March 2000, *see* 65 Fed. Reg. 16922 (Mar. 30, 2000) copy in Appendix 91 to this supplement. FDA has also changed its regulation with an interim rule that reflects the guidance. 65 Fed. Reg. 43233 (July 13, 2000). The change reflects the only court decision addressing this specific issue. See *TorPharm, Inc. v. Shalala*, Civ. No. 97-1925 (JR), 1997

§ 4.03[A] GENERIC AND INNOVATOR DRUGS

U.S. Dist. LEXIS 21983 (D.D.C. Sept. 15, 1997), *decision vacated as moot* (Apr. 9, 1998). This decision was vacated because it became moot while on appeal. The author represented intervenor GlaxoWellcome Inc. in that case.

Page 4-59. Change footnote 227 to read:

Id. See 21 C.F.R. 314.107(b)(3)(i)(A) (2002). In one case, the district court used this provision to truncate the 30-month period when it thought the patent holder had inappropriately listed a late-issued patent. That decision was, however, overturned on appeal as an inappropriate use of this provision. *See Andrx Pharmaceuticals, Inc. v. Biovail Corp.*, 276 F.3d 1368, 1376 (Fed. Cir. 2002) (finding that district court had improperly used this provision because of conduct in FDA proceedings rather than delays in the patent litigation). For a case in which the court extended the 30-month period because of delays attributed to the generic manufacturer, *see Eli Lilly Co. v. Zenith Gold Line Pharmaceuticals, Inc.*, 2001 WL 238090, 58 U.S.P.Q.2d 1543 (S.D. Ind. Mar. 8, 2001). An example of a case in which extension was denied is *Zeneca Limited v. Pharmachemie B.V.*, 16 F. Supp. 2d 112 (D. Mass. 1998).

Page 4-59. Add after the first full paragraph:

In an October 2002 proposal, FDA sought to reinterpret the law in this area in an important respect. FDA proposed that it would be able to approve an ANDA immediately, without waiting 45 days after the receipt of a notice relating to a Paragraph IV certification, in situations in which FDA concludes that no such notice need be sent. FDA proposed that, when an ANDA applicant amends its application to include a Paragraph IV certification with respect to a patent but that application already includes such a notice with respect to another patent, no patent notice need be submitted. In what many would regard as a tortured interpretation of the statutory scheme, FDA simply concludes that, with no notice ever being sent for such certifications, the statutory 30-month period would never begin with respect to such certifications.[227.1] Whether this portion of FDA's proposed regulation will be finalized and, if finalized, will withstand judicial review, remains unclear as of this writing.

[227.1] 67 Fed. Reg. 65448, 65455 (Oct. 24, 2002) (Appendix 92 to this supplement).

[B] Effects on Patent Infringement Litigation

Page 4-60. Change the first line of footnote 232 to read:

FDCA Sections 505(j)(5)(B), 505(c)(3)(C), 512(c)(2)(D), 21 U.S.C. 355(j)(5)(B), 355(c)(3)(C), 360b(c)(2)(D).

[C] Patents Not Subject to Certification

Page 4-60. Change the third sentence of the first paragraph through the end of the carryover paragraph to read:

That provision can be fairly read to allow patent infringement litigation based on process patents to be brought at the time of submission of an ANDA, should the patent holder learn of that submission. One court, however, has explicitly held that this provision applies only where there has been a paragraph IV submission challenging the patent, which would not occur for a process patent because such a patent would not be listed.[235] In some cases, the patent holder will learn of a potential infringement of a process patent because it also holds a product or use patent for the drug at issue. In others it may learn by some other means. In either case, a court might agree that a declaratory judgment on potential process patent infringement would be appropriate.[235.1]

---

[235] *Allergan, Inc. v. Alcon Laboratories, Inc.*, 200 F. Supp. 2d 1219, 1230 (C.D. Cal. 2002). There is also *dicta* in the Supreme Court decision in *Eli Lilly and Co. v. Medtronic, Inc.*, 496 U.S. 661, 678 (1990), that the act of infringement created by 35 U.S.C. 271(e)(2) consists of submitting an ANDA or 505(b)(2) NDA "containing the fourth type of certification" required by the statute. If one accepts that statement as accurately characterizing the law, then process patents, which would not be the subject of paragraph IV certifications because they would not be published by the FDA, would not form the basis for patent infringements under Section 271(e)(2). *See also Bristol-Myers Squibb Co. v. Royce Laboratories*, 69 F.3d 1130, 1131 (Fed. Cir. 1995), *cert. denied*, 516 U.S. 1067 (1996) ("Inclusion of a paragraph IV certification in an ANDA, however, is deemed an act of infringement").

[235.1] An example of a case in which the court found declaratory judgment jurisdiction in that circumstance is *Glaxo, Inc. v. Torpharm, Inc.*, No. 95 C 4686, 1997 WL 282742 (N.D. Ill. May 18, 1997). In a related but somewhat different situation, in which the patent at issue covered a use of the drug that had not been listed because it was not the approved use, Section 271(e)(2) was held not to support a suit alleging that the ANDA applicant would be inducing infringement of the unapproved use. *Allergan, Inc. v. Alcon Laboratories, Inc.*, 200 F. Supp. 2d 1219 (C.D. Cal. 2002). *See also Warner-Lambert Co. v. Apotex Corp.*, No. 98 C 4293, 2001 WL 1104618 (N.D. Ill. Sept. 14, 2001).

§ 4.04[A] GENERIC AND INNOVATOR DRUGS

Page 4-61. Add after the first full paragraph:

FDA's proposed change in its regulations to permit a generic applicant not to provide notice of a Paragraph IV patent challenge when it has previously made such a challenge with respect to a different patent on the same drug raises the question whether, should the innovator company become aware of the second Paragraph IV certification, it would be permitted to sue to block the approval based on that certification. FDA seems to believe that such a suit would be possible, but it does not, in the preamble to its proposed regulation, cite the patent provision, 35 U.S.C. 271(e)(2), specifically applicable to suits under the Waxman-Hatch Act.[238.1] While one can argue from the text of those provisions that such a suit should be possible, there has been confusing language about the limits of that provision that raise some uncertainty on this point.[238.2]

[238.1] 67 Fed. Reg. 65448, 65455 (Oct. 24, 2002) (Appendix 92 to this supplement).
[238.2] *See* Note 235 *supra* (in the main volume).

§ 4.04 PATENT EXTENSIONS

[A] Eligibility

Page 4-62. Replace the text following the first sentence of footnote 244, and the supporting citation, with the following:

At the time of passage, Title I did not apply to antibiotics (then approved under 21 U.S.C. 357), insulin (then approved under 21 U.S.C. 356) or biologicals (approved under the Public Health Service Act). The issue of the statute's applicability to antibiotics was arguable because of an FDA regulation stating that approved antibiotics would be treated as approved new drugs, and that issue was litigated in *Glaxo, Inc. v. Heckler*, 623 F. Supp. 69 (E.D.N.C. 1985). The FDA's interpretation was upheld by the court. The author represented the FDA in the initial hearing in that case. Subsequently, the separate provisions for approval of antibiotics and insulin have been deleted. *See* Section 4.02[I] of the main volume for discussion of the transition rule for antibiotics. New antibiotics are now covered by Title I.

DELAYING APPROVAL OF COMPETITIVE PRODUCTS § 4.04[E]

[C] Breadth of Extended Patent

Page 4-69. Change footnote 267 to read:

35 U.S.C. 156(b)(1). Note that, if several uses (*i.e.*, several indications) of the drug had been approved before the patent expired, the statute would allow extension of the patent for all such uses. This would, apparently, be true even though the first approval, which ended the regulatory review period for the drug, was for a limited use and approval of additional indications came later in supplemental NDAs or NADAs.

[D] Computing the Extension

[5] Making the Computation

Page 4-75. Change the last citation in footnote 296 to read:

37 C.F.R. 1.778(d)(1)(i) (2002) (animal drugs); 37 C.F.R. 1.779(d)(1)(i) (2002) (veterinary biological products).

Page 4-76. Change the second citation in footnote 298 to read:

37 C.F.R. 1.778(d)(2) (2002) (animal drugs); 37 C.F.R. 1.779(d)(2) (2002) (veterinary biological products).

[E] Patent Extension Application

[1] Content

Page 4-76. Add to footnote 299:

See also 37 C.F.R. 1.790 and 1.791 (2002), dealing with interim patent term extensions.

Page 4-77. Change the first sentence of the first full paragraph to the following:

The PTO regulations specify 15 different items that must be included within the application.

§ 4.04[E]   **GENERIC AND INNOVATOR DRUGS**

Page 4-78. Change the first full sentence of the carryover paragraph to read:

For drug products, there must be identification of each active ingredient and a statement, for each active ingredient, that the ingredient has not been previously approved; or, if it has been approved, the date of approval, the use for which it was approved, and the statute under which it was approved, must be supplied.

Page 4-78. Change the last two sentences of the carryover paragraph (retaining the footnotes) to read:

The application must contain the name, address, and telephone number of a contact person for the applicant,[314] the prescribed fee,[315] and two duplicate copies of the application papers.[316]

Page 4-78. Change footnote 316 to read:

37 C.F.R. 1.740(b) (2002).

Page 4-78. Delete footnote 317.

Page 4-79. Change the last sentence of the first full paragraph on this page to read:

The PTO regulations state the prescribed fees.

[2] Method of Processing

Page 4-80. Change the third textual sentence in footnote 326 to read:

The patent term extension amendment contains a provision that (properly read) prohibits delegation of authority to make due diligence determinations below the Office of the Commissioner of Food and Drugs. (Through a mistake in implementation of 1999 amendments that change references to the "Commissioner" of Patents and Trademarks to the "Director," the relevant provision now refers to the "Office of the Director of Food and Drugs." 35 U.S.C. 156(d)(2)(B)(i). Because the 1999 amendment, Pub. L. 106-113 § 4732(a)(10)(A) (1999), did not intend to make a substantive change in this provision, and since there is no "Director of Food and

DELAYING APPROVAL OF COMPETITIVE PRODUCTS § 4.04[F]

Drugs," this statute presumably retains its original meaning and is intended to refer to the Office of Commissioner of Food and Drugs.)

[3] Interim Extensions

[a] *Extension Prior to Approval*

Page 4-83. Change footnote 341 to read:

37 C.F.R. 1.790(a) (2002).

[F] URAA Patent Extensions

[1] Extensions and Transitional Provision

Page 4-85. Change the second sentence of footnote 350, and its supporting citation, to read:

Note that the statute does, however, provide some opportunity for extensions of patents to make up for time lost in certain procedures during the patent application process. *See* 35 U.S.C. 154(b).

[2] Issues Raised by the URAA

[a] *The Transitional Provision*

Page 4-88. Change footnote 362 to read:

FDCA Section 505(j)(4)(J), (K), 21 U.S.C. 355(j)(4)(J), (K).

Page 4-89. Change the initial citation in footnote 363 to read:

21 C.F.R. 314.94(a)(12)(viii)(C)(1) (2002).

Page 4-90. Change footnote 370 to read:

FDCA Section 505(c)(3)(B), (j)(5)(B)(ii), 21 U.S.C. 355(c)(3)(B), (j)(5)(B)(ii).

Page 4-92. Change footnote 382 to read:

At that time, FDA's regulations required delay of approval until patent litigation was resolved in the Court of Appeals, where, as in this case, the

§ 4.05[A]

patent holder had appealed an adverse District Court decision. 21 C.F.R. 314.107(e)(2)(ii) (1995) (since amended—*see* note 222.1 in this supplement, *supra*).

[b] The URAA and Waxman-Hatch Patent Extensions

Page 4-98. Change the second sentence on this page to read:

The court concluded that adding the Waxman-Hatch extension to the 20-year period would violate 35 U.S.C. 156(a)(2), which provides that a Waxman-Hatch extension may be given provided "the term of the patent has never been extended under subsection (e)(1) of this section."

§ 4.05 PATENT INFRINGEMENT LAW

[A] Testing to Obtain FDA Approval

Page 4-99. Insert after the first case citation in footnote 412:

; *see also Amgen, Inc. v. Hoechst Marion Roussel, Inc.*, 3 F. Supp. 2d 104 (D. Mass. 1998) (applying broad reading to a pharmaceutical patent case).

[B] Seeking Approval Prior to Patent Expiration

Page 4-101. Add after the first citation in footnote 418:

While the statute by its terms says that the filing is an act of infringement, when the issue is litigated the focus is on whether the drug that the ANDA applicant will ultimately seek to market would infringe the patent. *See Bayer AG v. Elan Pharmaceutical Research Corp.*, 212 F.3d 1241, 1248 (Fed. Cir. 2000).

Page 4-101. Replace the text of footnote 418 from the eighth line, beginning with "It is not . . . ," with the following:

After considerable litigation, the Federal Circuit resolved that the filing of an ANDA at FDA's Rockville, Maryland headquarters was not itself a basis for venue in the State of Maryland in a case brought in response to a patent challenge contained in an ANDA. *See Zeneca LTD. v. Mylan Pharmaceutical Inc.*, 173 F.3d 829 (Fed Cir. 1999).

DELAYING APPROVAL OF COMPETITIVE PRODUCTS § 4.05[C]

Page 4-102. Change the first citation in footnote 419 to the following:

35 U.S.C. 271(e)(2).

[C] Remedies

Page 4-103. Add to footnote 427:

Note that there is authority for the proposition that a jury trial will not be available in a case brought under this provision. *Tegal Corp. v. Tokyo Electron America Inc.*, 257 F.3d 1331, 1341 (Fed. Cir. 2001) ("a defendant, asserting only affirmative defenses and no counterclaims, does not have a right to a jury trial in a patent infringement suit if the only remedy sought by the plaintiff-patentee is an injunction."); *Pfizer Inc. v. Novopharm Ltd.*, 2001 WL 477163 (N.D. Ill. May 3, 2001) (holding that neither party is entitled to a jury trial in an action under § 271(e)(2) predicated solely on the filing of a Paragraph IV ANDA). If the defendant counterclaims for invalidity, district courts have both granted and denied jury trials. *Compare Glaxo Group Ltd. v. Apotex, Inc.*, 2001 WL 1246628 (N.D. Ill. Oct. 16, 2001) (ruling that where invalidity is raised as a counterclaim there is no right to a jury trial, as suits under § 271(e)(2) are inherently equitable) with *Warner-Lambert Co. v. Purepac Pharm. Co.*, 2001 WL 883232 (D.N.J. Mar. 30, 2001) (holding that defendant in a suit under § 271(e)(2) is entitled to a jury trial on its counterclaim of invalidity and non-infringement) and *Hoechst Marion Roussel, Inc. v. Par Pharm. Inc.*, 1996 WL 468593 (D.N.J. 1996) (granting jury trial demand in action under § 271(a) for declaratory judgment of patent invalidity).

CHAPTER 5
PUBLIC AVAILABILITY OF NDA DATA

§ 5.01 SAFETY AND EFFECTIVENESS DATA

Page 5-4. Replace the last two sentences of footnote 7 with the following:

In *Public Citizen Health Research Group v. FDA*, 185 F.3d 898 (D.C. Cir. 1999), the court held that Section 505(l) does not apply to data from INDs that have been abandoned. It thus overturned the decision of a District Court that had found that provision applicable to the data in the INDs in question and had gone on to find that "extraordinary circumstances" required a showing greater than the substantial competitive harm that is sufficient to prevent disclosures of confidential information under "Exemption 4" of the Freedom of Information Act, 5 U.S.C. 552(b)(4).

Page 5-4. Change the first sentence of the first full paragraph and its footnote to read:

In the absence of extraordinary circumstances, the FDA will release, if requested, any safety and effectiveness data in a BLA or in an ANDA when the Agency issues the approval of that application.[9]

[9] 21 C.F.R. 601.51(e)(1) (2002) (BLAs); 21 C.F.R. 314.430(f)(6) (2002) (ANDAs). It is more likely that the safety and effectiveness data in a BLA will ultimately be released than it is for NDA data, apparently because of the expectation that BLA data cannot be used to support approval of a generic product.

CHAPTER 6
POTENTIAL FOR GOVERNMENT COMPENSATION OF INNOVATORS

Page 6-1. Add at the end of the first paragraph:

The issue, in fact, assumes new relevance as Congress may be asked to consider a change in the law that would allow approvals of generic versions of drugs approved under biologic license applications.[2.1] Such a change in the law would raise the types of issues discussed here. Similarly, an unconstitutional takings analysis is directly relevant to the controversy over FDA's interpretation of the law to permit applicants submitting so-called 505(b)(2) NDAs to rely on data submitted by other applicants.[2.2]

[2.1] *See* Chapter 13 in this supplement, *infra.*
[2.2] *See* Section 3.05[A][3] of the main volume.

Page 6-2. Add to footnote 6:

For a discussion of the issue of taking trade secrets and an analysis of the *Monsanto* decision as it applies in situations in which revealing the trade secret was a condition of marketing, see *Philip Morris, Inc. v. Reilly*, Nos. 00-2425, 00-2449, 2001 WL 1215365 (1st Cir. Oct. 16, 2001).

Page 6-5. Change the last paragraph on this page to read:

The Waxman-Hatch Act was enacted in 1984, and no suit alleging an uncompensated taking resulting from the approval of an ANDA has ever been brought. In the case of an innovator that submitted data in its NDA prior to the 1984 amendments, however, such a suit is still theoretically possible. Moreover, as noted at the outset of this chapter, this issue may well be litigated should Congress, or the FDA without new authority from Congress, seek to approve generic versions of products first approved under biologics license applications.[19] Also, as noted, the issue of compensation for taking of intellectual property is raised by FDA's interpretation of the law with respect to 505(b)(2) NDAs. This intersection of constitutional law with the FDCA thus remains a live issue.

[19] Or first approved, prior to the development of biologic license applications, under "product license applications," the type of application that had previously been used to approve products under the Public Health Service Act.

Chapter 7
THE ORPHAN DRUG AMENDMENTS

§ 7.01 "ORPHAN DRUG" DESIGNATION

Page 7-2. Change footnote 5, after the initial citation, to read:

A list of orphan drug designations and of orphan drugs approved for marketing may be found on the Internet on ⟨www.fda.gov/orphan/designat/list.htm⟩.

Page 7-6. Change the second citation in footnote 23 to read:

FDCA § 526(c), 21 U.S.C. 360bb(c).

§ 7.02 ORPHAN DRUG EXCLUSIVITY

Page 7-7. Add to footnote 29:

In *Sigma-Tau Pharmaceuticals, Inc. v. Schwetz*, 288 F.3d 141 (4th Cir. 2002), plaintiff argued unsuccessfully that exclusivity should bar approval of a generic that was not labeled for the indication covered by exclusivity because circumstances made it obvious that the generic drug would be used for that indication. This decision underscores the limited incentive that the statute provides to develop orphan indications for a drug that may be marketed for other uses.

Page 7-8. Add to carryover footnote 30:

In *Baker Norton Pharmaceuticals, Inc. v. United States Food and Drug Administration*, 132 F. Supp. 2d 30 (D.D.C. 2001), the court rejected plaintiff's argument that the term "drug" means product and not, as FDA has interpreted the term, active moiety. Plaintiff had argued that exclusivity would block only another company's version of the same drug product and that a second company's product should be considered different if there was a functional difference between the two products. 132 F. Supp. at 37.

Pages 7-9 to 7-10. Change the carryover sentence to read:

FDA, in its regulations, decided to define the term "same drug" for purposes of this statute differently for small and large molecules.

Page 7-10. Insert footnote 37.1 callout in the third line of the first full paragraph:

... a "significant therapeutic advantage."[37.1]

[37.1] 21 C.F.R. 316.3(b)(3).

Page 7-10. Add to footnote 38:

A March 2002 FDA decision to approve Serono's version of beta-interferon despite exclusivity accorded to Biogen's beta-interferon product provides FDA guidance on several issues. Serono's product used a different dosage regimen than Biogen's and FDA, on the basis of a head-to-head trial, concluded that Serono's drug showed greater efficacy. In approving that drug, FDA concluded that clinical superiority could be shown by increased effectiveness and adequate (as opposed to "at least equal") safety or increased safety and adequate (as opposed to "at least equal") effectiveness, Memorandum from Marlene Haffner, M.D. to Jay Siegel, M.D., "Office of Orphan Products Development (OOPD) Analysis of Exclusivity Issues Raised in the Serono BLA for Rebif" at 3 (Mar. 7, 2002) (copy in Appendix 86). FDA noted that this approval was the first to break exclusivity on the basis of effectiveness and the first to rely on a head-to-head trial. *Id.* at 2. This approval also illustrated FDA's view that superior efficacy in one parameter is sufficient to show clinical superiority without a showing of superiority (or even that the drugs are comparable) with respect to other efficacy parameters. Memorandum from C. Rask et al to BLA STN 103780/2 File, "Comparative Study of Rebif to Avonex and Orphan Exclusivity" at 4 (March 7, 2002). The author's law firm represented Serono in its interactions with FDA on this matter.

Page 7-11. Change the second sentence on this page to read:

It can be argued that the resolution of the problem does not satisfy due process.

CHAPTER 8
DEBARMENT

§ 8.02 OVERVIEW

Page 8-2. Change the first sentence of footnote 2 to read:

The statute as enacted, Pub. L. No. 102-282, 106 Stat. 149 (1992), amended the Federal Food, Drug, and Cosmetic Act by adding FDCA Sections 306-308, 21 U.S.C. 335a 335c, by amending Section 505(j), 21 U.S.C. 355(j), and by adding new subsections (bb)-(ee) to Section 201, 21 U.S.C. 321.

§ 8.03 DEBARMENT

[B] Mandatory Debarment of Individuals

Page 8-5. Change the first sentence of footnote 15 and its accompanying citation to read:

The definition of "drug products" specifically includes not only drugs, but also animal drugs and drugs regulated under the biologics provision of the Public Health Service Act, FDCA Section 201(dd), 21 U.S.C. 321(dd).

Page 8-7. Change the last citation in carryover footnote 23 to read:

Landgraf v. USI Film Products, 511 U.S. 244, 280 (1994).

Page 8-7. Change footnote 25 to read:

FDCA Section 306(b)(2)(A)(i)(II), 21 U.S.C. 335a(b)(2)(A)(i)(II).

Page 8-7. Change the second sentence of footnote 26 to read:

Court decisions have accepted FDA's position. *See Bae v. Shalala*, 44 F.3d 489, 495 (7th Cir. 1995) (referring to statute as excluding individuals

§ 8.03[D] **GENERIC AND INNOVATOR DRUGS**

"with prior felony convictions"). *Compare DiCola v. Food and Drug Administration*, 77 F.3d 504, 506 n.* (D.C. Cir. 1996) (concluding that argument that the statute does not apply retroactively had been waived).

Page 8-7. Change footnote 27 to read:

59 Fed. Reg. at 55671-72; 59 Fed. Reg. 62399, 62401 (Dec. 5, 1994) (debarment of Atul Shah). Courts have agreed with FDA's position. *See, e.g., DiCola v. Food and Drug Administration*, 77 F.3d 506-07; *Bae v. Shalala*, 44 F.3d 492-93.

[D] Permissive Debarment of Individuals

[2] Fraudulent Activity

Page 8-10. Change the last sentence of the first full paragraph and its accompanying footnote to read:

In each case, however, FDA must find, on the basis of the conviction and of other information (which presumably need not be related to the conviction), that the individual has "demonstrated a pattern of conduct sufficient to find that there is reason to believe that such individual may violate requirements under [the Federal Food, Drug, and Cosmetic Act] relating to drug products."[38]

[38] FDCA Section 306(b)(2)(B)(iii), 21 U.S.C. 335a(b)(2)(B)(iii).

[3] Participation in Acts Leading to Conviction

Page 8-10. Change footnote 40 to read:

FDCA Section 306(b)(2)(B)(iii), 21 U.S.C. 335a(b)(2)(B)(iii).

[4] High Managerial Agent

Page 8-11. Change the first sentence of the second paragraph to read:

The term "high managerial agent" is defined by the statute to mean an officer or director of a corporation or association, a partner in a partnership, or any employee or agent of a corporation, association, or partnership whose duties are such that his or her conduct may "fairly be assumed to represent the policy of" the institution.

DEBARMENT § 8.04[A]

Page 8-11. Change the citation in footnote 43 to read:

FDCA Section 201(cc), 21 U.S.C. 321(cc).

[F] **Procedure**

Page 8-14. Change footnote 55 to read:

FDCA Section 306(i), 21 U.S.C. 335a(i).

[G] **Termination of Debarment**

[2] **Termination of Debarment of Individuals**

Page 8-17. Change footnote 65 to read:

FDCA Section 306(d)(4)(C), 21 U.S.C. 335a(d)(4)(C).

[H] **Judicial Review**

Page 8-18. Change footnote 67 to read:

See FDCA Section 306(b)(2)(B)(iii), 21 U.S.C. 335a(b)(2)(B)(iii), discussed in Section 8.03[D][3] of the main volume and this supplement, *supra.*

§ 8.04 **CIVIL PENALTIES**

[A] **Grounds for Imposition of Penalties**

Page 8-20. Change footnote 72 to read:

FDCA Section 201bb, 21 U.S.C. 321(bb).

CHAPTER 9
FDA FRAUD POLICY

§ 9.01 GENERALLY

Page 9-2. Add to footnote 4:

Also useful in understanding the guide is FDA Regulatory Procedures Manual, Chapter 10, Subchapter: Application Integrity Policy (Update No. 1, March 5, 1998). This document can be retrieved on FDA's Web site at ⟨www.fda.gov/ora/compliance_ref/rpm_new2/rpm10aip.html⟩ (visited December, 2002).

§ 9.02 APPLICABILITY AND EFFECT

Page 9-4. Change the first citation in footnote 10 to read:

FDCA Section 308(a)(1), 21 U.S.C. 335c(a)(1)

§ 9.03 ACTIONS REQUIRED

Page 9-5. Change footnote 12 to read:

56 Fed. Reg. 46191, 46200 (Sept. 10, 1991).

Chapter 10
ACCELERATED APPROVALS

§ 10.01 BACKGROUND

Page 10-2. Change the second through fourth sentences of footnote 1 to read:

That policy has been abandoned, and FDA simply classifies all applications as either "priority" or "standard." That classification affects FDA's review time commitments. *See* § 12.06 of the main volume. In 2002, Congress concluded that an application for a "priority countermeasure" should be considered a "priority drug or biological product" for purposes of the FDA performance goals. *See* Pub. L. 107-188, 116 Stat. 594, Section 122(c) (2002).

§ 10.03 EXPEDITED APPROVAL PROCEDURE

Page 10-10. Change the fifth and sixth sentences of the first paragraph to read:

FDA concluded that the statute essentially endorsed its prior efforts and, in September 1998, issued a guidance describing the various agency programs that it believes satisfy the fast track drug development objective of the statute.[34.1] This section will first discuss the 1997 statute in conjunction with the accelerated approval regulations and then, for completeness, will also address the Subpart E regulation procedures.

[34.1] FDA, "Guidance for Industry: Fast Track Drug Development Programs—Designation, Development, and Application Review (September 1998) (Appendix 87 to this supplement).

[A] Fast Track Products

Page 10-10. Add after the last sentence on this page:

In 2002, Congress amended the law further to state that FDA may designate a priority countermeasure to bioterrorism as a "fast track product"

§ 10.03[B]   GENERIC AND INNOVATOR DRUGS

prior to the submission of a request for designation by the sponsor or applicant or of an IND.[35.1] This statute permits the sponsor or applicant to decline such a designation, however.[35.2]

[35.1] Pub. L. 107-188, 116 Stat 594 (2002), Section 122(a).
[35.2] *Id.*

[1] Eligibility

Page 10-11. Change the first sentence of the second paragraph on this page to read:

A fast track product must also "demonstrate the potential to address unmet medical needs for" the life-threatening or serious condition for which it is intended.

[2] Standard of Approval

Page 10-12. Change footnote 46 to read:

21 C.F.R. 314.510 (2002); 21 C.F.R. 601.41 (2002).

Page 10-12. Add to the end of footnote 47:

57 Fed. Reg. 58947 (Dec. 11, 1992).

Page 10-12. Change the first citation in footnote 49 to read:

21 C.F.R. 314.510 (2002); 21 C.F.R. 601.41 (2002).

[B] Subpart E

Page 10-16. Change footnote 66 to read:

FDA references the Subpart E regulations in its guidance issued in response to the 1997 amendment. FDA, Guidance for Industry: Fast Track Drug Development Programs—Designation, Development, and Application Review at 1 (September 1998) (Appendix 87 to this supplement).

Page 10-17. Change the first full sentence on this page to read:

While comments were solicited on these interim rules, no significant changes were made in response to those comments.

Chapter 11
EXPORT AND IMPORT REQUIREMENTS

§ 11.01 INTRODUCTION

Page 11-2. Add after the second sentence of the first paragraph:

In 2000, Congress passed provisions that, though never implemented, were intended to facilitate reimportation into the United States of drugs sold abroad at lower prices.[1.1]

[1.1] Medicine Equity and Drug Safety Act of 2000, Pub. L. No. 106-387 § 745, 114 Stat. 1549A-35, adding to the statute FDCA § 804, 21 U.S.C. 384. As discussed below, this provision would go into effect only upon a certification from the Secretary of Health and Human Services that implementation would be both safe and cost-effective, and the Secretary refused to provide that certification.

§ 11.02 EXPORT REQUIREMENTS

[A] Approved Drugs

Page 11-3. Change the second sentence of the first full paragraph to read:

Congress, in passing the FDA Export Reform and Enhancement Act of 1996,[3] sought to address this problem, and FDA, in late 2001, issued a final rule that clarified the statute's provisions.[3.1]

[3] Pub. L. 104-134, signed Apr. 26, 1996.

[3.1] 66 Fed. Reg. 65429 (Dec. 19, 2001). The final rule implements the notification and recordkeeping requirements of the statute but the preamble discussions of the regulation provide some useful information on FDA's views of other provisions.

Pages 11-3 to 11-4. Replace the carryover paragraph, and its accompanying footnotes, with:

FDA has made clear its position that, if the drug, though sold for exactly the purposes approved in the United States, is labeled in the lan-

§ 11.02[B] GENERIC AND INNOVATOR DRUGS

guage of, or otherwise to meet the requirements of, a foreign country, it is not to be considered an FDA-approved drug.[5] Nevertheless, in accordance with the above-cited statutory provision, such a product may be legally exported, as long as it is sold only for the FDA-approved uses and is "accompanied" by the FDA-approved label. FDA clarified that it does not require the FDA-approved label to be affixed to each exported product but simply to be included in the export shipment.[6]

[5] 66 Fed. Reg. 65432.
[6] 66 Fed. Reg. 65437.

[B] Unapproved Drugs

[1] Approval in Country With Advanced Drug Regulatory System

Page 11-7. Change the second sentence of the second paragraph and footnote 22 to read:

FDA interprets this provision as requiring a notice when the first export to any favored country (which FDA refers to as a "listed" country), occurs, with no need to submit an additional notification for exports to other listed countries.[22] FDA states that the notice may identify the listed country to which the export is made but is not required to do so.[22.1]

[22] 66 Fed. Reg. 65441-65442.
[22.1] 21 C.F.R. 1.101(d)(iv), 66 Fed. Reg. 65448. FDA notes that, if the name of the listed country is not identified in the notification and FDA is required to communicate with the authorities in the countries to which the drug is exported, it will have to inspect the exporting company to obtain that information. 66 Fed. Reg. 65440. FDA thus seems to encourage identification of the listed country, though it acknowledges that the notification must be submitted only with respect to export to the first such country. 66 Fed. Reg. 65441. That leaves open the question of whether, if a company does decide to include the name of the listed country, it would then be required to submit another notification if it began export to an additional listed country.

Page 11-7. Change footnote 23 to read:

66 Fed. Reg. 65442.

Page 11-7. Change footnote 24 to read:

21 C.F.R. 1.101(d)(iv)(4), 66 Fed. Reg. 65448.

EXPORT AND IMPORT REQUIREMENTS § 11.02[B]

Page 11-7. Add after the first sentence of the third paragraph:

FDA has required that such records include the product's trade name, its generic name, a description of its strength and dosage form and lot or control number, the consignee's name and address, and the date of export and the quantity of drug exported.[25.1]

[25.1] 21 C.F.R. 1.101(e), 66 Fed. Reg. 65448. The records are to be kept at the site from which the drug was exported or manufactured and maintained for the same period that records subject to good manufacturing practice or quality systems regulations applicable to the product must be maintained. The records must be made available to FDA during an FDA inspection.

[3] Prerequisites for All Exports of Unapproved Human Drugs

Page 11-11. Add to footnote 37:

Records demonstrating compliance with this provision must be maintained and made available to FDA inspectors upon request. *See* 21 C.F.R. 1.101(b), 66 Fed. Reg. 65448. Note that records demonstrating lack of conflict with the laws of the importing country are required, by the regulation, to include either a letter from an appropriate foreign government agency stating that the product has marketing approval from the foreign government or does not conflict with that country's laws, or a notarized certification by a responsible company official in the United States that the product does not conflict with the laws of the importing country, including a statement that acknowledges criminal liability for any false certification. 21 C.F.R. 1.101(b)(2). This provision is, at the time of this writing, subject to a stay request. FDA has stated that a drug would not be considered to be sold or offered for sale in domestic commerce if the drug for export is labeled for a use not approved in the United States or is labeled solely in a foreign language with labeling that has not been approved by FDA. 66 Fed. Reg. 65437.

Page 11-11. Add at the end of footnote 38:

Note that, as respects animal drugs, the determination of imminent hazard may be made by the Secretary of Agriculture. *Id.*

[4] Export of Unapproved Animal Drugs

Page 11-12. Change the last sentence to read:

FDA has stated that it "is working on" an interpretation of what would be considered a banned animal drug, but has not, as of this writing stated its position on that point.[45.1]

[45.1] 63 Fed. Reg. 32219, 32222 (June 12, 1998).

[C] Drugs for Investigational Use

Page 11-12. Add to footnote 46:

FDA has proposed to amend this regulation. 67 Fed. Reg. 41642 (June 19, 2002).

Page 11-13. Change footnote 47 to read:

FDA has taken the position that export to any country other than the 25 favored countries, or transshipment through a favored country to a country not on the list, is not permitted by this provision, except that export to a principal investigator in a favored country would be permitted even if that investigator would then administer the investigational new drug in a country not on the favored country list. *See* 67 Fed. Reg. 41642, 41643-44 (June 19, 2002).

Page 11-13. Replace the last sentence in the carryover paragraph, and the accompanying footnote, with:

There is no requirement that the exporter notify FDA about the export, though it must maintain records of the export that would be subject to FDA inspection.[49]

[49] 21 C.F.R. 1.101(e), 66 Fed. Reg. 65429, 65448 (Dec. 19, 2001). *See also* 67 Fed. Reg. 41642, 41644 (June 19, 2002) (discussion of issue in preamble to proposed revision of 21 C.F.R. 312.110).

Page 11-13. Change footnote 51 to read:

21 C.F.R. 312.110(b)(2) (2002). Note that FDA has proposed to change this regulation to eliminate the requirement of FDA authorization prior to export. The proposed substitute provision would require the person seek-

EXPORT AND IMPORT REQUIREMENTS § 11.02[D]

ing to export an unapproved new drug for investigational use without an IND to a non-favored country to send a written certification to FDA at the time the drug is first exported that would describe the drug being exported, and identify the country or countries to which it is being exported. *See* proposed 21 C.F.R. 312.110(b)(4), 67 Fed. Reg. 41642, 41648 (June 19, 2002). This proposed regulation sets out the detailed requirements to justify export.

Page 11-13. Add to footnote 52:

Note, however, that FDA has proposed to change this regulation, 67 Fed. Reg. 41642 (June 19, 2002) and that change would, among other things, eliminate the requirement of prior FDA approval for such exports.

[D] Export of Unfinished Drugs

Page 11-14. Change footnote 54 to read:

FDA has acknowledged this fact, after initially proposing to require notification to FDA of such exports, *see* 66 Fed. Reg. 65429, 65441 (Dec. 19, 2001).

Page 11-14. Add at the end of footnote 55:

See 66 Fed. Reg. 65441 (discussion of FDA's view that, upon approval in one of the favored countries, notice should be provided to FDA of export under FDCA § 802(b)).

Page 11-14. Insert after the first full paragraph:

There is a special provision for partially processed biological products that allows their export with no restrictions so long as, at the time of export, they are not in a form applicable to patient use, are not intended for sale in the United States, and are intended for further manufacture, and so long as they are manufactured in conformance with good manufacturing practices or meet analogous international standards and satisfy the requirements for export applicable to FDA-regulated products generally.[55.1]

[55.1] Public Health Service Act § 351(h), 42 U.S.C. 262(h), incorporating the requirements of FDCA § 801(a)(1), 21 U.S.C. 381(a)(1). Additional recordkeeping requirements

§ 11.03[A]   GENERIC AND INNOVATOR DRUGS

for partially processed biological products are set out in 21 C.F.R. 1.101(c), 66 Fed. Reg. 65448.

§ 11.03   IMPORTS

[A]   Generally

Page 11-15. Add at the end of the section:

Note, however, that Congress in the year 2000 passed a bill permitting reimportation of drugs, including prescription drugs, into the United States under specified conditions. That law was conditioned on a demonstration to Congress by the Secretary of Health and Human Services that its implementation would be both safe and cost-effective, a demonstration that Secretaries in two successive administrations have declined to provide, leaving a statutory provision that has no effect.[59.1]

[59.1] The Medicine Equity and Drug Safety Act of 2000, Pub. L. No. 106-387 § 745, 114 Stat. 1549A-35, added to the laws FDCA § 804, 21 U.S.C. 384. As that provision required the demonstration by the Secretary referred to in the text, FDCA § 804(l), 21 U.S.C. 384(l), the law has no effect whatsoever. However, as of this writing there are continuing attempts to resuscitate the concept of reimportation of drugs manufactured in the United States, at least from Canada.

CHAPTER 12
PRESCRIPTION DRUG USER FEES

§ 12.01 INTRODUCTION

Page 12-2. Replace the first paragraph on this page with the following:

The Public Health Security and Bioterrorism Preparedness and Response Act of 2002 extended for five years the drug user fee provisions first enacted into law in 1992.[1]

[1] *See* Prescription Drug User Fee Act of 1992 Pub. L. 102-571 (1992), amended and extended for five years by the Food and Drug Administration Modernization Act of 1997, Pub. L. 105-115 (1997). The latest five-year extension began with the start of the fiscal year on October 1, 2002. Pub. L. 107-188, Section 508 (2002). The user fee provisions have been nearly universally considered a success. The 2002 statute modified the earlier legislation somewhat.

Page 12-2. Change the third sentence of the second paragraph to read:

Instead it is found in letters to congressional leaders, the most recent of which is a letter from Secretary of Health and Human Services Tommy Thompson.[2]

[2] This letter, and an incorporated document entitled "PDUFA Reauthorization Performance Goals and Procedures," are Appendices 88 and 89 to this supplement. The previous statement of goals is in Appendix 75 to the main volume.

Page 12-2. Delete the citation at the end of footnote 3.

§ 12.02 TYPES OF USER FEES

[A] Drug Application Fees

[1] Applications Affected

Page 12-3. Change footnote 7 to read:

FDCA Section 735(1), 21 U.S.C. 379g(1).

§ 12.02[A]   **GENERIC AND INNOVATOR DRUGS**

Page 12-3. Change the second citation in footnote 10 to read:

FDCA Section 736(c)(4), 21 U.S.C. 379h(c)(4)

Page 12-3. Change the second citation in footnote 11 to the following, and add the following text:

FDCA Section 736(c)(4), 21 U.S.C. 379h(c)(4). The former provision states that the lower fee shall be half of the amount of the higher fee referred to in the text.

Page 12-4. Replace the first full paragraph of the text, and its accompanying footnotes, with the following:

    Any drug that is designated as an "orphan drug"[13] is entitled to an exemption from the user fee requirement unless that application includes an indication for other than a rare disease or condition.[14] Note that a prior provision, which exempted from user fees supplements proposing to include a new indication for use in pediatric populations, has now been revoked.[15]

   [13] *See* FDCA Section 526(a)(1), 21 U.S.C. 360bb(a)(1). See Chapter 7 of the main volume for discussion of the Orphan Drug Amendments.
   [14] FDCA Section 736(a)(1)(E), 21 U.S.C. 379h(a)(1)(E).
   [15] The Best Pharmaceuticals for Children Act of 2001, Pub. L. 107-109, § 5, repealed this exemption.

Page 12-4. Change footnote 18 to read:

FDCA Section 736(a)(1)(F), 21 U.S.C. 379h(a)(1)(F).

[2] Amount of Fees

Page 12-5. Change the first paragraph, and its accompanying footnotes, to read:

    The statute identifies total revenue to be generated by user fees for fiscal years 2003 through 2007, dividing those totals essentially evenly in each of those years among the three types of fees—application/supplement, establishment, and product.[22] The amounts included in the statute are then to be adjusted to reflect the greater of the total percentage change in the Commerce Price Index for all urban consumers for the 12-month

PRESCRIPTION DRUG USER FEES § 12.02[B]

period ending June 30 of the previous fiscal year, or the total percentage change for the previous fiscal year in basic pay for federal employees.[23] A further adjustment is then made based on analysis of the workload of the agency in reviewing applications.[24] The FDA then establishes the application, product, and establishment fees based on the revenue amounts as adjusted.[25] For fiscal year 2003, the fee is $533,400 for applications requiring clinical data, and the fee is $266,700 for those not requiring clinical data and for supplements requiring clinical data.[26]

[22] FDCA Section 736(b), 21 U.S.C. 379h(b).
[23] FDCA Section 736(c)(1), 21 U.S.C. 379h(c)(1).
[24] FDCA Section 736(c)(2), 21 U.S.C. 379h(c)(2). For fiscal year 2007, there is a potential additional adjustment to provide an operating reserve for the first three months of fiscal year 2008. FDCA Section 736(c)(3), 21 U.S.C. 379h(c)(3).
[25] FDCA Section 736(c)(4), 21 U.S.C. 379h(c)(4). Establishment and product fees are discussed in the main volume in subsequent sections.
[26] 67 Fed. Reg. 50448 (Aug. 2, 2002).

[B] Prescription Drug Establishment Fee

Page 12-7. Delete from lines 6 to 7 of the first full paragraph:

large volume parenteral drug products approved before September 1, 1992

Page 12-7. Change sentences 2 through 4 of the third full paragraph to read:

That calculation is to provide a revenue amount specified in the statute, as adjusted for inflation and agency workload.[37] For the year 2003, FDA calculated that there would be 354 fee-paying establishments, and determined that the fee per establishment should be $209,900.[38]

[37] FDCA Section 736(b), (c), 21 U.S.C. 379h(b), (c).
[38] 67 Fed. Reg. 50448, 50450 (Aug. 2, 2002).

Pages 12-7 to 12-8. Delete the carryover paragraph and its accompanying footnote.

Page 12-8. Change the citation at the end of footnote 41 to read:

FDCA Section 510(j)(2), 21 U.S.C. 360(j)(2).

§ 12.02[C] GENERIC AND INNOVATOR DRUGS

[C] Prescription Drug Product Fee

Page 12-8. Change the second sentence of the first paragraph under this heading to read:

The fee is to be paid on or before October 1 of each year.

Page 12-8. Change footnote 44 to read:

FDCA Section 736(a)(3)(B), 21 U.S.C. 379h(a)(3)(B). The reference to abbreviated antibiotic applications and pre–Waxman-Hatch ANDAs was first added to the law in the 1997 reauthorization. Note that there should not, under current law, be BLAs for products covered by ANDAs. The 2002 amendments added a reference to an exemption for a drug listed in the FDA list of approved drugs with a potency described in terms of per 100 ml, presumably the result of successful special pleading by the manufacturer of a particular product.

Page 12-8 to 12-9. Change the carryover sentences to the end of the paragraph, and the accompanying footnotes, to read:

The fee is calculated by FDA to produce revenue amounts identified by the statute, and is subject to adjustment for inflation and workload changes.[45] For 2003, FDA set a product fee of $32,400 per product.[46] The fees would be expected to rise each year both because of adjustments for inflation and because the statute, for years 2003 through 2006, provides for an increased total amount to be earned by FDA each year. (The amounts for years 2006 and 2007 are the same.)

[45] FDCA Section 736(b), (c), 21 U.S.C. 379h(b), (c).
[46] 67 Fed. Reg. 50448, 50450 (Aug. 2, 2002).

§ 12.03 WAIVERS

Page 12-9. Delete the phrase numbered "(4)" in the first full paragraph and renumber phrase "(5)" as "(4)."

Page 12-9. Add to footnote 47:

In 2002, Congress deleted a provision that allowed a waiver for an NDA or supplement when charging the fee would be inequitable because a 505(b)(2) NDA filed by another applicant for a product containing the

PRESCRIPTION DRUG USER FEES § 12.05

same active ingredient could not be assessed fees because the application was not for a new molecular entity or new indication. Pub. L. 107-188, Section 504(d)(1)(B), (C). *Compare* FDCA Section 736(d)(1)(D) (2001).

Page 12-10. Change the second citation in footnote 51 to read:

See FDCA Section 736(a)(1)(D), (F), 21 U.S.C. 379h(a)(1)(D), (F).

Page 12-10. Delete all but the first two sentences of the first paragraph and the accompanying footnotes.

§ 12.05 CONDITION FOR CONTINUATION OF FEES

Page 12-10. Change the last two lines on this page to read:

Congress and the administration, as well as the pharmaceutical manufacturers who supported this legislation in 1992, 1997, and 2002,

Page 12-11. Change the first two full sentences on this page, and the accompanying footnote, to read:

To assure that that does not happen, the law provides that, if appropriations for salaries and expenses of FDA for a fiscal year (excluding amounts obtained through fees) are not equal to or greater than the amount of appropriations for FDA for fiscal year 1997 multiplied by an inflation adjustment factor, all fees for that year must be refunded.[56] Thus, should a future Congress or administration seek effectively to decrease the budget of FDA that comes from general revenues (by not keeping up with inflation), the fees for that year would have to be refunded.

[56] FDCA Section 736(f)(1), 21 U.S.C. 379h(f)(1). The adjustment factor is described in FDCA Section 735(8), 21 U.S.C. 379g(8).

Page 12-11. Change the first sentence in the first full paragraph, and its accompanying footnote, to read:

The total fees for a fiscal year may not exceed the total cost for that fiscal year for the resources allocated for the review of human drug applications.[57]

[57] FDCA Section 736(c)(5), 21 U.S.C. 379h(c)(5).

§ 12.06 GENERIC AND INNOVATOR DRUGS

Page 12-11. Add after the last sentence of the first full paragraph:

The 2002 amendments added to the description of the types of activities considered part of the process for the review of human drug applications specific reference to collecting, developing, and reviewing safety information on a drug during a period of time after approval, not to exceed three years.[59.1] FDA has interpreted this language as an endorsement of its use of user fee funds for risk management activities.

[59.1] FDCA Section 735(6)(F), 21 U.S.C. 379(g)(6)(F).

§ 12.06 THE QUID PRO QUO: FDA COMMITMENTS

Page 12-11. Change the paragraph under this heading, and its accompanying footnote, to read:

The user fee legislation was passed in 1992, and extended in 1997 and 2002, in exchange for a commitment from FDA to use the revenues to achieve specific goals in speeding the review of drug product approval applications. The 2002 "performance goals" were outlined in an enclosure to letters to Congress from Secretary of Health and Human Services Thompson.[60]

[60] Letters to Chairman and Ranking Minor Members of Committee on Health, Education, Labor, and Pensions, United States Senate, Committee on Energy and Commerce, Houses of Representatives from Tommy Thompson (June 4, 2002). The enclosure appears as Appendix 89 in this supplement.

[A] Application Review

Page 12-12. Replace the entire section, and its accompanying footnotes, with:

FDA in 2002 made commitments with respect to original NDA and BLA submissions and with respect to resubmissions after response letters. The resubmissions were divided into Class 1 resubmissions, comprising those with relatively straightforward changes, such as final printed labeling, safety update information, etc., and Class 2 resubmissions, which include other items, such as more significant data submissions and information requiring presentation to an advisory committee.[61] With respect to original NDAs and BLAs, FDA agreed to review and act on 90 percent of

— priority applications within six months of receipt;
— standard applications within ten months of receipt;

— Class 1 resubmitted applications within two months of receipt;
— Class 2 resubmitted applications within six months of receipt.

With respect to efficacy supplements (supplements containing efficacy information for which a new indication is sought), FDA agreed to review and act on 90 percent of:

— priority efficacy supplements within six months of receipt;
— standard efficacy supplements within ten months of receipt.

With respect to resubmitted efficacy supplements, the commitments change somewhat from year to year. In each year 90 percent of Class 2 resubmitted efficacy supplements are to be reviewed and acted on within six months of receipt. For Class 1 resubmitted efficacy supplements, the time permitted for FDA review and action on 90 percent of these supplements decreases from six months in fiscal year 2003, to four months in fiscal years 2004-2006, to two months in fiscal year 2007. In addition, a commitment is made to act on 30 percent of such applications within two months in 2003, 50 percent in 2004, 70 percent in 2005 and 80 percent in 2006, until the 90 percent goal is reached in 2007.

In addition, during each year FDA commits to reviewing and acting upon 90 percent of manufacturing supplements within six months of receipt and 90 percent of manufacturing supplements requiring prior approval within four months of receipt.[62]

[61] *See* Enclosure (Appendix 89) at 16.
[62] *Id.* at 1-3.

[B] Other Performance Goals

Page 12-13. Change footnote 63 to read:

Id. at 4-5.

Page 12-13. Change footnote 64 to read:

Id. at 5.

Page 12-13. Change the last sentence in the first full paragraph, and the accompanying footnote, to read:

FDA commits to provide answers to 90 percent of requests for appeals within 30 days of receipt of the written appeal.[65]

§ 12.06[B]   GENERIC AND INNOVATOR DRUGS

[65] *Id.* at 5.

Page 12-13. Change footnote 66 to read:

Id. at 6-7.

Page 12-13. Change footnote 67 to read:

Id. at 7.

Page 12-13. Change the last sentence in the second full paragraph to read:

In addition, FDA agrees to institute pilot programs to determine whether review letters for pre-submitted "reviewable units" of NDAs or BLAs would expedite the process or whether frequent scientific feedback and interactions during drug development would expedite the process.[68]

[68] *Id.* at 7-10.

Pages 12-13 to 12-14. Change the carryover paragraph and its accompanying footnotes to read:

In addition, FDA in this set of performance goals notes that user fees will be used to evaluate post-approval risk management studies or other measures, and commits to produce final guidance documents on risk assessment, risk management, and pharmacovigilance by the end of fiscal year 2004.[69] The goals also provide for the potential engagement by FDA of expert consultants, who may be nominated by the application sponsor, to participate in the agency's review of protocols for clinical studies for biotechnology products.[70] FDA commits to notify the sponsor, by letter, telephone, facsimile, or secure e-mail, of substantive deficiencies identified in the initial filings of an NDA, BLA, or efficacy supplement within 14 calendar days after the 60-day filing date of the application, with a goal of achieving such notifications within that time that increases from 50 percent of applications in 2003 to 70 percent in 2004 and 90 percent in fiscal years 2005 through 2007.[71]

[69] *Id.* at 10-11.
[70] *Id.* at 11-12.
[71] *Id.* at 12.

Chapter 13
FDA REGULATION OF BIOLOGIC DRUGS

§ 13.01   What is a Biologic?
§ 13.02   Biologic Approval Requirements
§ 13.03   Generic Biologics?

§ 13.01   WHAT IS A BIOLOGIC?

The biologics approval process has assumed increased importance in recent years, in part because many, though not all, products of biotechnology are regulated as biologics. Unfortunately it is not always simple to determine which products FDA will regulate as biologics. FDA has said that, as a general rule, biologics, in contrast to chemically synthesized drugs, are derived from living sources, such as humans, animals, plants and microorganisms.[1] Moreover, FDA says that most biologic products "are complex mixtures that are not easily identified or characterized."[2] But some products derived from living sources that are complex mixtures are not approved as biologics.[3]

The statutory definition states that: "'biological product' means a virus, therapeutic serum, toxin, antitoxin, vaccine, blood, blood component or derivative, allergenic product, *or analogous product*, or arsphenamine or derivative of arsphenamine (or any other trivalent organic arsenic

---

[1] *See* CBER, *Frequently Asked Questions*, ⟨http://www.FDA.gov/cber/faq.htm⟩ (visited July 10, 2002).
[2] *Id.*
[3] Conjugated estrogens is a prominent example.

compound), applicable to the prevention, treatment, or cure of a disease or condition of human beings."[4] What then is an "analogous product"? FDA's regulation explains that products (1) are analogous to viruses if they are prepared from or with a virus or an actually or potentially infectious agent; (2) are analogous to therapeutic serum if composed of whole blood or plasma or if they contain some organic constituent or product "other than a hormone or an amino acid," derived from whole blood, plasma, or serum; or (3) are analogous to a toxin or antitoxin, if intended, "irrespective of its source of origin," to prevent, treat, or cure a disease or injury through a specific immune process.[5] The quoted language highlights two aspects of the definition that are not intuitively apparent: Hormones and amino acids are not approved as biologics; drugs acting through a specific immune process are biologics. In each case, how the product is derived is irrelevant. Other examples of biologic-like drugs that are approved under Section 505 NDAs instead of BLAs may be found in an Inter-Center Agreement available on FDA's Web site.[6]

As would be expected, there are sometimes differences in view as to whether particular products are to be regulated as biologics or as non-biologic drugs. The agency does have a procedure for resolving disputes as to proper jurisdiction.[7] Sometimes, however, by choosing which Center to start with, companies can effectively steer a product that might fall under either definition to the regulatory framework that they desire.

§ 13.02 BIOLOGIC APPROVAL REQUIREMENTS

A biological product can be either a drug or a medical device. Depending on how it is classified, the testing of the biologic prior to approval is regulated under either the drug or medical device provisions of the

---

[4] Public Health Service Act, Section 351(i), 42 U.S.C. 262(i) (emphasis added) (Appendix 90 to this supplement). The definition was changed in 1997 and adds an explicit reference to "analogous product" to statutory language derived from the prior statute. *See* Pub. L. 105-115, Sec. 123(d) (1997). FDA and its predecessor agency had previously included such products by practice and regulation.

[5] 21 C.F.R. 600.3(h)(5).

[6] The decision whether a product will be reviewed under an NDA or a BLA is made in accordance with an InterCenter Agreement first published in 1991. InterCenter Agreement Between the Center for Drug Evaluation and Research and the Center for Biologics Evaluation and Research, (Oct. 25, 1991), *available at* ⟨www.fda.gov/oc/ombudsman/drug-bio.htm⟩.

[7] 21 C.F.R. 3.7 (2002).

FDA REGULATION OF BIOLOGIC DRUGS § 13.02

Federal Food, Drug, and Cosmetic Act.[8] Biologics, however, are approved by the Food and Drug Administration under Section 351 of the Public Health Service Act.[9] That approval is obtained by submission of a biologics approval application ("BLA").[10]

As a practical matter, the requirements for showing the safety and effectiveness of a biologic drug are similar, if not identical, to those that apply to non-biologic drugs approved under Federal Food, Drug, and Cosmetic Act Section 505(b)(1).[11] Thus, while the statutory provision applicable to biologics refers to the requirement that the product be "safe, pure, and potent,"[12] FDA has interpreted that provision as requiring the type of evidence of safety and effectiveness, including adequate and well-controlled investigations showing the product's effectiveness, that are required by statute for non-biologic drugs.[13]

There are, however, important differences between the regulation of biologics and that of non-biologic drugs. Those differences are related in part to history[14] and in part to the physical differences between most biologic products and the most common type of non-biologic drug. First, for biologic products, there is a greater regulatory focus on the process by which manufacture occurs. Indeed, until recently, a separate approval

---

[8] For drugs, FDCA Section 505(i), 21 U.S.C. 355(i) (investigational new drug applications ("INDs")); for devices, FDCA Section 520(g), 21 U.S.C. 360j(g) (investigational device exemptions ("IDEs")). *See* Public Health Service Act Section 351(j); 42 U.S.C. 262(j). Note, however, that the investigation is regulated by the FDA Center (Center for Drug Evaluation and Research or Center for Biologics Evaluation and Research) assigned to approve the marketing application. That Center approves the IND or IDE, as the case may be.

[9] 42 U.S.C. 262. All biologics must be approved before marketing. Biologics for veterinary use are approved by the Department of Agriculture rather than the FDA. *See* 21 U.S.C. 154.

[10] 21 C.F.R. 601.2 (2002).

[11] *Compare* 21 C.F.R. 314.50 (2002) (NDAs) *with* 21 C.F.R. 601.25 (BLAs).

[12] 42 U.S.C. 262(a)(2)(B)(i)(I).

[13] *Compare* 21 C.F.R. 314.126 (2002) (describing adequate and well-controlled investigation requirement for NDAs) *with* 21 C.F.R. 601.25(d)(2) (2002) (discussing BLA requirements and incorporating 21 C.F.R. 314.126, unless the controlled investigation requirement is waived).

[14] The Biologics Control Act of 1902 preceded the Pure Food and Drug Act, the first federal regulation of chemical drugs, by four years. FDA began to approve biologics only in 1972, when it absorbed the office of the National Institutes of Health, which had regulated biologics until then.

of the establishment at which the biologic is manufactured was required.[15] Second, there is no provision for approval of a generic version of a drug approved under the biologics approval provision without the submission of full safety and effectiveness data.

Many industry observers have, in the past, pointed to a third difference, a perceived divergence in regulatory philosophy between the different centers within the FDA that have been responsible for approving the different types of drugs. The Center for Biologics Evaluation and Research is believed by many (perhaps unfairly) to be more science-oriented than the Center for Drug Evaluation and Research. In September 2002, this perception became less important as FDA announced that responsibility for approval of BLAs for pharmaceutical biologics was being shifted to the latter Center. The announcement said that the transition would occur in 2003. The Biologics Center will continue to be responsible for vaccines.[16]

§ 13.03 GENERIC BIOLOGICS?

The innovator biologic industry has relied on the fact that FDA has never approved a "generic" biologic under the Public Health Service Act. Indeed, some have argued that the term "generic biologic" is a misnomer, since, unlike chemical drugs, it is considered impossible to make a true generic copy of a biologic product.[17] Nevertheless, the generic drug industry has expressed a strong interest in entering into this potentially lucrative market and some in Congress, at this writing, have stated their interest in exploring the concept.[18]

---

[15] FDA amended its biologics regulations in May 1996 to eliminate the former Establishment License Application ("ELA") and Product License Application ("PLA") and to create a combined BLA. The BLA is now referred to in the statute, as amended in 1997. Public Health Service Act Section 351(a)(1)(A), 42 U.S.C. 262(a)(1)(A) (Appendix 91 to this supplement).

[16] FDA News, "FDA to Consolidate Review Responsibilities for New Pharmaceutical Products" (Sept. 6, 2002).

[17] This author has, in fact, made this argument on occasion. Those who argue that there cannot be "generic biologics" sometimes use the term "follow-on biologics" to describe products that purport to copy approved biologics.

[18] For example, Senator Rockefeller has pushed for creation of a commission to study the issue. *See* S 2677, Section 103, 148 Cong. Rec. S 6019 (June 25, 2002). *See also* 148 Cong. Rec. S 7876-78 (Aug. 1, 2002) (statement of Senator Hatch urging FDA to consider mechanisms to approve generic versions of biologics).

§ 13.03

Because under FDCA Section 505 FDA approves some products that would seem to be covered by the statute's biologic definition, some have argued that FDA could simply reclassify a particular biologic as a Section 505 drug in order to permit approval of a generic version pursuant to a "505(b)(2) NDA."[19] Such a reclassification would have dubious support in the statute, and if FDA attempted to approve under Section 505 a generic version of a product approved under a biologic license application, litigation would certainly ensue.

Another approach sometimes discussed would be for FDA to reinterpret the Public Health Service Act to allow generic products to be approved under that Act under a "paper BLA" procedure.[20] However, that would require permitting the sponsor of the generic product to rely on the data in the file of the innovator. The necessary data would include trade secret manufacturing information as well as the results of safety and effectiveness testing. Reliance on the former to approve a generic competitor seems clearly to be an unconstitutional taking of property.[21] Some also may argue that permitting the generic sponsor to rely on the safety and effectiveness testing of the innovator would constitute such a taking, though that argument is complicated by the fact that such tests are generally publicly released upon approval of the innovator.[22] Note that legislative changes to permit "generic biologics" would face the same constitutional issues.

The shift of responsibility for approval of BLAs for pharmaceutical biologics to the FDA's Center for Drug Evaluation and Research may ultimately have important consequences on the question of whether there

---

[19] *See, e.g.*, Generic Pharmaceutical Association (GPhA) materials for Jan. 30, 2002 meeting with FDA, at 16. *See* Section 3.05 of the main volume for a discussion of so-called 505(b)(2) NDAs.

[20] Generic Pharmaceutical Association (GPhA) Materials for Jan. 30, 2002, meeting with FDA at 17.

[21] See Chapter Six of the main volume for discussion of constitutional taking issues.

[22] The policy of releasing such data was justified on the grounds that there could not be a generic version of a biological product that would rely on those data (the "data afford no competitive advantage because, unlike the situation with new drugs, no competitor can utilize it to gain approval for his product," 39 Fed. Reg. 44602, 44641 (Dec. 24, 1974)). There would thus be a good argument that the submission of the data with the understanding that they would be released after approval was conditioned on the expectation that the release of the data would not lead to generic approval and was explicitly not a submission that granted permission to FDA or any member of the public to rely on those data to obtain approval of a competing product.

§ 13.03   GENERIC AND INNOVATOR DRUGS

ever can be "generic biologics." Those administering the Center for Biologics Evaluation and Research are considered supportive of the view that the importance of the manufacturing process for such products makes a "generic biologic" difficult if not impossible.[23] At the same time, the sister Center for Drug Evaluation and Research is believed to be going forward with efforts to facilitate approval of generic versions of the biologic-type products approved under section 505(b)(1).[24] In announcing the shift of responsibilities to the latter Center, FDA said that the move would not affect "current" FDA policy on "generic biologics."[25] Over the longer term, however, that may in fact be its result.

---

[23] *See* FDC Reports, June 4, 2001 at 8 (statement of CBER Director Dr. Zoon). *Cf.* a 1999 statement by the Director of FDA's Office of Orphan Products Development: "The Center for Biologics Evaluation and Research has no means of establishing that two biological products from different sponsors can be expected to have the same effectiveness and safety." Nov. 8, 1999, letter from Marlene Haffner, M.D., to Alan Bennet, Esq. Note that those within FDA who discount the importance of process as a disqualification for generic or follow-on biological products refer to the adoption of so-called "comparability protocols" that have permitted innovator manufacturers to change their process for manufacturing a biological product from the one used in making the product during the clinical trials of the biologic. *See* 21 C.F.R. 601.12(e) (2002). Supporters of the innovator view counter that such changes make sense only when the manufacturer has access to the full manufacturing process for the original product and has a history of experience with a product, neither of which would apply to a potential generic manufacturer. It is also noteworthy that innovator companies seeking to use comparability protocols have found that FDA has required considerable data to support such protocols, so that they are not in fact widely used.

[24] At this writing, guidances are reportedly being prepared for potential generic versions of human growth hormone and human insulin. For an early description of the drug Center's approach, involving potential 505(b)(2) NDAs, *see* "FDA Generic Recombinant Protein Approval Process Will Use 'Paper' NDAs," *Health News Daily* (Mar. 30, 1999).

[25] FDA News, "FDA to Consolidate Review Responsibilities for New Pharmaceutical Products" (Sept. 6, 2002).

APPENDIX 85

Guidance for Industry—Applications
Covered by Section 505(b)(2)

Guidance for Industry

Applications Covered by Section 505(b)(2)

DRAFT GUIDANCE

This guidance document is being distributed for comment purposes only.

Comments and suggestions regarding this draft document should be submitted within 60 days of publication of the *Federal Register* notice announcing the availability of the draft guidance. Submit comments to Dockets Management Branch (HFA-305), Food and Drug Administration, 5630 Fishers Lane, rm. 1061, Rockville, MD 20857. All comments should be identified with the docket number listed in the notice of availability that publishes in the *Federal Register*.

For questions on the content of the draft document contact Khyati Roberts, (301) 594-6779.

U. S. Department of Health and Human Services
Food and Drug Administration
Center for Drug Evaluation and Research (CDER)
October 1999

GENERIC AND INNOVATOR DRUGS

Guidance for Industry

Applications Covered by Section 505(b)(2)

DRAFT GUIDANCE

For additional copies, contact:

Drug Information Branch
Division of Communications Management, HFD-210
Center for Drug Evaluation and Research (CDER)
5600 Fishers Lane
Rockville, MD 20857
(Tel) 301-827-4573
http://www.fda.gov/cder/guidance/index.htm

U.S. Department of Health and Human Services
Food and Drug Administration
Center for Drug Evaluation and Research (CDER)
October 1999

APPENDIX 85

Table of Contents

I. WHAT IS THE PURPOSE OF THIS GUIDANCE? 1

II. WHAT IS A 505(B)(2) APPLICATION? 2
    A. WHAT TYPE OF INFORMATION *CAN* AN APPLICANT RELY ON? 2
    B. WHAT KIND OF APPLICATION CAN BE SUBMITTED AS A 505(B)(2) APPLICATION? 3

III. WHAT ARE SOME EXAMPLES OF 505(B)(2) APPLICATIONS? 4

IV. WHAT CAN'T BE SUBMITTED AS 505(B)(2) APPLICATIONS? 6

V. WHY DOES IT MATTER IF AN NDA IS A 505(B)(2) APPLICATION? 6

VI. PATENT AND EXCLUSIVITY PROTECTIONS THAT COULD AFFECT A 505(B)(2) APPLICATION 7
    A. WHAT TYPE OF PATENT AND/OR EXCLUSIVITY PROTECTION IS A 505(B)(2) APPLICATION ELIGIBLE FOR? 7
    B. WHAT COULD DELAY THE APPROVAL OR FILING OF A 505(B)(2) APPLICATION? 7

VII. WHAT SHOULD BE INCLUDED IN 505(B)(2) APPLICATIONS? 7

REFERENCES 10

GLOSSARY 11

GENERIC AND INNOVATOR DRUGS

Draft - Not for Implementation

GUIDANCE FOR INDUSTRY[1]

Applications Covered by Section 505(b)(2)

I. WHAT IS THE PURPOSE OF THIS GUIDANCE?

This guidance identifies the types of applications that are covered by section 505(b)(2) of the Federal Food, Drug, and Cosmetic Act (the Act). A 505(b)(2) application is a new drug application (NDA) described in section 505(b)(2) of the Act. It is submitted under section 505(b)(1) of the Act and approved under section 505(c) of the Act. This guidance also provides further information and amplification regarding FDA's regulations at 21 CFR 314.54.

Section 505 of the Act describes three types of new drug applications: (1) an application that contains full reports of investigations of safety and effectiveness (section 505(b)(1)); (2) an application that contains full reports of investigations of safety and effectiveness but where at least some of the information required for approval comes from studies not conducted by or for the applicant and for which the applicant has not obtained a right of reference (section 505(b)(2)); and (3) an application that contains information to show that the proposed product is identical in active ingredient, dosage form, strength, route of administration, labeling, quality, performance characteristics, and intended use, among other things, to a previously approved product (section 505(j)). Note that a supplement to an application is a new drug application.

Section 505(b)(2) was added to the Act by the Drug Price Competition and Patent Term Restoration Act of 1984 (Hatch-Waxman Amendments). This provision expressly permits FDA to rely, for approval of an NDA, on data not developed by the applicant. Sections 505(b)(2) and (j) together replaced FDA's *paper NDA policy*, which had permitted an applicant to rely on studies published in the scientific literature to demonstrate the safety and effectiveness of duplicates of certain post-1962 pioneer drug products (see 46 FR 27396, May 19, 1981). Enactment of the generic drug approval provision of the Hatch-Waxman Amendments ended the need for approvals of duplicate drugs through the paper NDA process by permitting approval under 505(j) of duplicates of approved drugs (listed

---

[1]This guidance has been prepared by the Center for Drug Evaluation and Research (CDER) at the Food and Drug Administration. This guidance document represents the Agency's current thinking on the types of applications that may be submitted pursuant to section 505(b)(2) of the Act. It does not create or confer any rights for or on any person and does not operate to bind FDA or the public. An alternative approach may be used if such approach satisfies the requirements of the applicable statute, regulations, or both.

APPENDIX 85

Draft - Not for Implementation

drugs) on the basis of chemistry and bioequivalence data, without the need for evidence from literature of effectiveness and safety. Section 505(b)(2) permits approval of applications other than those for duplicate products and permits reliance for such approvals on literature or on an Agency finding of safety and/or effectiveness for an approved drug product.

Definitions for specific terms used throughout this guidance are given in the Glossary.

II. WHAT IS A 505(B)(2) APPLICATION?

A 505(b)(2) application is one for which one or more of the investigations relied upon by the applicant for approval "were not conducted by or for the applicant and for which the applicant has not obtained a right of reference or use from the person by or for whom the investigations were conducted" (21 U.S.C. 355(b)(2)).

A. What type of information *can* an applicant rely on?

What type of information can an applicant rely on in an application that is based upon studies "not conducted by or for the applicant and for which the applicant has not obtained a right of reference?"

1. Published literature

An applicant should submit a 505(b)(2) application if approval of an application will rely to any extent on published literature (a *literature-based* 505(b)(2)). If the applicant has not obtained a right of reference to the raw data underlying the published study or studies, the application is a 505(b)(2) application; if the applicant obtains a right of reference to the raw data, the application may be a full NDA (i.e., one submitted under section 505(b)(1)). An NDA will be a 505(b)(2) application if any of the specific information necessary for approval is obtained from literature or from another source to which the applicant does not have a right of reference, even if the applicant also conducted clinical studies to support approval. Note, however, that this does not mean *any* reference to published general information (e.g., about disease etiology, support for particular endpoints, methods of analysis) or to general knowledge causes the application to be a 505(b)(2) application. Rather, reference should be to specific information (clinical trials, animal studies) necessary to the approval of the application.

2. The Agency's finding of safety and effectiveness for an approved drug

An applicant should submit a 505(b)(2) application for a change in a drug when approval of the application relies on the Agency's previous finding of safety and/or effectiveness for a drug. This mechanism, which is embodied in a regulation at 21 CFR 314.54, essentially makes the Agency's conclusions that would support the approval of

Draft - Not for Implementation

a 505(j) application available to an applicant who develops a modification of a drug. Section 314.54 permits a 505(b)(2) applicant to rely on the Agency's finding of safety and effectiveness for an approved drug to the extent such reliance would be permitted under the generic drug approval provisions at section 505(j). This approach is intended to encourage innovation in drug development without requiring duplicative studies to demonstrate what is already known about a drug while protecting the patent and exclusivity rights for the approved drug.

It is possible that an applicant could submit a 505(b)(2) application that relies both on literature and upon the Agency's finding of safety and effectiveness for a previously approved drug product (e.g., to support a new claim).

B. What kind of application can be submitted as a 505(b)(2) application?

1. New chemical entity (NCE)/new molecular entity (NME)

A 505(b)(2) application may be submitted for an NCE when some part of the data necessary for approval is derived from studies not conducted by or for the applicant and to which the applicant has not obtained a right of reference. For an NCE, this data is likely to be derived from published studies, rather than FDA's previous finding of safety and effectiveness of a drug. If the applicant had a right of reference to all of the information necessary for approval, even if the applicant had not conducted the studies, the application would be a considered a 505(b)(1) application.

2. Changes to previously approved drugs

For changes to a previously approved drug product, an application may rely on the Agency's finding of safety and effectiveness of the previously approved product, coupled with the information needed to support the change from the approved product. The additional information could be new studies conducted by the applicant or published data. This use of section 505(b)(2), described in the regulations at 21 CFR 314.54, was intended to encourage innovation without creating duplicate work and reflects the same principle as the 505(j) application: it is wasteful and unnecessary to carry out studies to demonstrate what is already known about a drug. The approach was described in a letter to industry dated April 10, 1987, from Dr. Paul D. Parkman, then Acting Director of the Center for Drugs and Biologics. This guidance helps to clarify and amplify the approaches stated in the April 10, 1987, letter and in the regulations.

An applicant should file a 505(b)(2) application if it is seeking approval of a change to an approved drug that would not be permitted under section 505(j), because approval will require the review of clinical data. However, section 505(b)(2) applications should

APPENDIX 85

Draft - Not for Implementation

not be submitted for duplicates of approved products that are eligible for approval under 505(j) (see 21 CFR 314.101(d)(9)).

In addition, an applicant may submit a 505(b)(2) application for a change in a drug product that is eligible for consideration pursuant to a suitability petition under Section 505(j)(2)(C) of the Act. In the preamble to the implementing regulations for the Hatch-Waxman amendments to the Act, the Agency noted that an application submitted pursuant to section 505(b)(2) of the Act is appropriate even when it could also be submitted in accordance with a suitability petition as defined at section 505(j)(2)(C) of the Act (see 57 FR 17950; April 28, 1992).

III. WHAT ARE SOME EXAMPLES OF 505(B)(2) APPLICATIONS?

Following are examples of changes to approved drugs for which 505(b)(2) applications should be submitted. Please note that in particular cases, changes of the type described immediately below may not require review of information other than BA or BE studies or data from limited confirmatory testing.[2] In those particular cases, approval of the drug may also be sought in a 505(j) application based on an approved suitability petition as described in section 505(j)(2)(C) of the Act. The descriptions below address the situation in which the application should be filed as a 505(b)(2) application because approval of the application will require review of studies beyond those that can be considered under section 505(j). Some or all of the additional information could be provided by literature or reference to past FDA findings of safety and effectiveness for approved drugs, or it could be based upon studies conducted by or for the applicant or to which it has obtained a right of reference.

- *Dosage form.* An application for a change of dosage form, such as a change from a solid oral dosage form to a transdermal patch, that relies to some extent upon the Agency's finding of safety and/or effectiveness for an approved drug.

- *Strength.* An application for a change to a lower or higher strength.

- *Route of administration.* An application for a change in the route of administration, such as a change from an intravenous to intrathecal route.

- *Substitution of an active ingredient in a combination product.* An application for a change in one of the active ingredients of an approved combination product for another active ingredient that has or has not been previously approved.

Following are additional examples of applications that may be accepted pursuant to section 505(b)(2) of the Act. Some or all of the additional information could be provided by the literature or reference to

---

[2] Limited confirmatory testing is explained in further detail in 54 FR 288872, 28880 (July 10, 1989) and 57 FR 17950, 17957-58 (April 28, 1992).

4

83

GENERIC AND INNOVATOR DRUGS

Draft - Not for Implementation

past FDA findings of safety and effectiveness for approved drugs, or it could be based on studies conducted by or for the applicant or to which it has obtained a right of reference.

- *Formulation.* An application for a proposed drug product that contains a different quality or quantity of an excipient(s) than the listed drug where the studies required for approval are beyond those considered limited confirmatory studies appropriate to a 505(j) application.

- *Dosing regimen.* An application for a new dosing regimen, such as a change from twice daily to once daily.

- *Active ingredient.* An application for a change in an active ingredient such as a different salt, ester, complex, chelate, clathrate, racemate, or enantiomer of an active ingredient in a listed drug containing the same active moiety.

- *New molecular entity.* In some cases a new molecular entity may have been studied by parties other than the applicant and published information may be pertinent to the new application. This is particularly likely if the NME is the prodrug of an approved drug or the active metabolite of an approved drug. In some cases, data on a drug with similar pharmacologic effects could be considered critical to approval.

- *Combination product.* An application for a new combination product in which the active ingredients have been previously approved individually.

- *Indication.* An application for a not previously approved indication for a listed drug.

- *Rx/OTC switch.* An application to change a prescription (Rx) indication to an over-the-counter (OTC) indication.

- *OTC monograph.* An application for a drug product that differs from a product described in an OTC monograph (21 CFR 330.11), such as a nonmonograph indication or a new dosage form.

- *Naturally derived or recombinant active ingredient.* An application for a drug product containing an active ingredient(s) derived from animal or botanical sources or recombinant technology where clinical investigations are necessary to show that the active ingredient is the same as an active ingredient in a listed drug.

- *Bioequivalence.* Generally, an application for a pharmaceutically equivalent drug product must be submitted under section 505(j) of the Act and the proposed product must be shown to be bioequivalent to the reference listed drug (21 CFR 314.101(d)(9)). Applications for proposed drug products where the rate (21 CFR 314.54(b)(2)) and/or extent (21 CFR 314.54(b)(1)) of absorption exceed, or are otherwise different from, the 505(j) standards for bioequivalence compared to a listed drug may be submitted pursuant to section 505(b)(2) of the

APPENDIX 85

Draft - Not for Implementation

Act. Such a proposed product may require additional clinical studies to document safety and efficacy at the different rate and extent of delivery. Generally, the differences in rate and extent of absorption should be reflected in the labeling of the 505(b)(2) product. The proposed product does not need to be shown to be clinically *better* than the previously approved product; however, a 505(b)(2) application should not be used as a route of approval for poorly bioavailable generic drug products unable to meet the 505(j) standards for bioequivalence. If the proposed product is a duplicate of an already approved product, it should not be submitted as a 505(b)(2) application (21 CFR 314.101(d)(9)).

For example, a 505(b)(2) application would be appropriate for a controlled release product that is bioinequivalent to a reference listed drug where:

1. The proposed product is at least as bioavailable as the approved pharmaceutically equivalent product (unless it has some other advantage, such as smaller peak/trough ratio); or

2. The pattern of release of the proposed product, although different, is at least as favorable as the approved pharmaceutically equivalent product.

IV. WHAT CAN'T BE SUBMITTED AS 505(B)(2) APPLICATIONS?

- An application that is a duplicate of a listed drug and eligible for approval under section 505(j) (see 21 CFR 314.101(d)(9)); or,

- An application in which the *only* difference from the reference listed drug is that the extent to which the active ingredient(s) is absorbed or otherwise made available to the site of action is less than the listed drug (21 CFR 314.54(b)(1)); or,

- An application in which the *only* difference from the reference listed drug is that the rate at which its active ingredient(s) is absorbed or otherwise made available to the site of action is *unintentionally* less than that of the listed drug (21 CFR 314.54(b)(2)).

V. WHY DOES IT MATTER IF AN NDA IS A 505(B)(2) APPLICATION?

Unlike a full NDA for which the sponsor has conducted or obtained a right of reference to all the data essential to approval, the filing or approval of a 505(b)(2) application may be delayed due to patent or exclusivity protections covering an approved product. Section 505(b)(2) applications must include patent certifications described at 21 CFR 314.50(i) and must provide notice of certain patent certifications to the NDA holder and patent owner under 21 CFR 314.52.

GENERIC AND INNOVATOR DRUGS

Draft - Not for Implementation

VI. PATENT AND EXCLUSIVITY PROTECTIONS THAT COULD AFFECT A 505(B)(2) APPLICATION

A. What type of patent and/or exclusivity protection is a 505(b)(2) application eligible for?

A 505(b)(2) application may itself be granted 3 years of Waxman-Hatch exclusivity if one or more of the clinical investigations, other than BA/BE studies, was essential to approval of the application and was conducted or sponsored by the applicant (21 CFR 314.50(j); 314.108(b)(4) and (5)). A 505(b)(2) application may also be granted 5 years of exclusivity if it is for a new chemical entity (21 CFR 314.50(j); 314.108(b)(2)). A 505(b)(2) application may also be eligible for orphan drug exclusivity (21 CFR 314.20-316.36) or pediatric exclusivity (section 505A of the Act).

A 505(b)(2) application must contain information on patents claiming the drug or its method of use (21 CFR 314.54(a)(1)(v)).

B. What could delay the approval or filing of a 505(b)(2) application?

Approval or filing of a 505(b)(2) application, like a 505(j) application, may be delayed because of patent and exclusivity rights that apply to the listed drug (21 CFR 314.50(i), 314.107, and 314.108 and section 505A of the Act). This is the case even if the application also includes clinical investigations supporting approval of the application.

VII. WHAT SHOULD BE INCLUDED IN 505(B)(2) APPLICATIONS?

The Act (sections 505(b)(1) and (b)(2)) and FDA regulations (21 CFR 314.54) distinguish between 505(b)(1) and (b)(2) applications. Although the two types of applications must meet the same standards for approval (see section 505(b) and (c) of the Act), they differ in source of information to support safety and effectiveness, the patent certification requirements, BA/BE evidence, exclusivity bars, and processing within the FDA. The requirements for 505(b)(1) and 505(b)(2) applications are described at 21 CFR 314.50. Additional requirements for certain 505(b)(2) applications are described at 21 CFR 314.54.

A 505(b)(2) application should include the following:

- Identification of those portions of the application that rely on information the applicant does not own or to which the applicant does not have a right of reference (for example, for reproductive toxicity studies).

- If the 505(b)(2) seeks to rely on the Agency's previous finding of safety or efficacy for a listed drug or drugs, identification of any and all listed drugs by established name, proprietary name (if

APPENDIX 85

Draft - Not for Implementation

any), dosage form, strength, route of administration, name of the listed drug's sponsor, and the application number (21 CFR 314.54(a)(1)(iii)). Even if the 505(b)(2) application is based solely upon literature and does not rely expressly on an Agency finding of safety and effectiveness for a listed drug, the applicant must identify the listed drug(s) on which the studies were conducted, if there are any. If the 505(b)(2) application is for an NCE and the 505(b)(2) applicant is not relying on literature derived from studies of an approved drug, there may not be a listed drug. If there is a listed drug that is the pharmaceutical equivalent to the drug proposed in the 505(b)(2) application, that drug should be identified as the listed drug.

- Information with respect to any patents that claim the drug or the use of the drug for which approval is sought (21 CFR 314.50(h)). This patent information will be published in the Orange Book when the application is approved.

- Information required under 314.50(j) if the applicant believes it is entitled to marketing exclusivity (21 CFR 314.54(a)(1)(vii)).

- A patent certification or statement as required under section 505(b)(2) of the Act with respect to any relevant patents that claim the listed drug and that claim any other drugs on which the investigations relied on by the applicant for approval of the application were conducted, or that claim a use for the listed or other drug (21 CFR 314.54(a)(1)(vi)).

  If there is a listed drug that is the pharmaceutical equivalent of the drug proposed in the 505(b)(2) application, the 505(b)(2) applicant should provide patent certifications for the patents listed for the pharmaceutically equivalent drug. Patent certifications should specify the exact patent number(s), and the exact name of the listed drug or other drug even if all relevant patents have expired.

- If an application is for approval of a new indication, and not for the indications approved for the listed drug, a certification so stating (21 CFR 314.54(a)(1)(iv).

- A statement as to whether the listed drug(s) identified above have received a period of marketing exclusivity (21 CFR 314.108(b)). If a listed drug is protected by exclusivity, filing or approval of the 505(b)(2) application may be delayed.

- A Bioavailability/Bioequivalence (BA/BE) study comparing the proposed product to the listed drug (if any).

- Studies necessary to support the change or modification from the listed drug or drugs (if any). Complete studies of safety and effectiveness may not be necessary if appropriate bridging studies are found to provide an adequate basis for reliance upon FDA's finding of safety and effectiveness of the listed drug(s).

Draft - Not for Implementation

Before submitting the application, the applicant should submit a plan to the appropriate new drug evaluation division identifying the types of bridging studies that should be conducted. The applicant should also identify those components of its application for which it expects to rely on FDA's finding of safety and effectiveness of a previously approved drug product. The division will critique the plan and provide guidance.

APPENDIX 85

Draft - Not for Implementation

REFERENCES

April 10, 1987, letter from then Acting Director of the Center for Drugs and Biologics to all NDA and ANDA holders and applicants.

"Abbreviated New Drug Application Regulations; Proposed Rule," *Federal Register*. Vol. 54, No. 130, Monday, July 10, 1989, page 28872.

"Abbreviated New Drug Regulations; Final Rule," *Federal Register*. Vol. 57, No. 82, Tuesday, April 28, 1992, page 17950.

"Abbreviated New Drug Application Regulations; Patent and Exclusivity Provisions; Final Rule," *Federal Register*. Vol. 59, No. 190, Monday, October 3, 1994, page 50338.

GENERIC AND INNOVATOR DRUGS

Draft - Not for Implementation

GLOSSARY

505(b)(2) application: an application submitted under section 505(b)(1) of the Act for a drug for which one or more of the investigations relied on by the applicant for approval of the "application were not conducted by or for the applicant and for which the applicant has not obtained a right of reference or use from the person by or for whom the investigations were conducted" (21 U.S.C. 355(b)(2)).

Active ingredient: "any component that is intended to furnish pharmacological activity or other direct effect in the diagnosis, cure, mitigation, treatment, or prevention of disease, or to affect the structure or any function of the body of man or of animals. The term includes those components that may undergo chemical change in the manufacture of the drug product and be present in the drug product in a modified form intended to furnish the specified activity or effect" (21 CFR 60.3(b)(2)).

Active moiety: "the molecule or ion, excluding those appended portions of the molecule that cause the drug to be an ester, salt (including a salt with hydrogen or coordination bonds), or other noncovalent derivative (such as a complex, chelate, or clathrate) of the molecule, responsible for the physiological or pharmacological action of the drug substance" (21 CFR 314.108(a)).

Investigations relied on for approval: those without which the application cannot be approved (i.e., animal and human safety tests as well as clinical investigations of effectiveness).

Listed drug: "a new drug product that has an effective approval under section 505(c) of the act for safety and effectiveness or under section 505(j) of the act, which has not been withdrawn or suspended under section 505(e)(1) through (e)(5) or (j)(5) of the act, and which has not been withdrawn from sale for what FDA has determined are reasons of safety or effectiveness. Listed drug status is evidenced by the drug product's identification as a drug with an effective approval in the current edition of FDA's "Approved Drug Products with Therapeutic Equivalence Evaluations" (the list) or any current supplement thereto, as a drug with an effective approval. A drug product is deemed to be a listed drug on the date of effective approval of the application or abbreviated application for that drug product" (21 CFR 314.3(b)).

Literature: published reports of well-controlled studies that support safety or effectiveness; proposed and final monographs published in the *Federal Register*; the data supporting a *Federal Register* notice announcing a product's safety and/or effectiveness.

Orange Book: *Approved Drug Products with Therapeutic Equivalence Evaluations* and any current supplement to the publication.

Pharmaceutical equivalent or duplicate: "drug products that contain identical amounts of the identical active drug ingredient, i.e., the same salt or ester of the same therapeutic moiety, in identical dosage forms, but not necessarily containing the same inactive ingredients, and that meet the identical compendial or other applicable standard of identity, strength, quality, and purity, including potency and,

11

APPENDIX 85

Draft - Not for Implementation

where applicable, content uniformity disintegration times and/or dissolution rates" (21 CFR 320.1(c)). Products with different mechanisms of release can be considered to be pharmaceutical equivalents or duplicates.

Referenced listed drug: "the listed drug identified by FDA as the drug product upon which an applicant relies in seeking approval of its abbreviated application" (21 CFR 314.3(b)).

Right of reference or use: "the authority to rely upon, and otherwise use, an investigation for the purpose of obtaining approval of an application, including the ability to make available the underlying raw data from the investigation for FDA audit, if necessary" (21 CFR 314.3(b)).

Sponsors have the right of reference to any studies: (1) they conduct, (2) that are conducted for them, or (3) for which they formally obtain a documented *right of reference*.

An applicant is not considered to have a *right of reference* to published studies, because the applicant does not have access to the raw data. However, if the raw data are in the public domain, a right of reference is unnecessary.

Suitability petition: A citizen petition submitted to the Agency seeking permission to file an abbreviated new drug application for a change from a listed drug in dosage form, strength, route of administration, or active ingredient in a combination product. (See section 505(j)(2)(C) of the Act)

APPENDIX 86

March 7, 2002 Memorandum to Jay Siegel, Office of Therapeutics Research and Review (CBER), from Marlene E. Haffner, Office of Orphan Products Development, Food and Drug Administration

DEPARTMENT OF HEALTH & HUMAN SERVICES	Public Health Service Food and Drug Administration Orphan Products Development

Memorandum

DATE: March 7, 2002

FROM: Marlene E. Haffner, MD, MPH, RADM USPHS, Director

SUBJECT: Office of Orphan Products Development (OOPD) Analysis of Exclusivity Issues Raised in the Serono BLA for Rebif

TO: Jay Siegel, MD, Director, Office of Therapeutics Research and Review, CBER

and

BLA STN 10378 / 0 FILE

Background

The Orphan Drug Act (the Act) grants seven years of exclusive marketing rights to a specific drug[1] for a specific orphan indication. The marketing exclusivity bars FDA approval during this period of the "same drug" from another sponsor for the same orphan indication. Experience has shown that this exclusivity is one of the strongest incentives in the Act for encouraging research and development of treatments for rare diseases and conditions. The importance FDA places on appropriately maintaining the value of the exclusivity incentive of the Act is reflected in the implementing regulations at 21 CFR Part 316. These same regulations also recognize the equally important need to accommodate improvements in a drug, so as to make available treatments that provide significant medical benefit.

The "Same Drug"

The orphan drug regulations adopt a definition of "same drug" that recognizes the need to give meaning to orphan exclusivity and recognition to significant therapeutic advances. Therefore, the regulations create a presumption that two drugs with similar physical/chemical characteristics are the same, and that exclusivity granted to one drug will block approval of the subsequent drug for the same indication. However, this presumption may be overcome by evidence to show that, despite the physical/chemical

---

[1] The Orphan Drug Act applies to both drugs approved under Section 505 of the Food, Drug, and Cosmetic Act (FDCA), and to biological products licensed under section 351 of the Public Health Service Act (PHSA). The interferon-beta products at issue are regulated under Section 351 of the PHSA. Most biological products licensed under the PHSA also meet the definition of "drug" under the FDCA. The term "drug" is used through this memo to discuss the principles of the Orphan Drug Act and the regulations.

GENERIC AND INNOVATOR DRUGS

similarity, the subsequent drug is clinically superior, and therefore is not barred by the exclusivity. Even though differences in formulation, dose, or other product characteristics by themselves do not render a drug different (that is, not the "same drug") within the orphan drug regulations, they may result in a drug being found to be different if the difference makes it clinically superior, in that it provides a significant therapeutic advantage over the product with exclusivity. The courts have found that FDA's interpretation and application of these concepts are consistent with the Orphan Drug Act. *See Baker-Norton Pharmaceuticals, Inc. v. FDA and Bristol-Myers Squibb*, 132 F.Supp. 2d 30 (D.D.C. 2001); *Berlex Laboratories, Inc. v. FDA*, 942 F.Supp. 19 (D..D.C. 1996).

Interferon beta Products

The orphan drug issues associated with the exclusivity and approval of the multiple interferon beta products for the treatment of relapsing-remitting multiple sclerosis are an example of the need to balance the value of the orphan exclusivity incentive with the availability of improved treatments for patients. The Office of Orphan Products Development (OOPD) has worked closely with CBER in the resolution of these matters. CBER's comprehensive review of the comparative study of Rebif to Avonex and orphan exclusivity describes the regulatory history of these drug products and the related orphan drug issues. OOPD believes this review correctly describes and applies the orphan drug regulations to the comparison between Biogen's Avonex and Serono's Rebif. Only a few points warrant additional discussion.

Head-to-Head Trials

Because of the agency's commitment to maintain the value of the exclusivity incentive, the requirements for demonstrating clinical superiority are stringent. The regulations require head-to-head trials in most cases for a demonstration of increased effectiveness. The requirements for safety comparisons are somewhat less rigorous because comparisons of profound adverse events may be made without a direct head-to-head clinical trial. Direct comparison trials are the standard because they eliminate the use of anecdotal evidence and prevent "apples and oranges" comparisons of dissimilar factors. However, they place a significant financial and technical burden on the sponsor of a second product. The rigor of this requirement is probably best illustrated by the fact that in the nineteen years the Act has been in existence, this matter involving multiple interferon beta treatments for relapsing-remitting multiple sclerosis is the first instance where a sponsor has attempted to challenge the exclusivity of a product by showing that its drug was more effective in a direct comparison trial.

It is also important to note that, until review of the Rebif/Avonex data, no drug product had been determined to be a different drug as a result of a head-to-head comparative trial. Avonex was found to be a different product than Betaseron based on a comparison of the safety findings in two different studies used in the approval process of two different drugs. This was possible because of the distinct nature of the adverse event at issue, and the marked difference between the two products with respect to the severity of the adverse event. However, there is no doubt Serono's study has met the more stringent standard of the type of study necessary to assess comparative efficacy.

APPENDIX 86

Clinical Superiority

The orphan drug regulations clearly separate the categories of effectiveness and safety for purposes of showing clinical superiority, allowing the Agency to distinguish between two drugs by a finding of superiority in either of these categories. There is no additional requirement that the subsequent product, although clinically superior in one parameter, must also be shown to be at least equal in all others. This would set an inappropriate and nearly impossible burden (in terms of clinical trial design) on the sponsor of a second product. A more meaningful standard is a significant therapeutic benefit in terms of increased effectiveness and adequate safety, or increased safety and adequate effectiveness. The balancing of risks and benefits embodied in a drug product as a whole is done when the agency determines whether the drug may be approved for the particular use.

There is also a third approach described in the regulations for showing a significant therapeutic advantage. This requires a demonstration that, in an unusual case where neither greater effectiveness or safety has been shown, a drug otherwise makes a major contribution to patient care. This analysis may involve multiple aspects of the drug product, since the benefit to the patient is likely to be greater convenience or less discomfort, and the very term "major contribution to patient care" implies a more global assessment. So, for example, an assessment of the safety or effectiveness of the new form of the subsequent product might be considered in determining whether the drug made a major contribution to patient care. However, even in this instance, there can not be an infinite number of comparison criteria if this provision of the regulation is to be meaningful.

Given the conclusions in CBER's review, and the considerations above, OOPD believes that Serono has met the burden of establishing Rebif as not "the same drug" as Avonex because it is clinically superior in terms of efficacy. OOPD agrees that the data show a significant difference in the number of exacerbations between patients treated with Avonex and those treated with Rebif. The use of exacerbations also is a clinically meaningful measurement because these episodes represent significant suffering and hardship to the patients. As described in detail in CBER's review memorandum, the number of exacerbations is an endpoint used to establish efficacy for multiple interferon beta products and thus is well-recognized as clinically meaningful. Moreover, OOPD agrees with the CBER conclusion that the magnitude of the benefit in terms of reduced exacerbations in patients treated with Rebif represents a significant therapeutic advantage.

GENERIC AND INNOVATOR DRUGS

Safety

The difference in adverse events between Avonex and Rebif is real. For example, the injection-site necrosis observed with Rebif is not observed with Avonex. However, the adverse events do not appear to pose a serious limitation on Rebif's use. Both Rebif and Avonex would represent reasonable alternatives for the prescribing physicians and their patients.

Conclusion

OOPD concurs with CBER that Serono's Rebif may be approved for treatment of relapsing remitting multiple sclerosis because it is not the same drug as Biogen's Avonex.

APPENDIX 86

cc: OPD Precedent file
J.Fritz, OPD HF35
OTRR:BLA STN 10378 / 0 file

APPENDIX 87

Guidance for Industry—
Fast Track Drug Development Programs—
Designation, Development, and Application Review

Guidance for Industry
Fast Track Drug Development Programs – Designation, Development, and Application Review

U.S. Department of Health and Human Services
Food and Drug Administration
Center for Drug Evaluation and Research (CDER)
Center for Biologics Evaluation and Research (CBER)
September 1998

Procedural 9

Guidance for Industry
Fast Track Drug Development Programs – Designation, Development, and Application Review

Comments and suggestions regarding this document should be submitted within 90 days of publication in the *Federal Register* of the notice announcing the availability of the guidance. All comments should be identified with the docket number provided at the beginning of the notice. Submit comments to the Dockets Management Branch (HFA-305), Food and Drug Administration, 12420 Parklawn Dr., rm. 1-23, Rockville, MD 20857.

After the comment period closes, comments should be provided in writing to the Center for Drug Evaluation and Research (CDER), Food and Drug Administration, 5600 Fishers Lane, Rockville, MD 20857; or Center for Biologics Evaluation and Research (CBER), 1401 Rockville Pike, Rockville, MD 20852-1448.

Additional copies are available from:
The Drug Information Branch (HFD-210), Center for Drug Evaluation and Research (CDER),
5600 Fishers Lane, Rockville, MD 20857 (Tel) 301-827-4573
http://www.fda.gov/cder/guidance/index.htm
or
Office of Communication, Training, and Manufacturers Assistance (HFM-40),
Center for Biologics Evaluation and Research (CBER)
1401 Rockville Pike, Rockville, MD 20852-1448,
http://www.fda.gov/cber/guidelines.htm; (Fax) 888-CBERFAX or 301-827-3844
(Voice Information) 800-835-4709 or 301-827-1800

APPENDIX 87

TABLE OF CONTENTS

I. INTRODUCTION 1

II. CRITERIA FOR QUALIFICATION AS A FAST TRACK DRUG
   DEVELOPMENT PROGRAM 3
   A. Serious or Life-Threatening Condition 3
   B. Demonstrating the Potential to Address Unmet Medical Needs 6

III. PROCESS FOR THE DESIGNATION OF A DRUG AS A PRODUCT IN A FAST
    TRACK DRUG DEVELOPMENT PROGRAM 7
    A. Timing of Submission 7
    B. Where to Send a Fast Track Designation Submission 8
    C. Content of a Fast Track Designation Submission 8
    D. FDA Response 9
    E. Continued Designation as a Fast Track Drug Development Program 9

IV. PROGRAMS FOR EXPEDITING DEVELOPMENT AND REVIEW 10
    A. Meetings 10
    B. Written Correspondence 11
    C. Review Programs 12
    D. Dispute Resolution 16

FIGURE I: Scheme for Determining Fast Track 17

APPENDIX 1: Section 112 of the
Food and Drug Administration Modernization Act of 1997 18

APPENDIX 2: Procedures for Drugs Intended to Treat
Life-Threatening and Severely Debilitating Illnesses 20

APPENDIX 3: Priority Review Policies 21

APPENDIX 4: Accelerated Approval of New Drugs and Biological Products for
Serious or Life-Threatening Illnesses 22

GUIDANCE FOR INDUSTRY[1]
Fast Track Drug Development Programs – Designation, Development, and Application Review

I. INTRODUCTION

The fast track programs of the Food and Drug Administration (FDA) are designed to facilitate the development and expedite the review of new drugs that are intended to treat serious or life-threatening conditions and that demonstrate the potential to address unmet medical needs (fast track products). This document provides guidance to industry on FDA's fast track programs and, in doing so, is intended to meet the requirement of section 112(b) of the Food and Drug Administration Modernization Act of 1997 (the Modernization Act) (P.L. 105-115) (Appendix 1). Section 112 of the Modernization Act amends the Federal Food, Drug, and Cosmetic Act (the Act) by adding new section 506 (21 U.S.C. 356) and directs FDA to issue guidance describing its policies and procedures pertaining to fast track products. Section 506 authorizes FDA to take actions appropriate to facilitate the development and expedite the review of an application for such a product. These actions are not limited to those specified in the fast track provision but also encompass existing FDA programs to facilitate development and review of products for serious and life-threatening conditions. Such programs include (a) the procedures described in the 1988 interim rule "Procedures for Drugs Intended to Treat Life-Threatening and Severely Debilitating Illnesses" (21 CFR 312.80 through 312.88 (Subpart E)), in which FDA formalized certain procedures to facilitate the development of promising therapies (Appendix 2), and (b) the priority review procedures of the Center for Biologics Evaluation and Research (CBER) (SOPP 8405, *Complete Review and Issuance of Action Letters* (June 11, 1998)) and the Center for Drug Evaluation and Research (CDER) (MAP 6020.3, *Priority Review Policy* (April 22, 1996)) (Appendix 3).

Under the Subpart E regulations for investigational new drugs (Appendix 2), drug development is considered a continuum from early preclinical and clinical studies through submission of a marketing application. The regulations emphasize the critical nature of close early communication between the Agency and a sponsor, outline procedures such as pre-IND and end of phase 1 meetings as methods to improve the efficiency of preclinical and clinical development, and focus on efforts by the Agency and sponsor to reach early agreement on the design of the major clinical efficacy studies that will be needed to support approval.

---

[1] This guidance has been prepared by the Fast Track Working Group comprising individuals in the Center for Biologics Evaluation and Research (CBER) and the Center for Drug Evaluation and Research (CDER) at the Food and Drug Administration. This guidance document represents the Agency's current thinking on the policies and procedures that pertain to fast track products. It does not create or confer any rights for or on any person and does not operate to bind FDA or the public. An alternative approach may be used if such approach satisfies the requirements of the applicable statute, regulations, or both.

APPENDIX 87

CBER and CDER have longstanding policies that describe criteria for review priority classification of marketing applications. Products regulated by CBER are eligible for priority review if they provide a significant improvement in the safety or effectiveness of the treatment, diagnosis, or prevention of a serious or life-threatening disease (CBER SOPP 8405) (see Appendix 3). Products regulated by CDER are eligible for priority review if they provide a significant improvement compared to marketed products in the treatment, diagnosis, or prevention of a disease; eligibility is not limited to drugs for a serious or life-threatening disease (CDER MAP 6020.3) (see Appendix 3). A fast track product would ordinarily meet either Center's criteria for priority review. Note, however, that an NDA or BLA sponsor need not seek fast track designation to be eligible for priority review.

The Modernization Act specifically permits FDA to:

1. Approve a marketing application under section 505(c) of the Act or section 351 of the Public Health Service Act "upon a determination that the product has an effect on a clinical endpoint or on a surrogate endpoint that is reasonably likely to predict clinical benefit." This, in effect, codifies in statute FDA's Accelerated Approval Rule (Appendix 4), made final in 1992, which allows expedited marketing of certain new drugs or biological products intended to treat serious or life-threatening illnesses and that appear to provide meaningful therapeutic benefits to patients compared with existing treatments.[2] Under this rule, "FDA may grant marketing approval for a new drug [or biological] product on the basis of adequate and well-controlled trials establishing that the drug [or biological] product has an effect on a surrogate endpoint that is reasonably likely, based on epidemiologic, therapeutic, pathophysiologic, or other evidence, to predict clinical benefit or on the basis of an effect on a clinical endpoint other than survival or irreversible morbidity."[3] Where an accelerated approval is based upon a surrogate endpoint or on an effect on a clinical endpoint other than survival or irreversible morbidity, post-marketing studies are ordinarily required "to verify and describe the drug's clinical benefit and to resolve remaining uncertainty as to the relation of the surrogate endpoint upon which approval was based to clinical benefit, or the observed clinical benefit to ultimate outcome" (57 FR 58942, December 11, 1992).

2. Accept for review portions of a marketing application prior to receipt of the complete application.

---

[2] See 21 CFR Part 314, Subpart H (Accelerated Approval of New Drugs for Serious or Life-Threatening Illnesses) and 21 CFR Part 601, Subpart E (Accelerated Approval of Biological Products for Serious or Life-Threatening Illnesses).

[3] 21 CFR 314.510 and 601.41. The accelerated approval regulations give FDA flexibility with respect to the types of endpoints that can be relied on to support marketing approval, but do not affect the quantity or quality of evidence needed to demonstrate substantial evidence of effectiveness. Any endpoint considered appropriate to be relied on to support approval, whether a surrogate endpoint or a clinical endpoint, must be supported by substantial evidence of effectiveness. Section 506 of the Act, in incorporating the language of the accelerated approval regulations, affirms FDA's authority to base marketing approval on data other than clinical efficacy data directly establishing an effect on the ultimate clinical outcome (57 FR 58942 at 58946, December 11, 1992).

GENERIC AND INNOVATOR DRUGS

Fast track programs should be distinguished from expanded access programs for investigational drugs such as the Treatment Investigational New Drug (IND) regulations (52 FR 19466, May 22, 1987; codified as 21 CFR 312.34). Fast track is intended to facilitate development and expedite review of drugs to treat serious and life-threatening conditions so that an approved product can reach the market expeditiously. Expanded access programs such as Treatment IND are intended to facilitate access to investigational drugs prior to approval for patients with serious and life-threatening conditions and without therapeutic alternatives.

In this guidance, the Agency will discuss the regulations, policies, and procedures related to facilitating development and expediting review of promising therapies for serious and life-threatening conditions for which there is an unmet medical need. This guidance will seek to clarify the criteria and processes for designation of fast track products and to present a coherent, integrated description of the diverse activities and policies that can facilitate development and expedite review of drugs that demonstrate the potential to advance the treatment of serious and life-threatening illnesses.

II. CRITERIA FOR QUALIFICATION AS A FAST TRACK DRUG DEVELOPMENT PROGRAM

Section 506(a)(1) of the Act states that a drug designated as a fast track product is intended for the treatment of a serious or life-threatening condition and demonstrates the potential to address unmet medical needs for the condition. The fast track classification thus does not apply to a product alone, but applies to a combination of the product and specific indication for which it is being studied. The indication, for the purposes of this document, includes both the condition for which the drug is intended (e.g., heart failure) and the anticipated or established benefits of use (e.g., improved exercise tolerance, decreased hospitalization, increased survival).[4] It is therefore the development program for a specific drug for a specific indication that will receive fast track designation. Such a program is referred to in this document as a *fast track drug development program* and the criteria involved in designation are represented in Figure 1. These criteria are more fully described below.

A. Serious or Life-Threatening Condition

This section of the document provides specific guidance regarding how the Agency intends to determine whether a condition is serious and whether a drug is intended to treat a serious condition. All conditions meeting the definition of life-threatening as set forth at 21 CFR

---

[4] The specific benefit being studied, and what is to be shown about that benefit, could affect fast track designation. For example, an anti-fungal agent under development to treat a life-threatening, systemic fungal infection not adequately treated by existing therapy would be eligible for fast track, but if the same anti-fungal were being developed to treat only a non-serious, superficial fungal infection or a systemic infection that was treatable with existing therapy, and without an attempt to show that it fills an unmet need, the anti-fungal agent would not be eligible for fast track. If both development programs were occurring simultaneously, only the development program for the life-threatening infection would receive fast track designation.

3

APPENDIX 87

312.81(a) would also be serious conditions. Because the benefits of fast track designation apply to products for serious conditions as well as to products for life-threatening conditions, distinction between the two categories of conditions with regard to eligibility for fast track programs is unnecessary. Therefore, in the following discussion, all references to serious conditions will include life-threatening conditions.

1. Whether a condition is serious

As discussed in the preamble to the proposed accelerated approval rule (57 FR 13234, April 15, 1992), determination of the seriousness of a condition:

> ... is a matter of judgment, but generally is based on its impact on such factors as survival, day-to-day functioning, or the likelihood that the disease, if left untreated, will progress from a less severe condition to a more serious one. Thus, acquired immunodeficiency syndrome (AIDS), all other stages of human immunodeficiency virus (HIV) infection, Alzheimer's dementia, angina pectoris, heart failure, cancer, and many other diseases are clearly serious in their full manifestations. Further, many chronic illnesses that are generally well-managed by available therapy can have serious outcomes [such as] ... inflammatory bowel disease, asthma, rheumatoid arthritis, diabetes mellitus, systemic lupus erythematosus, depression, psychoses, and many other diseases.

For a condition to be serious, the condition should be associated with morbidity that has substantial impact on day-to-day functioning. Short-lived and self-limiting morbidity will usually not be sufficient but the morbidity need not be irreversible, providing it is persistent or recurrent.

2. Whether the drug is intended to treat a serious condition

For a product to be in a fast track drug development program, it must not only be used in patients with a serious condition, it must be intended to treat a serious aspect of that condition. Thus, in making a fast track determination, FDA will assess whether the development program is designed to demonstrate an effect on a serious aspect of the condition. The following examples illustrate FDA's approach:

 a. A therapeutic product that is directed at some aspect of a serious condition would be considered to treat a serious condition if it is being evaluated for effects on a serious manifestation(s) or serious symptom(s) of the condition.

 b. A diagnostic product would be considered to treat a serious condition if it is being evaluated directly for its impact on a serious aspect of the condition or if it is being evaluated for its ability to improve diagnosis or detection of the condition and scientific data provide a strong basis for a

4

GENERIC AND INNOVATOR DRUGS

        presumption that the improvements in diagnosis or detection of the condition will lead to improved outcome.

c. A preventive product would be considered to treat a serious condition if (i) it is being evaluated for its ability to prevent a serious manifestation(s) of the condition, or (ii) it is being studied for its ability to prevent the condition and it is scientifically reasonable to assume that prevention of the condition would prevent its serious consequences.

d. A product that is intended to ameliorate or prevent a side effect of therapy of a condition would be considered to treat a serious condition if the side effect is serious (e.g., serious infections in patients receiving immunosuppressive therapy).

e. A product that is intended, and is being studied for its ability, to treat a condition while avoiding the side effects of currently accepted treatments of the condition may be considered to treat a serious condition if such side effects are serious (e.g., a less myelosuppressive treatment for a tumor or an anti-inflammatory drug that does not cause gastrointestinal bleeding). The potential for a new drug to avoid the serious sequelae of existing drugs would qualify that drug development program for fast track designation only in limited circumstances. Many therapies, even those intended to treat non-serious conditions, are associated with rare, serious, adverse reactions, and new therapies, despite initial hopes, often are associated with their own set of serious reactions. Nonetheless, some adverse reactions are significant public health problems, and the development of therapies that do not cause such serious reactions would merit close attention. The Agency may designate the development of such a therapy as a fast track drug development program when (i) currently accepted therapy is widely used despite an unavoidable serious risk, (ii) serious outcomes are a significant public health issue, and (iii) the new therapy shows significant potential to have a substantially improved overall safety profile with at least similar efficacy.

Many conditions not generally considered to be serious have rare or distant serious sequelae (e.g., urinary tract infections or duodenal ulcers). Product development programs for such conditions could be designated as fast track if the sponsor specifically designs the development program to demonstrate an effect on those serious sequelae. Conversely, some conditions that are generally considered to be serious have non-serious manifestations requiring symptomatic therapy (e.g., insomnia associated with schizophrenia, skin discoloration from Addison's disease, alopecia with lupus, subcutaneous nodules from rheumatoid arthritis). The Agency will not generally designate as fast track a development program for a product whose effect has been measured in terms of non-serious manifestations unless the product's effect on those manifestations is reasonably likely to predict benefit on a serious manifestation.

APPENDIX 87

B. Demonstrating the Potential to Address Unmet Medical Needs

Section 506(a) of the Act further requires that the drug demonstrate the potential to address unmet medical needs. Thus, in designating a fast track drug development program, the Agency will determine whether the drug has a potential to address unmet medical needs and whether the development program is designed to evaluate this potential.

    1. Evaluation of whether the drug development plan addresses unmet medical needs

An unmet medical need is a medical need that is not addressed adequately by an existing therapy.

        a. Where there is no available therapy for the condition

If no therapy exists for a serious condition, there is an obvious unmet medical need and a new treatment effective in that condition would meet this aspect of the criteria for fast track designation.

        b. Where there is available therapy for the condition

When therapies exist for a condition, the developmental program for the new agent would address unmet medical needs if it evaluated any of the following:

            i. Improved effect(s) on serious outcomes of the condition that are affected by alternate therapies (e.g., superiority of the new drug used alone or in combination with other therapies in an active controlled trial assessing an endpoint reflecting serious morbidity).

            ii. Effect(s) on serious outcomes of the condition not known to be affected by the alternatives (e.g., progressive disability in multiple sclerosis when the alternative treatments have shown an effect on exacerbations but have not shown an effect on progressive disability).

            iii. Ability to provide benefit(s) in patients who are unable to tolerate or are unresponsive to alternative agents (e.g., an antipsychotic agent that is effective in people failing standard therapy), or an ability to be used effectively in combination with other critical agents that cannot be combined with available therapy.

            iv. Ability to provide benefit(s) similar to those of alternatives while avoiding serious toxicity that is present in existing therapies, or avoiding less serious toxicity that is common and causes discontinuation of treatment of a serious disease.

6

GENERIC AND INNOVATOR DRUGS

v. Ability to provide benefit(s) similar to those of alternatives but with improvement in some factor, such as compliance or convenience, that is shown to lead to improved effects on serious outcomes.[5]

2. Demonstration of the drug's potential

The type of information needed to demonstrate the potential of a drug to address unmet medical needs will depend on the stage of drug development. Data that become available during clinical development should support the drug's potential to address unmet medical needs and the development plan should be designed to assess this potential. The Agency will rely on summaries of available data to determine whether the potential to address unmet medical needs has been demonstrated.

Before human studies begin, the potential for a drug to address unmet medical needs will be based on pharmacologic and animal model data. At this stage, there may be little evidence of effectiveness of the drug in humans and the potential will be largely theoretical. For later fast track designation, but still prior to the completion of the principal controlled trials, available clinical data should begin to confirm or be consistent with the potential to address unmet medical needs. Still later in the development of a drug, the Agency will normally consider whether the clinical data from controlled and uncontrolled trials, as summarized by the sponsor, support the potential of the drug to address unmet medical needs. At this later stage in development, when an alternate therapy is available, the Agency's determination will also be based on whether the new therapy has been evaluated by comparison with the existing therapy, usually by direct comparison in clinical trials.

III. PROCESS FOR THE DESIGNATION OF A DRUG AS A PRODUCT IN A FAST TRACK DRUG DEVELOPMENT PROGRAM

The general procedures applicable to the submission and review of fast track designation requests are described below.

A. Timing of Submission

A sponsor may submit a request for fast track designation at the time of original submission of its IND, or at any time thereafter prior to receiving marketing approval of its BLA or NDA. Note that the IND and potential fast track designation may be discussed prior to an IND submission in a pre-IND meeting, but a decision on designation would await submission of the IND. Although benefits associated with fast track designation may occur throughout the drug development

---

[5] Although improved convenience alone could be considered an improvement in therapy, a product will generally qualify as being in a fast track drug development program only if it is reasonable to believe or is demonstrated that greater convenience will lead to better compliance and better compliance will lead to a favorable effect on serious outcomes, and only if the potential effect on serious outcomes is being assessed in clinical trials.

APPENDIX 87

process, from the early IND submission to evaluation of a marketing application, as a practical matter, requests should ordinarily occur no later than the sponsor's pre-BLA/NDA meeting with the Agency, as many of the benefits of fast track designation will no longer be applicable after that time.

B. Where to Send a Fast Track Designation Submission

A request for fast track designation should be submitted as an amendment to the sponsor's IND in triplicate with Form FDA 1571 attached or, if the request is simultaneous with submission of the original IND, should accompany the IND. The request for fast track designation should identify the sponsor's contact person, including the person's address, telephone number, and fax number. The IND or amendment should be submitted to the attention of the appropriate division in CBER or CDER and should have a cover letter that clearly identifies the submission as a "Request for Fast Track Designation." In the unusual situation where a request is made after the filing of a BLA or NDA, the request should be submitted to the BLA or NDA with a Form FDA 356h.

C. Content of a Fast Track Designation Submission

   1.   In general

The submission in support of a request for fast track designation should establish that the criteria necessary for designation are met, i.e., (i) that the drug is intended to treat a serious or life threatening condition (see section II.A. above), and (ii) that the drug has the potential to address unmet medical needs and this potential is being evaluated in the planned drug development program (see section II.B. above). The sponsor should identify the serious condition and the unmet medical needs, provide a plausible basis for the assertion that the drug has the potential to address such unmet medical needs, and include in the development plan (at a level of detail appropriate to the stage of development) trials designed to evaluate this potential.

   2.   Discussion and supporting documentation

To facilitate FDA review, a submission for fast track designation should contain all discussion and supporting documentation needed to permit a reviewer to assess whether the criteria for fast track designation are met without having to refer to information located elsewhere, yet should also not be voluminous. The amount of discussion and supporting documentation needed to show that the criteria are met will vary. For example, little explanation or supporting documentation may be needed to establish that studying the drug in the treatment of a fatal condition with no approved treatment would qualify if the endpoint were mortality. It will usually be necessary to submit more extensive explanation and supporting documentation to show that for a non-fatal condition, serious or life threatening aspects of the condition will be studied. Where acceptable therapy for the condition already exists, still more extensive discussion and supporting documentation may be needed to establish that the new therapy has the potential to fill a medical need not met by existing therapy.

8

Any data or published reports that support assertions made in the discussion section of the fast track submission and that have not previously been submitted to the sponsor's IND should be included in the submission. Supporting data already contained in the sponsor's IND generally need only be summarized in the fast track submission with reference to its location in the IND. For assertions made in the submission that are consistent with accepted medical knowledge, the sponsor does not need to include references to clinical data or other external sources. If a sponsor references a large number of sources, a list of those references should be included.

D. FDA Response

FDA will respond to a request for fast track designation within 60 calender days of receipt of the request.

1. Designation letter

If the Agency determines that the criteria for designation as a fast track drug development program have been met, the designation letter will (i) state that fast track designation is granted for development of the product for use in treating the specific serious or life-threatening condition, (ii) point out the need for the sponsor to design and perform studies that can show whether the product fulfills unmet medical needs, and (iii) alert the sponsor that the drug development program is expected to continue to meet the criteria for fast track designation (see section III.E. below).

2. Non-designation letter

A non-designation letter would reflect a determination that the request was incomplete or that the drug development program failed to meet the criteria for fast track designation. The non-designation letter will explain the reasons for the Agency's decision. FDA will respond to a subsequent request for fast track designation after a non-designation determination within 60 calendar days of receiving the subsequent request.

E. Continued Designation as a Fast Track Drug Development Program

It is foreseeable that, for certain products in fast track drug development programs, it will become apparent over the course of drug development that the development programs do not continue to meet the criteria for fast track designation. A product in a fast track development program may not continue to meet the criteria if the drug no longer (i) demonstrates a potential to address unmet medical needs, or (ii) is being studied in a manner that would show the product is able to treat a serious or life-threatening condition and fulfills unmet medical needs. It may no longer demonstrate a potential to address unmet needs, for example, if a new product were approved that addressed the same needs, or if emerging clinical data failed to show that the product in a fast track development program had the anticipated advantage over existing therapy. For products in fast track drug development programs, the Agency expects that the appropriateness of considering particular drug development plans as part of the fast track program will be discussed

APPENDIX 87

and evaluated during the drug development process, including at the end of phase 2 meeting and the pre-BLA/NDA meeting. If the sponsor recognizes that the fast track drug development program will no longer be pursued, the sponsor should inform the Agency of this change in plans.

When fast track designation is no longer supported by emerging data or the designated drug development program is no longer being pursued, the Agency may choose to send a letter notifying the sponsor that the program is no longer classified as a fast track drug development program.

IV. PROGRAMS FOR EXPEDITING DEVELOPMENT AND REVIEW

It is important to distinguish between fast track designation itself and the specific programs that are available to a sponsor or applicant of a product in a fast track drug development program under section 506(a) of the Act. A sponsor or applicant may apply for fast track designation at any time in the development process from the original submission of an IND until the BLA or NDA is approved by the Agency (see section III.A.). A product designated as being in a fast track drug development program would be eligible for consideration for some or all of the programs outlined below.

It is also important to recognize that, with the exception of the submission of portions of a BLA/NDA before submission of the entire application,[6] the programs described below have been established in regulations under authority separate from section 506 of the Act. Therefore, products that are not in drug development programs that have been designated as fast track may also be able to take advantage of these programs.

A. Meetings

Appropriately timed meetings between the regulated industry and FDA are a critical aspect of efficient drug development. Sponsors of products in fast track drug development programs should be in regular contact with the appropriate reviewing division to ensure that the evidence necessary to support marketing approval will be developed and presented in a format conducive to an efficient review. Specifically, the following are strongly recommended:

1. Pre-IND consultation so that (i) appropriate preclinical studies can be performed to demonstrate the potential to address unmet medical needs and to support introduction of the product into human trials, (ii) phase 1 studies can be optimally designed to support further product development, (iii) overall development strategy can be considered, and (iv) issues regarding the potential for fast track designation may be discussed.

---

[6] Current FDA regulations do not provide for Agency review of portions of a BLA or NDA prior to the submission of the complete application, except a complete Chemistry, Manufacturing, and Controls (CMC) section can be submitted to an NDA 90 to 120 days before the anticipated submission of the remainder of the NDA under 21 CFR 314.50(d)(1)(iv).

GENERIC AND INNOVATOR DRUGS

2. An end of phase 1 meeting because, as discussed in 21 CFR 312.82 (see Appendix 3), the first phase 2 controlled trials in life-threatening or severely debilitating illnesses may provide sufficient data on safety and effectiveness to support approval, with later development of more extensive safety data, dose response information, and other information in post marketing studies. It is critical that early trials with mortality/major morbidity endpoints be discussed before implementation to reach agreement on study design, including the statistical plan.

3. An end of phase 2 meeting to ensure that agreement between FDA and the sponsor has been reached on the design of the principal controlled trials intended to provide evidence of safety and efficacy. As noted in the paragraph above (section A.2.), for some fast track drug development programs, a meeting with much the same purpose will occur at the end of early clinical testing and may be referred to as "end of phase ½ meeting."[7] Note that the standard of evidence applicable to principal controlled trials is set forth at 21 CFR 314.126 (see also the FDA guidance document, *Providing Clinical Evidence of Effectiveness for Human Drug and Biological Products* (May, 1998)).

4. A pre-BLA/NDA meeting to discuss and achieve agreement on critical issues including:

    - Whether preliminary evidence of effectiveness was seen in the principal controlled trials intended to provide evidence of effectiveness.
    - Structure, content, and timing of submission of the BLA or NDA.
    - Structure and content of any electronic submissions.
    - Structure, content, and timing of submission of portions of an application for marketing approval, if such submission is appropriate.
    - Readiness for, and proposed timing of, preapproval inspections.
    - Potential for, and proposed timing of, advisory committee presentation if applicable.

5. A meeting may be scheduled to discuss labeling issues as early in the review process as appropriate.

B. **Written Correspondence**

1. In addition to meeting minutes, described in CBER SOPP 8101.1 (*Scheduling Meetings with Regulated Industry*) and CDER MAP 4512.1 (*Formal Meetings Between CDER and External Constituents* (March 7, 1996)), the following should be provided to the sponsor by FDA:

    - Timely comments on the design of the proposed principal controlled

---

[7] Functionally, the end of phase ½ meeting is an end of phase 2 meeting that occurs at the end of phase 1.

APPENDIX 87

clinical trials that are to provide the basis for the Agency's determination of the safety and effectiveness of the product.

- End of phase 1 and/or end of phase 2 letters commenting on the adequacy of phase 2/3 development plans.

2. In addition to the usual information contained in premeeting packages described in CBER SOPP 8101.1 and CDER MAP 4512.1, the sponsor should provide the following to FDA:

- Responses to FDA questions about any clinical trials that are to form the basis for the Agency's determination of the safety and effectiveness of the product.
- At the earliest possible time, protocols of any clinical trials that are not being carried out under an IND (i.e., foreign studies) and that will form the basis for the Agency's determination of the safety and effectiveness of the product.
- In meeting packages for meetings held after initial fast track designation, a discussion of how accumulated data and study plans continue to demonstrate that the product and the development plan meet the criteria for fast track designation.
- If submission of portions of an incomplete application is sought, a written request for this kind of submission and a proposed schedule for submission (see IV.C.2. below).
- As soon as possible, if there are plans to study a surrogate endpoint suitable for review under the accelerated approval provisions, a discussion of and support for the proposed endpoint.

C. Review Programs

Sponsors of products in fast track drug development programs may be considered for one or more of the following procedures regarding marketing applications.

1. Priority review of BLAs and NDAs

Because fast track products are intended to treat serious or life-threatening conditions and must demonstrate the potential to address unmet medical needs for such conditions, a BLA or NDA for a product in a fast track drug development program ordinarily will be eligible for priority review (CBER SOPP 8405, CDER MAP 6020.3) (see Appendix 3).

2. Submission of portions of an application

   a. Submitting portions of a BLA/NDA

   Section 506(c) of the Act provides that FDA may consider for review portions of a

12

GENERIC AND INNOVATOR DRUGS

marketing application before the complete BLA or NDA is submitted. Filing may only occur if the applicant provides a schedule for submission of information necessary to make the application complete and pays any fees that may be required under section 736 of the Act (i.e., user fees).

After the sponsor submits to the IND a preliminary evaluation of data from the clinical trials, the Agency may consider accepting portions of an application if (i) the clinical trials that would form the basis for the Agency's determination of the safety and effectiveness of the product and that would support drug labeling are nearing completion or have been completed, (ii) the Agency agrees that the product continues to meet the criteria for fast track designation, and (iii) the Agency agrees that preliminary evaluation of the clinical data supports a determination that the product may be effective.

A sponsor seeking to submit portions of an application should (i) provide a schedule for submission of the portions of the BLA or NDA and receive FDA agreement to accept portions of the application and agreement that the schedule is acceptable <u>before</u> making any submission under the schedule, and (ii) pay any applicable user fee to the Agency at the time the first portion of the BLA or NDA is submitted. The pre-BLA/NDA meeting should be used to obtain preliminary agency agreement on the proposal. At the meeting, the sponsor and the reviewing division should discuss the data that will be used to support effectiveness, the schedule for submission of each portion of the BLA or NDA, and a description of portions of the application to be submitted separately. A request to submit portions of an application ordinarily should be included in the information package for the pre-BLA/NDA meeting. If a sponsor seeks to submit portions of an application under these procedures after the pre-BLA/NDA meeting, the sponsor should request submission and submit a proposed schedule for submission of portions of an application to the IND as soon as possible.

A request for submission of portions of an application should be submitted as an amendment to the IND for the product in a fast track drug development program in triplicate with Form FDA 1571 attached. The cover letter to the amendment should clearly identify the amendment as "Request for Submission of Portions of an Application." A sponsor may apply for fast track designation and submission of portions of a BLA or NDA at the same time. These requests should be submitted as <u>one</u> amendment to the IND.

FDA will respond to a request for submission of portions of an application by letter to the sponsor. Any changes in an agreement to accept portions of an application will also be in writing.

b. Portions of an application eligible for early submission

Generally, the Agency will accept for submission only a complete section of a BLA

13

APPENDIX 87

or NDA, such as the entire CMC section, toxicology section, or clinical section (Form FDA 356h may be a useful guide to items in a BLA or NDA). It is expected that a section submitted for review will be in a form adequate to have been included in a complete BLA or NDA submission. Drafts should not be included in a submission; if final reports need to be updated, the applicant should submit a formal amendment to the BLA or NDA with the revised information. Occasionally, the Agency may, in its discretion, accept less than a complete section (e.g., a CMC section lacking final consistency lot data and long term stability data; an acute toxicology section lacking chronic toxicology data; or final study reports for some or all of the principal controlled trials without integrated summaries) if it determines that such a subsection would constitute a reviewable unit and would be useful in making the review process more efficient overall. The company should confirm that these subsections are final reports. The Agency and the sponsor should work together at the time of the pre-BLA/NDA meeting to clearly define the parameters of accepting an incomplete section and to determine whether FDA could conduct a meaningful review of the submission prior to receiving the missing information.

c. Submission of the user fee

Section 506(c)(1) of the Act requires a sponsor to pay any fee that may be required under section 736 of the Act before FDA may commence review of any portion of an application. The applicant should submit Form FDA 3397 with any applicable user fee and should follow the same procedures as those followed when a complete application is submitted.

d. Commencement of review

Acceptance of a portion of an application by the Agency does not necessarily mean that review will commence or proceed prior to the receipt of a complete application. Actual commencement and scheduling of review will depend on many factors, including staffing, workload, competing priorities, time line for completion of applications, and the perceived efficiency of commencing review before the complete submission.

e. Calculation of review time

The review clock will not begin until the applicant informs the Agency that a complete BLA or NDA has been submitted. Following notification that the application is complete, the Agency will make a filing determination within the usual time (see 21 CFR 314.101 and CBER SOPP 8404, *Refuse to File Guidance for Product License Applications and Establishment License Applications* (June 11, 1993)).

3. Accelerated Approval

GENERIC AND INNOVATOR DRUGS

Applicants whose products are in fast track drug development programs may seek traditional approval based on data demonstrating an effect on clinically meaningful endpoints or well-established surrogate endpoints. Alternatively, they may seek approval under the accelerated approval regulations (Appendix 4). If an applicant seeks approval of a product in a fast track drug development program based on evidence of an effect on a less than well-established surrogate endpoint, FDA may grant accelerated approval based on a determination that the effect on the surrogate endpoint is reasonably likely to predict clinical benefit (21 CFR 314.510 and 601.41). Drug approval under the accelerated approval regulations may also be based on demonstrated clinical effects that are not the desired ultimate benefit but are reasonably likely to predict such benefit (e.g., improved exercise tolerance in refractory heart failure might be considered reasonably likely to predict ultimate benefit) (21 CFR 314.510 and 601.41).

Section 506(b) essentially codifies in statute FDA's accelerated approval regulations. A surrogate endpoint was defined in the preamble to the accelerated approval rule (57 FR 13234 at 13235, April 15, 1992) as "a laboratory or physical sign that is used in therapeutic trials as a substitute for a clinically meaningful endpoint that is a direct measure of how a patient feels, functions, or survives and that is expected to predict the effect of the therapy." Although some surrogate endpoints are recognized as well-established and have long been a basis for approval (e.g., change in blood pressure or cholesterol), the accelerated approval rule allows reliance in specific circumstances on a "surrogate endpoint that, while 'reasonably likely' to predict clinical benefit, is not so well-established as the surrogates ordinarily used as bases of approval in the past" (57 FR 58942 at 58944, December 11, 1992). To meet the statutory standard for approval, which requires the submission of "substantial evidence" to demonstrate effectiveness, "there must be evidence from adequate and well-controlled studies showing that the drug will have [its claimed] effect...[8] That effect will, in this case, be an effect on a surrogate endpoint...." (57 FR 58943-44).

With respect to approval based on clinical endpoints other than survival or irreversible morbidity, the preamble to the final accelerated approval rule pointed out that such approval would usually be considered (like other approvals based on a clinical finding) under traditional procedures, i.e., not under accelerated approval. Approval based on clinical endpoints other than survival or irreversible morbidity would "be considered under the accelerated approval regulations only when it is essential to determine effects on survival or irreversible morbidity in order to confirm the favorable risk/benefit judgment that led to approval" (57 FR 58946). The following examples illustrate types of clinical endpoints that could be a basis for approval with a requirement for further studies under the provisions of the Modernization Act and the accelerated approval rule:

---

[8] Under current law, as amended by section 115(a) of the Modernization Act, the Agency may, in some circumstances, consider "data from one adequate and well-controlled clinical investigation and confirmatory evidence ... to constitute substantial evidence." See the FDA guidance document, *Providing Clinical Evidence of Effectiveness for Human Drugs and Biological Products* (May, 1998).

APPENDIX 87

- Clinical endpoints measuring short-term benefit in a chronic condition where short-term benefit per se does not outweigh risk and where durability of benefit is uncertain but expected.

- Clinical endpoints measuring lesser symptoms or signs of a serious disease (e.g., weight loss, appearance) when the resulting benefits do not per se outweigh risks but are expected to lead to a favorable effect on ultimate outcome, which would outweigh risks.

- Clinical endpoints measuring substantial benefits otherwise suitable for ordinary approval but where there exists a significant but limited concern that the treatment may adversely effect ultimate outcome. Where such concerns are minimal, ordinary approval would be used. Where the concerns are substantial, data regarding ultimate outcome would be required pre-approval. Between these extremes, accelerated approval may be considered.

D. Dispute Resolution

An FDA determination under the fast track program may be appealed to the reviewing division. If the sponsor is not satisfied with the response provided by the FDA component, the sponsor may elect to pursue the Agency's procedures for internal review or dispute resolution (see 21 CFR 10.75, 312.48, and 314.103).

Figure 1   **Scheme for Determining Fast Track**

Not Fast Track ← No ← Is Some Aspect of the Condition Serious or Life-Threatening? II.A.1.

↓ Yes

Potentially Fast Track

Not Fast Track ← No ← Does the Drug Show Potential to Treat a Serious Aspect of the Condition? II.A.2.

↓ Yes

Potentially Fast Track

Not Fast Track ← No ← Is the Drug Development Program Designed to Determine Whether the Drug will Effect a Serious Aspect of the Condition? II.A.2.

↓ Yes

Potentially Fast Track

Is There any Approved Treatment for the Serious or Life-Threatening Aspect of the Condition Being Studied? II.B.1.a, II.B.2 → No → Fast Track Designation

↓ Yes

Potentially Fast Track

Not Fast Track ← No ← Is A Medical Need Unmet by Available Treatments Being Studied? II.B.1.b, II.B.2

↓ Yes

Fast Track Designation

17

APPENDIX 87

APPENDIX 1: Section 112 of the
Food and Drug Administration Modernization Act of 1997

SEC. 112. EXPEDITING STUDY AND APPROVAL OF FAST TRACK DRUGS.

(a) IN GENERAL- Chapter V (21 U.S.C. 351 et seq.), as amended by section 125, is amended by inserting before section 508 the following:
'SEC. 506. FAST TRACK PRODUCTS.
'(a) DESIGNATION OF DRUG AS A FAST TRACK PRODUCT-
'(1) IN GENERAL- The Secretary shall, at the request of the sponsor of a new drug, facilitate the development and expedite the review of such drug if it is intended for the treatment of a serious or life-threatening condition and it demonstrates the potential to address unmet medical needs for such a condition. (In this section, such a drug is referred to as a 'fast track product'.)
'(2) REQUEST FOR DESIGNATION- The sponsor of a new drug may request the Secretary to designate the drug as a fast track product. A request for the designation may be made concurrently with, or at any time after, submission of an application for the investigation of the drug under section 505(i) or section 351(a)(3) of the Public Health Service Act.
'(3) DESIGNATION- Within 60 calendar days after the receipt of a request under paragraph (2), the Secretary shall determine whether the drug that is the subject of the request meets the criteria described in paragraph (1). If the Secretary finds that the drug meets the criteria, the Secretary shall designate the drug as a fast track product and shall take such actions as are appropriate to expedite the development and review of the application for approval of such product.
'(b) APPROVAL OF APPLICATION FOR A FAST TRACK PRODUCT-
'(1) IN GENERAL- The Secretary may approve an application for approval of a fast track product under section 505(c) or section 351 of the Public Health Service Act upon a determination that the product has an effect on a clinical endpoint or on a surrogate endpoint that is reasonably likely to predict clinical benefit.
'(2) LIMITATION- Approval of a fast track product under this subsection may be subject to the requirements--
'(A) that the sponsor conduct appropriate post-approval studies to validate the surrogate endpoint or otherwise confirm the effect on the clinical endpoint; and
'(B) that the sponsor submit copies of all promotional materials related to the fast track product during the preapproval review period and, following approval and for such period thereafter as the Secretary determines to be appropriate, at least 30 days prior to dissemination of the materials.
'(3) EXPEDITED WITHDRAWAL OF APPROVAL- The Secretary may withdraw approval of a fast track product using expedited procedures (as prescribed by the Secretary in regulations which shall include an opportunity for an informal hearing) if--

GENERIC AND INNOVATOR DRUGS

`(A) the sponsor fails to conduct any required post-approval study of the fast track drug with due diligence;
`(B) a post-approval study of the fast track product fails to verify clinical benefit of the product;
`(C) other evidence demonstrates that the fast track product is not safe or effective under the conditions of use; or
`(D) the sponsor disseminates false or misleading promotional materials with respect to the product.

`(c) REVIEW OF INCOMPLETE APPLICATIONS FOR APPROVAL OF A FAST TRACK PRODUCT-
`(1) IN GENERAL- If the Secretary determines, after preliminary evaluation of clinical data submitted by the sponsor, that a fast track product may be effective, the Secretary shall evaluate for filing, and may commence review of portions of, an application for the approval of the product before the sponsor submits a complete application. The Secretary shall commence such review only if the applicant--
`(A) provides a schedule for submission of information necessary to make the application complete; and
`(B) pays any fee that may be required under section 736.
`(2) EXCEPTION- Any time period for review of human drug applications that has been agreed to by the Secretary and that has been set forth in goals identified in letters of the Secretary (relating to the use of fees collected under section 736 to expedite the drug development process and the review of human drug applications) shall not apply to an application submitted under paragraph (1) until the date on which the application is complete.

`(d) AWARENESS EFFORTS- The Secretary shall--
`(1) develop and disseminate to physicians, patient organizations, pharmaceutical and biotechnology companies, and other appropriate persons a description of the provisions of this section applicable to fast track products; and
`(2) establish a program to encourage the development of surrogate endpoints that are reasonably likely to predict clinical benefit for serious or life-threatening conditions for which there exist significant unmet medical needs.'.

(b) GUIDANCE- Within 1 year after the date of enactment of this Act, the Secretary of Health and Human Services shall issue guidance for fast track products (as defined in section 506(a)(1) of the Federal Food, Drug, and Cosmetic Act) that describes the policies and procedures that pertain to section 506 of such Act.

APPENDIX 87

APPENDIX 2: Procedures for Drugs Intended to Treat Life-Threatening and Severely Debilitating Illnesses

21 CFR Parts 312 and 314
Investigational New Drug, Antibiotic and Biological Drug Product Regulations;
Procedures for Drugs Intended to Treat Life-Threatening
and Severely Debilitating Illnesses; Interim Rule
(53 *Federal Register* 41516, October 21, 1998)

(Attachment provided separately)

GENERIC AND INNOVATOR DRUGS

APPENDIX 3: Priority Review Policies

Center for Biologics Evaluation and Research
Manual of Standard Operating Procedures and Policies
SOPP 8405, *Complete Review and Issuance of Action Letters*, June 11, 1998

Center for Drug Evaluation and Research
Manual of Policies and Procedures
MAP 6020.3, *Priority Review Policy*, April 22, 1996

(Attachment provided separately)

APPENDIX 87

APPENDIX 4: Accelerated Approval of New Drugs and Biological Products for Serious or Life-Threatening Illnesses

21 CFR 314 and 601
New Drug, Antibiotic, and Biological Drug Product Regulations;
Accelerated Approval; Final Rule
(57 *Federal Register* 58942, December 11, 1992)

(Attachment provided separately)

APPENDIX 88

June 4, 2002 letter from Tommy Thompson, Food and Drug Administration, re: the Prescription Drug User Fee Act of 1992

U.S. Food and Drug Administration

TEXT OF THE JUNE 4, 2002 LETTER TRANSMITTING THE PDUFA III PERFORMANCE GOALS AND PROCEDURES

As you are aware, the Prescription Drug User Fee Act of 1992 (PDUFA), as reauthorized by the Food and Drug Administration Modernization Act of 1997, expires at the end of Fiscal Year 2002. Under PDUFA, the additional revenues generated from fees paid by the pharmaceutical and biological prescription drug industries have been used to expedite the process for the review of prescription drugs, in accordance with performance goals that were developed by the Food and Drug Administration (FDA) in consultation with PDUFA stakeholders.

FDA has worked with various stakeholders, including representatives from consumer, patient, and health provider groups, and the pharmaceutical and biological prescription drug industries, to develop a reauthorization proposal for PDUFA that would build upon and enhance the success of the program. Title 5, Subtitle A, of the Public Health Security and Bioterrorism Preparedness and Response Act of 2002, as passed by the House on May 22, 2002, and by the Senate on May 23, 2002, reflects the fee mechanisms and other improvements developed in these discussions. The performance goals referenced in Section 502 are specified in the enclosure to this letter, entitled "PDUFA Reauthorization Performance Goals and Procedures." I believe they represent a realistic projection of what FDA can accomplish with industry cooperation and both the additional resources identified in the bill and annual FDA appropriations that fully cover the costs of pay and inflation increases for the drug and biologics review process each year.

This letter and the enclosed goals document pertain only to Title 5, Subtitle A (Prescription Drug User Fees) of H.R. 3448, the Public Health Security and Bioterrorism Preparedness and Response Act of 2002. OMB has advised that there is no objection to the presentation of these views from the standpoint of the Administration's program. We appreciate the support of you and your staffs, the assistance of other Members of the Committee, and that of the Appropriations Committees, in the reauthorization of this vital program.

Since

Tomr

Thompson

Enclosure

Identical Letters to the Chairman and Ranking Minority Members of:
Committee on Health, Education, Labor, & Pensions, United States Senate
Committee on Energy and Commerce, House of Representatives

APPENDIX 89

Prescription Drug User Fee Act of 1992, Reauthorization, performance goals and procedures (June 19, 2002)

U.S. Food and Drug Administration

ENCLOSURE

PDUFA REAUTHORIZATION PERFORMANCE GOALS AND PROCEDURES

The performance goals and procedures of the FDA Center for Drug Evaluation and Research (CDER) and the Center for Biologics Evaluation and Research (CBER), as agreed to under the reauthorization of the prescription drug user fee program in the [cite statute] are summarized as follows:

I. REVIEW PERFORMANCE GOALS - FISCAL YEAR 2003 THROUGH 2007

A. NDA/BLA Submissions and Resubmissions:

Review and act on 90 percent of standard original NDA and BLA submissions filed during fiscal year within 10 months of receipt.

1. Review and act on 90 percent of priority original NDA and BLA submissions filed during fiscal year within 6 months of receipt.
2. Review and act on 90 percent of Class 1 resubmitted original applications filed during fiscal year within 2 months of receipt.
3. Review and act on 90 percent of Class 2 resubmitted original applications filed during fiscal year within 6 months of receipt.

Original Efficacy Supplements:

1. Review and act on 90 percent of standard efficacy supplements filed during fiscal year within 10 months of receipt.
2. Review and act on 90 percent of priority efficacy supplements filed during fiscal year within 6 months of receipt.

Resubmitted Efficacy Supplements:

Fiscal Year 2003:

1. Review and act on 90 percent of Class 1 resubmitted efficacy supplements filed during fiscal year 2003 within 6 months of receipt and review and act on 30 percent within 2 months of receipt.
2. Review and act on 90 percent of Class 2 resubmitted efficacy supplements filed during fiscal year 2003 within 6 months of receipt.

Fiscal Year 2004:

1. Review and act on 90 percent of Class 1 resubmitted efficacy supplements filed during fiscal year 2004 within 4 months and review and act on 50 percent within 2 months of receipt.
2. Review and act on 90 percent of Class 2 resubmitted original applications filed

during fiscal year 2000 within 6 months of receipt.

Fiscal Year 2005:

1. Review and act on 90 percent of Class 1 resubmitted efficacy supplements filed during fiscal year 2005 within 4 months of receipt and review and act on 70 percent within 2 months of receipt.
2. Review and act on 90 percent of Class 2 resubmitted efficacy supplements within 6 months of receipt.

Fiscal Year 2006

1. Review and act on 90 percent of Class 1 resubmitted efficacy supplements filed during fiscal year 2006 within 4 months of receipt and review and act on 80 percent within 2 months of receipt.
2. Review and act on 90 percent of Class 2 resubmitted efficacy supplements within 6 months of receipt.

Fiscal Year 2007:

1. Review and act on 90 percent of Class 1 resubmitted efficacy supplements filed during fiscal year 2007 within 2 months of receipt.
2. Review and act on 90 percent of Class 2 resubmitted efficacy supplements within 6 months of receipt.

Original Manufacturing Supplements:

1. Review and act on 90 percent of manufacturing supplements filed during fiscal year within 6 months of receipt and review and act on 90 percent of manufacturing supplements requiring prior approval within 4 months of receipt.

These review goals are summarized in the following tables:

ORIGINAL and RESUBMITTED NDAs/BLAs:

SUBMISSION COHORT	STANDARD	PRIORITY
Original Applications	90% IN 10 MO	90% IN 6 MO
Class 1 Resubmissions	90% IN 2 MO	90% IN 2 MO
Class 2 Resubmissions	90% IN 6 MO	90% IN 6 MO

ORIGINAL and RESUBMITTED EFFICACY SUPPLEMENTS:

APPENDIX 89

SUBMISSION COHORT	STANDARD	PRIORITY
Original Efficacy Supplements	90% In 10 MO	90% IN 6 MO

RESUBMITTED EFFICACY SUPPLEMENTS

SUBMISSION COHORT	CLASS 1	CLASS 2
FY 2003	90% IN 6 MO/30% IN 2 MO	90% IN 6 MO
FY 2004	90% IN 4 MO/50% IN 2 MO	90% IN 6 MO
FY 2005	90% IN 4 MO/70% IN 2 MO	90% IN 6 MO
FY 2006	90% IN 4 MO/80% IN 2 MO	90% IN 6 MO
FY 2007	90% IN 2 MO	90% IN 6 MO

MANUFACTURING SUPPLEMENTS

SUBMISSION COHORT	MANUFACTURING SUPPLEMENTS NO PRIOR APPROVAL ("CHANGES BEING EFFECTED" OR "30-DAY SUPPLEMENTS")	MANUFACTURING SUPPLEMENTS THAT DO REQUIRE PRIOR APPROVAL
FY 2003 – 2007	90% IN 6 MO	90% IN 4 MO

II. NEW MOLECULAR ENTITY (NME) PERFORMANCE GOALS

A. The performance goals for standard and priority original NMEs in each submission cohort will be the same as for all of the original NDAs (including NMEs) in each submission cohort but shall be reported separately.

GENERIC AND INNOVATOR DRUGS

B. For biological products, for purposes of this performance goal, all original BLAs will be considered to be NMEs.

III. MEETING MANAGEMENT GOALS

A. Responses to Meeting Requests

1. Procedure: Within 14 calendar days of the Agency's receipt of a request from industry for a formal meeting (i.e., a scheduled face-to-face, teleconference, or videoconference) CBER and CDER should notify the requester in writing (letter or fax) of the date, time, and place for the meeting, as well as expected Center participants.

2. Performance Goal: FDA will provide this notification within 14 days for 90% in FY 2003 - 2007.

B. Scheduling Meetings

1. Procedure: The meeting date should reflect the next available date on which all applicable Center personnel are available to attend, consistent with the component's other business; however, the meeting should be scheduled consistent with the type of meeting requested. If the requested date for any of these types of meetings is greater than 30, 60, or 75 calendar days (as appropriate) from the date the request is received by the Agency, the meeting date should be within 14 calendar days of the date requested.

Type A Meetings should occur within 30 calendar days of the Agency receipt of the meeting request.

Type B Meetings should occur within 60 calendar days of the Agency receipt of the meeting request.

Type C Meetings should occur within 75 calendar days of the Agency receipt of the meeting request.

2. Performance goal: 90% of meetings are held within the timeframe (based on cohort year of request) from FY 03 to FY 07.

C. Meeting Minutes

1. Procedure: The Agency will prepare minutes which will be available to the sponsor 30 calendar days after the meeting. The minutes will clearly outline the important agreements, disagreements, issues for further discussion, and action items from the meeting in bulleted form and need not be in great detail.

APPENDIX 89

2. Performance goal: 90% of minutes are issued within 30 calendar days of date of meeting (based on cohort year of meeting) in FY 03 to FY 07.

D. Conditions

For a meeting to qualify for these performance goals:

1. A written request (letter or fax) should be submitted to the review division; and

2. The letter should provide:

   a. A brief statement of the purpose of the meeting;

   b. A listing of the specific objectives/outcomes the requester expects from the meeting;

   c. A proposed agenda, including estimated times needed for each agenda item;

   d. A listing of planned external attendees;

   e. A listing of requested participants/disciplines representative(s) from the Center;

   f. The approximate time that supporting documentation (i.e., the "backgrounder") for the meeting will be sent to the Center (i.e., "x" weeks prior to the meeting, but should be received by the Center at least 2 weeks in advance of the scheduled meeting for Type A meetings and at least 1 month in advance of the scheduled meeting for Type B and Type C meetings); and

3. The Agency concurs that the meeting will serve a useful purpose (i.e., it is not premature or clearly unnecessary). However, requests for a "Type B" meeting will be honored except in the most unusual circumstances.

IV. CLINICAL HOLDS

A. Procedure: The Center should respond to a sponsor's complete response to a clinical hold within 30 days of the Agency's receipt of the submission of such sponsor response.

B. Performance goal: 90% of such responses are provided within 30 calendar days of the Agency's receipt of the sponsor's response in FY 03 to FY07 (cohort of date of receipt).

GENERIC AND INNOVATOR DRUGS

V. MAJOR DISPUTE RESOLUTION

A. Procedure: For procedural or scientific matters involving the review of human drug applications and supplements (as defined in PDUFA) that cannot be resolved at the divisional level (including a request for reconsideration by the Division after reviewing any materials that are planned to be forwarded with an appeal to the next level), the response to appeals of decisions will occur within 30 calendar days of the Center's receipt of the written appeal.

B. Performance goal: 90% of such answers are provided within 30 calendar days of the Center's receipt of the written appeal in FY 03 to FY 07.

C. Conditions

1. Sponsors should first try to resolve the procedural or scientific issue at the Division level. If it cannot be resolved at that level, it should be appealed to the Office Director level (with a copy to the Division Director) and then, if necessary, to the Deputy Center Director or Center Director (with a copy to the Office Director).

2. Responses should be either verbal (followed by a written confirmation within 14 calendar days of the verbal notification) or written and should ordinarily be to either deny or grant the appeal.

3. If the decision is to deny the appeal, the response should include reasons for the denial and any actions the sponsor might take in order to persuade the Agency to reverse its decision.

4. In some cases, further data or further input from others might be needed to reach a decision on the appeal. In these cases, the "response" should be the plan for obtaining that information (e.g., requesting further information from the sponsor, scheduling a meeting with the sponsor, scheduling the issue for discussion at the next scheduled available advisory committee).

5. In these cases, once the required information is received by the Agency (including any advice from an advisory committee), the person to whom the appeal was made, again has 30 calendar days from the receipt of the required information in which to either deny or grant the appeal.

6. Again, if the decision is to deny the appeal, the response should include the reasons for the denial and any actions the sponsor might take in order to persuade the Agency to reverse its decision.

7. N.B. If the Agency decides to present the issue to an advisory committee and there are not 30 days before the next scheduled advisory committee, the issue will be presented at the following scheduled committee meeting in order to allow conformance with advisory committee administrative procedures.

VI. SPECIAL PROTOCOL QUESTION ASSESSMENT AND AGREEMENT

A. Procedure: Upon specific request by a sponsor (including specific questions that the sponsor desires to be answered), the agency will evaluate certain protocols and issues to assess whether the design is adequate to meet scientific and regulatory requirements identified by the sponsor.

1. The sponsor should submit a limited number of specific questions about the protocol design and scientific and regulatory requirements for which the sponsor seeks agreement (e.g., is the dose range in the carcinogenicity study adequate, considering the intended clinical dosage; are the clinical endpoints adequate to support a specific efficacy claim).

2. Within 45 days of Agency receipt of the protocol and specific questions, the Agency will provide a written response to the sponsor that includes a succinct assessment of the protocol and answers to the questions posed by the sponsor. If the agency does not agree that the protocol design, execution plans, and data analyses are adequate to achieve the goals of the sponsor, the reasons for the disagreement will be explained in the response.

3. Protocols that qualify for this program include: carcinogenicity protocols, stability protocols, and Phase 3 protocols for clinical trials that will form the primary basis of an efficacy claim. (For such Phase 3 protocols to qualify for this comprehensive protocol assessment, the sponsor must have had an end of Phase 2/pre-Phase 3 meeting with the review division so that the division is aware of the developmental context in which the protocol is being reviewed and the questions being answered.)

4. N.B. For products that will be using Subpart E or Subpart H development schemes, the Phase 3 protocols mentioned in this paragraph should be construed to mean those protocols for trials that will form the primary basis of an efficacy claim no matter what phase of drug development in which they happen to be conducted.

5. If a protocol is reviewed under the process outlined above and

agreement with the Agency is reached on design, execution, and analyses and if the results of the trial conducted under the protocol substantiate the hypothesis of the protocol, the Agency agrees that the data from the protocol can be used as part of the primary basis for approval of the product. The fundamental agreement here is that having agreed to the design, execution, and analyses proposed in protocols reviewed under this process, the Agency will not later alter its perspective on the issues of design, execution, or analyses unless public health concerns unrecognized at the time of protocol assessment under this process are evident.

B. Performance goal: 90% of special protocols assessments and agreement requests completed and returned to sponsor within timeframes (based on cohort year of request) from FY 03 to FY 07.

VII. CONTINOUS MARKETING APPLICATION

To test whether providing early review of selected applications and additional feedback and advice to sponsors during drug development for selected products can further shorten drug development and review times, FDA agrees to conduct the following two pilot programs:

A. Pilot 1 – Discipline Review Letters for Pre-Submitted "Reviewable Units" of NDAs/BLAs

1. This pilot applies to drugs and biologics that have been designated to be Fast Track drugs or biologics, pursuant to section 112 of the FDA Modernization Act (21 U.S.C. 506), have been the subject of an End-of-Phase 2 and/or a Pre-NDA/BLA meeting, and have demonstrated significant promise as a therapeutic advance in clinical trials.
2. For drugs and biologics that meet these criteria, FDA may enter into an agreement with the sponsor to accept pre-submission of one or more "reviewable units"of the application in advance of the submission of the complete NDA/BLA.
3. If following an initial review FDA finds a "reviewable unit" to be substantially complete for review (i.e., after a "filing review" similar to that performed on an NDA/BLA), FDA will initiate a review clock for the complete review of the "reviewable unit" of the NDA/BLA. The review clock would start from the date of receipt of the "reviewable unit."
4. To be considered fileable for review under paragraph 3, a "reviewable unit" must be substantially complete when submitted to FDA. Once a "reviewable unit" is "filed" by FDA, except as provided in paragraph 5 below, only minor information amendments submitted in response to FDA inquiries or requests and routine stability and safety updates will be considered during the review cycle.
5. Major amendments to the "reviewable unit" are strongly discouraged. However, in rare cases, and with prior agreement, FDA may accept and consider for review a major amendment to a "reviewable unit." To accommodate these rare cases, a major amendment to a "reviewable unit" submitted within the last three months of a 6-month review cycle may, at FDA's discretion, trigger a 3-month extension of the review clock for the "reviewable unit" in question. In no case, however, would a

APPENDIX 89

      major amendment be accepted for review and the review clock for the "reviewable unit" extended if the extended review clock for the "reviewable unit" exceeded the review clock for the complete NDA/BLA. (See paragraph 10 below).

6. After completion of review of the "reviewable unit" of the NDA/BLA by the appropriate discipline review team, FDA will provide written feedback to the sponsor of the review findings in the form of a discipline review letter (DRL).
7. The DRL will provide feedback on the individual "reviewable unit" from the discipline review team, and not final, definitive decisions relevant to the NDA/BLA.
8. If an application is to be presented to an advisory committee, the final DRL on the "reviewable unit" may be deferred pending completion of the advisory committee meeting and internal review and consideration of the advice received.
9. The following performance goals will apply to review of "reviewable units" of an NDA/BLA for Fast Track drugs and biologics that are submitted in advance of the complete NDA/BLA under this pilot program: a. Discipline review team review of a "reviewable unit" for a Fast Track drug or biologic will be completed and a DRL issued within 6 months of the date of the submission for 30% of "reviewable units" submitted in FY04; b. Discipline review team review of a "reviewable unit" for a Fast Track drug or biologic will be completed and a DRL issued within 6 months of the date of the submission for 50% of "reviewable units" submitted in FY05; c. Discipline review team review of a "reviewable unit" for a Fast Track drug or biologic will be completed and a DRL issued within 6 months of the date of the submission for 70% "reviewable units" submitted in FY06, and d. Discipline review team review of a "reviewable unit: for a Fast Track drug or biologic will be completed and a DRL letter issued within 6 months of the date of the submission for 90% of "reviewable units" submitted in FY07.
10. If the complete NDA/BLA is submitted to FDA while a 6-month review clock for a "reviewable unit" is still open, FDA will adhere to the timelines and performance goals for both the "reviewable unit" and the complete NDA/BLA. For example, if a "reviewable unit" is submitted in January and the complete NDA/BLA is submitted in April, the review goal for the "reviewable unit" will be July and the review goal for the complete NDA/BLA will be October.
11. Any resubmission or amendment of a "reviewable unit" submitted by the sponsor in response to an FDA discipline review letter will not be subject to the review timelines and performance goals proposed above. FDA review of such resubmissions and amendments in advance of submission of the complete NDA/BLA will occur only as resources allow.
12. This pilot program is limited to the initial submission of an NDA/BLA and is not applicable to a resubmission in response to an FDA complete response letter following the complete review of an NDA/BLA.
13. Guidance: FDA will develop and issue a joint CDER/CBER guidance on how it intends to implement this pilot program by September 30, 2003. The guidance will describe the principles, processes, and procedures that will be followed during the pilot program. The guidance also will define what subsections of a complete technical section would be considered an acceptable "reviewable unit" for pre-submission and review and how many individual "reviewable units" from one or more technical sections of an NDA/BLA can be pre-submitted and reviewed subject to separate review clocks under this program at any given time. The pilot program will be implemented in FY 2004, after the final guidance is issued and will continue through FY 2007.

GENERIC AND INNOVATOR DRUGS

B. Pilot 2 – Frequent Scientific Feedback and Interactions During Drug Development

1. This pilot applies to drugs and biologics that have been designated to be Fast Track drugs or biologics pursuant to section 112 of the FDA Modernization Act (21 U.S.C. 508), that are intended to treat serious and/or life-threatening diseases, and that have been the subject of an end-of-phase 1 meeting. The pilot program is limited to one Fast Track product in each CDER and CBER review division over the course of the pilot program.
2. For drugs and biologics that meet these criteria, FDA may enter into an agreement with the sponsor to initiate a formal program of frequent scientific feedback and interactions regarding the drug development program. The feedback and interactions may take the form of regular meetings between the division and the sponsor at appropriate points during the development process, written feedback from the division following review of the sponsor's drug development plan, written feedback from the division following review of important new protocols, and written feedback from the division following review of study summaries or complete study reports submitted by the sponsor.
3. Decisions regarding what study reports would be reviewed as summaries and what study reports would be reviewed as complete study reports under this pilot program would be made in advance, following discussions between the division and the sponsor of the proposed drug development program. In making these decisions, the review division will consider the importance of the study to the drug development program, the nature of the study, and the potential value of limited (i.e., based on summaries) versus more thorough division review (i.e., based on complete study reports).
4. Guidance: FDA will develop and issue a joint CDER/CBER guidance on how it intends to implement this pilot program by September 30, 2003. The guidance will describe the principles, processes, and procedures that will be followed during the pilot program. The pilot program will be implemented in FY 2004, after the final guidance is issued and will continue through FY 2007. The full (unredacted) study report will be provided to the FDA Commissioner and a version of the study report redacted to remove confidential commercial information or other information exempt from disclosure, will be made available to the public.

C. Evaluation of the Pilot Programs

1. In FY 2004, FDA will contract with an outside expert consultant(s) to evaluate both pilot programs.
2. The consultant(s) will develop an evaluation study design that identifies key questions, data requirements, and a data collection plan, and conduct a comprehensive study of the pilot programs to help assess the value, costs, and impact of these programs to the drug development and review process. A preliminary report will be generated by the consultant by the end of FY06.

VIII. PRE- AND PERI-NDA/BLA RISK MANAGEMENT PLAN ACTIVITIES

a. Submission and Review of pre-NDA/BLA meeting packages:

A pre-NDA/BLA meeting package may include a summary of relevant safety

APPENDIX 89

information and industry questions/discussion points regarding proposed risk management plans and discussion of the need for any post-approval risk management studies. The elements of the proposal may include:

1. assessment of clinical trial limitations and disease epidemiology 2. assessment of risk management tools to be used to address known and potential risks 3. suggestions for phase 4 epidemiology studies, if such studies are warranted 4. proposals for targeted post-approval surveillance (this would include attempts to quantify background rates of risks of concern and thresholds for actions) The pre-NDA/BLA meeting package will be reviewed and discussed by the review divisions as well as the appropriate safety group in CDER or CBER.

b. **Pre-NDA/BLA meeting with industry:** This meeting may include a discussion of the preliminary risk management plans and proposed observational studies, if warranted, as outlined above. Participants in this meeting will include product safety experts from the respective Center. The intent of these discussions will be for FDA to get a better understanding of the safety issues associated with the particular drug/biologic and the proposed risk management plans, and to provide industry with feedback on these proposals so that they can be included in the NDA/BLA submission. It is the intent of this proposal that such risk management plans and the discussions around them would focus on specific issues of concern, either based on already identified safety issues or reasonable potential focused issues of concern.

c. **Review of NDA/BLA:** The NDA/BLA submitted by industry may include the proposed risk management tools and plans, and protocols for observational studies, based on the discussions that began with the pre-NDA/BLA meeting, as described above, and may be amended as appropriate to further refine the proposal. These amendments would not normally be considered major amendments. Both the review division and the appropriate safety group will be involved in the review of the application and will try to communicate comments regarding the risk management plan as early in the review process as practicable, in the form of a discipline review letter. Items to be included in the risk management plan to assure FDA of the safety and efficacy of the drug or biologic are to be addressed prior to approval of an application. The risk management plan may contain additional items that can be used to help refine the risks and actions (e.g., background rates and observational studies) and these items may be further defined and completed after approval in accordance with time frames agreed upon at the time of product approval.

d. **Peri-Approval Submission of Observational Study Reports and Periodic Safety Update Reports (PSURs):** For NDA/BLA applications, and supplements containing clinical data, submitted on or after October 1, 2002, FDA may use user fees to review an applicant's implementation of the risk management plan for a period of up to two years post-approval for most products and for a period of up to three years for products that require risk management beyond standard labeling (e.g., a black box or bolded warning, medication guide, restricted distribution). This period is defined for purposes of the user fee goals as the peri-approval period. Issues that arise during implementation of the risk management plan (e.g., whether the plan is effective) will be reported to FDA either in the form of a PSUR or in a periodic or annual report (21 CFR 314.80 and 314.81) (ICH Guidance E2C, Clinical Safety Data Management: Periodic Safety Update Reports for Marketed Drugs) and addressed during the peri-approval period through discussions between the applicant and FDA. PSURs may be submitted and reviewed semi-annually for the first two or three years

GENERIC AND INNOVATOR DRUGS

post approval to allow adequate time for implementation of risk management plans.

For drugs approved under PDUFA III, FDA may use user fees to independently evaluate product utilization for drugs with important safety concerns, using drug utilization databases, for the first three years post approval. The purpose of such utilization evaluations is to evaluate whether these products are being used in a safe manner and to work pro-actively with companies during the peri-approval period to accomplish this. FDA will allocate $70,900,000 in user fees over 5 years to the activities covered in this section. FDA will track the specific amounts of user fees spent on these activities and will include in its annual report to Congress an accounting of this spending.

e. **Guidance Document Development:** By the end of Fiscal Year 04, CDER and CBER will jointly develop final guidance documents that address good risk assessment, risk management, and pharmacovigilance practices.

IX. INDEPENDENT CONSULTANTS FOR BIOTECHNOLOGY CLINICAL TRIAL PROTOCOLS

A. Engagement of Expert Consultant: During the development period for a biotechnology product, a sponsor may request that FDA engage an independent expert consultant, selected by FDA, to participate in the Agency's review of the protocol for the clinical studies that are expected to serve as the primary basis for a claim.

B. Conditions

1. The product must be a biotechnology product (for example, DNA plasmid products, synthetic peptides of fewer than 40 amino acids, monoclonal antibodies for in vivo use, and recombinant DNA-derived products) that represents a significant advance in the treatment, diagnosis or prevention of a disease or condition, or have the potential to address an unmet medical need;
2. The product may not have been the subject of a previously granted request under this program;
3. The sponsor must submit a written request for the use of an independent consultant, describing the reasons why the consultant should be engaged (e.g., as a result of preliminary discussions with the Agency the sponsor expects substantial disagreement over the proposed protocol); and
4. The request must be designated as a "Request for Appointment of Expert Consultant" and submitted in conjunction with a formal meeting request (for example, during the end-of-Phase II meeting or a Type A, meeting).

C. Recommendations for Consultants: The sponsor may submit a list of recommended consultants for consideration by the Agency. The selected consultant will either be a special government employee, or will be retained by FDA under contract. The consultant's role will be advisory to FDA and FDA will remain responsible for making scientific and regulatory decisions regarding the clinical protocol in question.

D. Denial of Requests: FDA will grant the request unless the Agency determines that engagement of an expert consultant would not serve a useful purpose (for example it is clearly premature). FDA will engage the services of an independent consultant, of FDA's

APPENDIX 89

choosing, as soon as practicable. If the Agency denies the request, it will provide a written rationale to the requester within 14 days of receipt.

E. Performance Goal Change: Due to the time required to select and screen the consultant for potential conflicts of interest and to allow the consultant sufficient time to review the scientific issues involved, the performance goals for scheduling the formal meeting (see section III) may be extended for an additional sixty (60) days.

F. Evaluation: During FY 2006, FDA will conduct a study to evaluate the costs and benefits of this program for both sponsors and the Agency.

X. FIRST CYCLE REVIEW PERFORMANCE PROPOSAL

A. Notification of Issues Identified during the Filing Review

1. Performance Goal: For original NDA/BLA applications and efficacy supplements, FDA will report substantive deficiencies identified in the initial filing review to the sponsor by letter, telephone conference, facsimile, secure e-mail, or other expedient means.
2. The timeline for such communication will be within 14 calendar days after the 60 day filing date.
3. If no deficiencies were noted, FDA will so notify the sponsor.
4. FDA's filing review represents a preliminary review of the application and is not indicative of deficiencies that may be identified later in the review cycle.
5. FDA will provide the sponsor a notification of deficiencies prior to the goal date for 50% of applications in FY 2003, 70% in FY 2004, and 90% in FY 2005, FY2006, and FY 2007.

B. Good Review Management Principles Guidance: FDA will develop a joint CDER-CBER guidance on Good Review Management Principles (GRMPs), and publish final guidance by the end of FY 2003. The Good Review Management Principles will address, among other elements, the following:

1. The filing review process, including communication of issues identified during the filing review that may affect approval of the application.
2. Ongoing communication with the sponsor during the review process (in accordance with 21 CFR 314.102(a)), including emphasis on early communication of easily correctable deficiencies (21 CFR 314.102(b)).
3. Appropriate use of Information Request and Discipline Review letters, as well as other informal methods of communication (phone, fax, e-mail).
4. Anticipating/planning for a potential Advisory Committee meeting.
5. Completing the primary reviews – allowing time for secondary and tertiary reviews prior to the action goal date.
6. Labeling feedback – planning to provide labeling comments and scheduling time for teleconferences with the sponsor in advance of the action goal date

C. Training: FDA will develop and implement a program for training all review personnel, including current employees as well as future new hires, on the good review management principles.

GENERIC AND INNOVATOR DRUGS

D. Evaluation: FDA will retain an independent expert consultant to undertake a study to evaluate issues associated with the conduct of first cycle reviews.

1. The study will be designed to assess current performance and changes that occur after the guidance on GRMPs is published. The study will include collection of various types of tracking data regarding actions that occur during the first cycle review, both from an FDA and industry perspective (e.g., IR letters, DR letters, draft labeling comments from FDA to the sponsor, sponsor response to FDA requests for information).
2. The study will also include an assessment of the first cycle review history of all NDAs for NMEs and all BLAs during PDUFA 3. This assessment will include a more detailed evaluation of the events that occurred during the review process with a focus on identifying best practices by FDA and industry that facilitated the review process.
3. The study will also include an assessment of the effectiveness of the training program implemented by FDA.
4. FDA will develop a statement of work for the study and will provide the public an opportunity to review and comment on the statement of work before the study is implemented. The consultant will prepare annual reports of the findings of the study and a final study report at the end of the 5-year study period. The full (un-redacted) study reports will be provided to the FDA Commissioner and a version of the study reports redacted to remove confidential commercial information or other information exempt from disclosure, will be made available to the public.
5. Development and implementation of the study of first cycle review performance will be a component of the Performance Management Plan conducted out of the Office of the Commissioner (see section X).
6. Administrative oversight of the study will rest in the Office of the Commissioner. The Office of the Commissioner will convene a joint CDER/CBER review panel on a quarterly basis as a mechanism for ongoing assessment of the application of Good Review Management Principles to actions taken on original NDA/BLA applications.

XI. IMPROVING FDA PERFORMANCE MANAGEMENT

A. Performance Fund: The Commissioner will use at least $7 million over five years of PDUFA III funds for initiatives targeted to improve the drug review process.

1. Funds would be made available by the Commissioner to the Centers based both on identified areas of greatest need for process improvements as well as on achievement of previously identified objectives.
2. Funds also could be used by the FDA Commissioner to diagnose why objectives are not being met, or to examine areas of concern.
3. The studies conducted under this initiative would be intended to foster: a. Development of programs to improve access to internal and external expertise b. Reviewer development programs, particularly as they relate to drug review processes, c. Advancing science and use of information management tools d. Improving both inter- and intra-Center consistency, efficiency, and effectiveness e. Improved reporting of management objectives f. Increased accountability for use of

APPENDIX 89

user fee revenues g. Focused investments on improvements in the process of drug review h. Improved communication between the FDA and industry
4. In deciding how to spend these funds, the Commissioner would take into consideration how to achieve greater harmonization of capabilities between CDER and CBER.

B. First Two Initiatives: Two specific initiatives will begin early in PDUFA III and supported from performance management initiative funds 1) evaluation of first cycle review performance, and 2) process review and analysis within the two centers.

1. First Cycle Review Performance See the First Cycle Review Performance (See section X. for details on this proposed study).
2. Process Review and Analysis
   a. In FY 2003, FDA will contract with an outside consultant to conduct a comprehensive process review and analysis within CDER and CBER. This review will involve a thorough analysis of information utilization, review management, and activity cost.
   b. The review is expected to take from 18-24 months, although its duration will depend on the type and amount of complexity of the issues uncovered during the review.
   c. The outcome of this review will be a thorough documentation of the process, a re-map of the process indicating where efficiencies can be gained, activity-based project accounting, optimal use of review tools, and a suggested path for implementing the recommendations.
   d. FDA would anticipate delivery of a report of the consultant's findings and recommendations in FY 2004-2005. The agency would consider these recommendations in planning any redesign or process reengineering to enhance performance.
3. Further Studies

In subsequent years of PDUFA III, FDA may develop other study plans that will focus on further analysis of program design, performance features and costs, to identify potential avenues for further enhancement. Future studies would be likely to include a comprehensive re-analysis of program costs following the implementation of new PDUFA III review initiatives and the adoption of any process changes following the recommendations of the year 1 and 2 studies.

XII. ELECTRONIC APPLICATIONS AND SUBMISSIONS - GOALS

a. The Agency will centralize the accountability and funding for all PDUFA Information Technology initiatives/activities for CBER, CDER, ORA and OC under the leadership of the FDA CIO. The July 2001 HHS IT 5-year plan states that infrastructure consolidation across the department should be achieved, including standardization. The Agency CIO will be responsible for ensuring that all PDUFA III IT infrastructure and IT investments support the Agency's common IT goals, fit into a common computing environment, and follow good IT management practices.
b. The Agency CIO will chair quarterly briefings on PDUFA IT issues to periodically review and evaluate the progress of IT initiatives against project milestones, discuss alternatives when projects are not progressing, and review proposals for new initiatives. On an annual basis, an assessment will be conducted of progress against

GENERIC AND INNOVATOR DRUGS

PDUFA III IT goals and, established program milestones, including appropriate changes to plans. A documented summary of the assessment will be drafted and forwarded to the Commissioner A version of the study report redacted to remove confidential commercial or security information, or other information exempt from disclosure, will be made available to the public. The project milestones, assessment and changes will be part of the annual PDUFA III IT report.

c. FDA will implement a common solution in CBER, CDER, ORA and OC for the secure exchange of content including secure e-mail, electronic signatures, and secure submission of, and access to application components.

d. FDA will deliver a single point of entry for the receipt and processing of all electronic submissions in a highly secure environment. This will support CBER, CDER, OC and ORA. The system should automate the current electronic submission processes such as checking the content of electronic submissions for completeness and electronically acknowledging submissions.

e. FDA will provide a specification format for the electronic submission of the Common Technical Document (e-CTD), and provide an electronic review system for this new format that will be used by CBER, CDER and ORA reviewers. Implementation should include training to ensure successful deployment. This project will serve as the foundation for automation of other types of electronic submissions. The review software will be made available to the public. .

f. Within the first 12 months, FDA will conduct an objective analysis and develop a plan for consolidation of PDUFA III IT infrastructure and desktop management services activities that will assess and prioritize the consolidation possibilities among CBER, CDER, ORA and OC to achieve technical efficiencies, target potential savings and realize cost efficiencies. Based upon the results of this analysis, to the extent appropriate, establish common IT infrastructure and architecture components according to specific milestones and dates. A documented summary of the analysis will be forwarded to the Commissioner. A version of the study report redacted to remove confidential commercial or security information, or other information exempt from disclosure, will be made available to the public.

g. FDA will implement Capability Maturity Model (CMM) in CBER, CDER, ORA and OC for PDUFA IT infrastructure and investments, and include other industry best practices to ensure that PDUFA III IT products and projects are of high quality and produced with optimal efficiency and cost effectiveness. This includes development of project plans and schedules, goals, estimates of required resources, issues and risks/mitigation plans for each PDUFA III IT initiative.

h. Where common business needs exist, CBER, CDER, ORA and OC will use the same software applications, such as eCTD software, and COTS solutions.

i. Within six months of authorization, a PDUFA III IT 5-year plan will be developed. Progress will be measured against the milestones described in the plan.

XIII. ADDITIONAL PROCEDURES

A. Simplification of Action Letters

To simplify regulatory procedures, CBER and CDER intend to amend their regulations and processes to provide for the issuance of either an "approval" (AP) or a "complete response" (CR) action letter at the completion of a review cycle for a marketing application.

APPENDIX 89

B. Timing of Sponsor Notification of Deficiencies in Applications

To help expedite the development of drug and biologic products, CBER and CDER intend to submit deficiencies to sponsors in the form of an "information request" (IR) letter when each discipline has finished its initial review of its section of the pending application.

XIV. DEFINITIONS AND EXPLANATION OF TERMS

A. The term "review and act on" is understood to mean the issuance of a complete action letter after the complete review of a filed complete application. The action letter, if it is not an approval, will set forth in detail the specific deficiencies and, where appropriate, the actions necessary to place the application in condition for approval.

B. A major amendment to an original application, efficacy supplement, or resubmission of any of these applications, submitted within three months of the goal date, extends the goal date by three months. A major amendment to a manufacturing supplement submitted within two months of the goal date extends the goal date by two months.

C. A resubmitted original application is a complete response to an action letter addressing all identified deficiencies.

D. Class 1 resubmitted applications are applications resubmitted after a complete response letter (or a not approvable or approvable letter) that include the following items only (or combinations of these items):

1. Final printed labeling

2. Draft labeling

3. Safety updates submitted in the same format, including tabulations, as the original safety submission with new data and changes highlighted (except when large amounts of new information including important new adverse experiences not previously reported with the product are presented in the resubmission)

4. Stability updates to support provisional or final dating periods

5. Commitments to perform Phase 4 studies, including proposals for such studies

6. Assay validation data

7. Final release testing on the last 1-2 lots used to support approval

8. A minor reanalysis of data previously submitted to the application

(determined by the agency as fitting the Class 1 category)

9. Other minor clarifying information (determined by the Agency as fitting the Class 1 category)

10. Other specific items may be added later as the Agency gains experience with the scheme and will be communicated via guidance documents to industry.

E. Class 2 resubmissions are resubmissions that include any other items, including any item that would require presentation to an advisory committee.

F. A Type A Meeting is a meeting which is necessary for an otherwise stalled drug development program to proceed (a "critical path" meeting).

G. A Type B Meeting is a 1) pre-IND, 2) end of Phase 1 (for Subpart E or Subpart H or similar products) or end of Phase 2/pre-Phase 3, or 3) a pre- NDA/BLA meeting. Each requestor should usually only request 1 each of these Type B meetings for each potential application (NDA/BLA) (or combination of closely related products, i.e., same active ingredient but different dosage forms being developed concurrently).

H. A Type C Meeting is any other type of meeting.

I. The performance goals and procedures also apply to original applications and supplements for human drugs initially marketed on an over-the-counter (OTC) basis through an NDA or switched from prescription to OTC status through an NDA or supplement.

PDUFA Home
FDA Home Page | Search | A-Z Index | Site Map | Contact FDA

FDA/Website Management Staff
Web page created by smc 2002-JUN-19.

APPENDIX 90

Section 262, Public Health Service Act (biologics license), 42 U.S.C. 262

U.S. Food and Drug Administration

From the U.S. House of Representatives Downloadable U.S. Code
[uscode.house.gov]
[Laws in effect as of January 5, 1999]

[CITE: 42USC262]

TITLE 42 - THE PUBLIC HEALTH AND WELFARE
    CHAPTER 6A - PUBLIC HEALTH SERVICE
    SUBCHAPTER II - GENERAL POWERS AND DUTIES
    Part F - Licensing of Biological Products and Clinical Laboratories
    subpart 1 - biological products

-HEAD-
    Sec. 262. Regulation of biological products

-STATUTE-
    (a) Biologics license
        (1) No person shall introduce or deliver for introduction into
interstate commerce any biological product unless -
            (A) a biologics license is in effect for the biological
    product; and
            (B) each package of the biological product is plainly marked
    with -
                (i) the proper name of the biological product contained in
        the package;
                (ii) the name, address, and applicable license number of the
        manufacturer of the biological product; and
                (iii) the expiration date of the biological product.
        (2)(A) The Secretary shall establish, by regulation, requirements
for the approval, suspension, and revocation of biologics licenses.
            (B) The Secretary shall approve a biologics license application -
                (i) on the basis of a demonstration that -
                    (I) the biological product that is the subject of the
        application is safe, pure, and potent; and
                    (II) the facility in which the biological product is
        manufactured, processed, packed, or held meets standards
        designed to assure that the biological product continues to be
        safe, pure, and potent; and
                (ii) if the applicant (or other appropriate person) consents to
        the inspection of the facility that is the subject of the
        application, in accordance with subsection (c) of this section.
        (3) The Secretary shall prescribe requirements under which a
biological product undergoing investigation shall be exempt from
the requirements of paragraph (1).
    (b) Falsely labeling or marking package or container; altering
        label or mark
    No person shall falsely label or mark any package or container of
any biological product or alter any label or mark on the package or
container of the biological product so as to falsify the label or
mark.
    (c) Inspection of establishment for propagation and preparation
    Any officer, agent, or employee of the Department of Health and
Human Services, authorized by the Secretary for the purpose, may
during all reasonable hours enter and inspect any establishment for
the propagation or manufacture and preparation of any biological
product.
    (d) Recall of product presenting imminent hazard; violations
        (1) Upon a determination that a batch, lot, or other quantity of
a product licensed under this section presents an imminent or

GENERIC AND INNOVATOR DRUGS

substantial hazard to the public health, the Secretary shall issue an order immediately ordering the recall of such batch, lot, or other quantity of such product. An order under this paragraph shall be issued in accordance with section 554 of title 5.

(2) Any violation of paragraph (1) shall subject the violator to a civil penalty of up to $100,000 per day of violation. The amount of a civil penalty under this paragraph shall, effective December 1 of each year beginning 1 year after the effective date of this paragraph, be increased by the percent change in the Consumer Price Index for the base quarter of such year over the Consumer Price Index for the base quarter of the preceding year, adjusted to the nearest 1/10 of 1 percent. For purposes of this paragraph, the term ''base quarter'', as used with respect to a year, means the calendar quarter ending on September 30 of such year and the price index for a base quarter is the arithmetical mean of such index for the 3 months comprising such quarter.

(e) Interference with officers

No person shall interfere with any officer, agent, or employee of the Service in the performance of any duty imposed upon him by this section or by regulations made by authority thereof.

(f) Penalties for offenses

Any person who shall violate, or aid or abet in violating, any of the provisions of this section shall be punished upon conviction by a fine not exceeding $500 or by imprisonment not exceeding one year, or by both such fine and imprisonment, in the discretion of the court.

(g) Construction with other laws

Nothing contained in this chapter shall be construed as in any way affecting, modifying, repealing, or superseding the provisions of the Federal Food, Drug, and Cosmetic Act (21 U.S.C. 301 et seq.).

(h) Exportation of partially processed biological products

A partially processed biological product which -

(1) is not in a form applicable to the prevention, treatment, or cure of diseases or injuries of man;

(2) is not intended for sale in the United States; and

(3) is intended for further manufacture into final dosage form outside the United States,

shall be subject to no restriction on the export of the product under this chapter or the Federal Food, Drug, and Cosmetic Act (21 U.S.C. 301 et. seq.) if the product is manufactured, processed, packaged, and held in conformity with current good manufacturing practice requirements or meets international manufacturing standards as certified by an international standards organization recognized by the Secretary and meets the requirements of section 801(e)(1) of the Federal Food, Drug, and Cosmetic Act (21 U.S.C. 381(e)).

(i) ''Biological product'' defined

In this section, the term ''biological product'' means a virus, therapeutic serum, toxin, antitoxin, vaccine, blood, blood component or derivative, allergenic product, or analogous product, or arsphenamine or derivative of arsphenamine (or any other trivalent organic arsenic compound), applicable to the prevention, treatment, or cure of a disease or condition of human beings.

(j) Application of Federal Food, Drug, and Cosmetic Act

The Federal Food, Drug, and Cosmetic Act (21 U.S.C. 301 et seq.) applies to a biological product subject to regulation under this section, except that a product for which a license has been approved under subsection (a) shall not be required to have an approved application under section 505 of such Act (21 U.S.C. 355).

APPENDIX 91

Guidance for Industry — Court Decisions, ANDA Approvals, and 180-Day Exclusivity Under the Hatch-Waxman Amendments to the Federal Food, Drug, and Cosmetic Act (March 2000)

Guidance for Industry

Court Decisions, ANDA Approvals, and 180-Day Exclusivity Under the Hatch-Waxman Amendments to the Federal Food, Drug, and Cosmetic Act

U.S. Department of Health and Human Services
Food and Drug Administration
Center for Drug Evaluation and Research (CDER)
Procedural

March 2000

Guidance for Industry

Court Decisions, ANDA Approvals, and 180-Day Exclusivity Under the Hatch-Waxman Amendments to the Federal Food, Drug, and Cosmetic Act

Comments and suggestions regarding this document should be submitted within 90 days of publication in the *Federal Register* of the notice announcing the availability of the guidance. All comments should be identified with the docket number provided at the beginning of the notice. Submit comments to the Dockets Management Branch (HFA-305), Food and Drug Administration, 12420 Parklawn Dr., rm. 1-23, Rockville, MD 20857.

After the comment period closes, comments should be provided in writing to the Center for Drug Evaluation and Research (CDER), Food and Drug Administration, 5600 Fishers Lane, Rockville, MD 20857.

Additional copies of this Guidance are available from:

Office of Training and Communications
Division of Communications Management
Drug Information Branch, HFD-210
Center for Drug Evaluation and Research
Food and Drug Administration
5600 Fishers Lane, Rockville, MD 20857
(Phone 301-827-4573)
Internet: http://www.fda.gov/cder/guidance/index.htm.

APPENDIX 91

TABLE OF CONTENTS

I. WHY IS FDA ISSUING THIS GUIDANCE? 1

II. STATUTORY AND REGULATORY BACKGROUND 2
    A. ANDA APPROVALS AND COURT DECISION 2
    B. 180-DAY EXCLUSIVITY AND DECISION OF A COURT 2

III. LITIGATION, CURRENT ISSUES, AND AGENCY POSITION 2

IV. EFFECT ON ANDA APPROVALS AND 180-DAY EXCLUSIVITY 4
    A. NEW DEFINITION OF *COURT* 4
    B. IMPLEMENTATION OF NEW DEFINITION OF *COURT* 4

GENERIC AND INNOVATOR DRUGS

Guidance for Industry[1]

Court Decisions, ANDA Approvals, and 180-Day Exclusivity Under the Hatch-Waxman Amendments to the Federal Food, Drug, and Cosmetic Act

I.   WHY IS FDA ISSUING THIS GUIDANCE?

This guidance is being issued in response to recent litigation and is intended to provide guidance to the pharmaceutical industry regarding (1) the timing of approval of abbreviated new drug applications (ANDAs) following an unsuccessful patent infringement action by the patent owner or new drug application (NDA) holder and (2) the start of 180 days of generic drug exclusivity.

FDA's interpretation of two provisions of the Federal Food, Drug, and Cosmetic Act (the Act) have been affected by recent court decisions interpreting the phrase "decision of a court" or "court decision." Section 505(j)(5)(B)(iii) of the Act governs the approval of ANDAs when the patent owner or NDA holder has brought a timely patent infringement action in response to the ANDA applicant's notice of filing of a paragraph IV certification to a listed patent. Section 505(j)(5)(B)(iv) of the Act governs the eligibility for and timing of 180-day exclusivity. The regulations implementing these statutory provisions are found at 21 CFR 314.107. Certain aspects of these regulations have been successfully challenged in *TorPharm, Inc. v. Shalala* and *Mylan Pharmaceuticals, Inc. v. Shalala*.[2] This guidance describes the Agency's response to those court decisions.

---

[1] This guidance has been prepared by the Office of Generic Drugs in the Center for Drug Evaluation and Research (CDER) at the Food and Drug Administration. This guidance represents the Agency's current thinking on sections 505(j)(5)(B)(iii)(I) and (iv) of the Act. It does not create or confer any rights for or on any person and does not operate to bind FDA or the public. An alternative approach may be used if such approach satisfies the requirements of the applicable statutes, regulations, or both.

[2] *TorPharm, Inc. v. Shalala,* No. 97-1925, 1997 U.S. Dist. LEXIS 21983 (D.D.C. Sep. 15, 1997), *appeal withdrawn and remanded,* 1998 U.S. App. LEXIS 4681 (D.C. Cir. Feb. 5, 1998); *vacated* No. 97-1925 (D.D.C. Apr. 9, 1998); *Mylan Pharmaceuticals, Inc. v. Shalala,* No. 99-2995, slip op. (D.D.C. Jan. 4, 2000).

APPENDIX 91

II. STATUTORY AND REGULATORY BACKGROUND

A. ANDA Approvals and Court Decision

The concept of a court decision is used in two important places in section 505(j) of the Act — in the provision governing the timing of ANDA approvals and in the 180-day exclusivity provision. There is a 30-month statutory bar to approval of an ANDA that is the subject of patent infringement litigation except if "before the expiration of such period the court decides that such patent is invalid or not infringed, the approval will be made effective on the date of the *court decision*" (section 505(j)(5)(B)(iii)(I) (emphasis added)). In implementing this provision, FDA interpreted *court* to mean "the court that enters final judgment from which no appeal can be or has been taken" (21 CFR 314.107(e)(1) (1999)). The Agency's reasons for adopting this interpretation are discussed in the preambles to the proposed and final rules implementing the 1984 Drug Price Competition and Patent Term Restoration Act.[3]

B. 180-Day Exclusivity and Decision of a Court

Certain court decisions are also important for 180-day generic drug exclusivity. FDA's interpretation of *court* in the court decision described in Section 505(j)(5)(B)(iii)(I) was influenced by the role such a decision plays in 180-day exclusivity. The 180-day period of exclusivity can begin on either (1) the date of first commercial marketing or (2) "the date of *a decision of a court* ... holding the patent which is the subject of the [paragraph IV] certification to be invalid, or not infringed, whichever is earlier" (section 505(j)(5)(B)(iv) (emphasis added)). As described in the preambles to the implementing regulations, FDA believed that for the 180-day exclusivity to have real meaning for the eligible ANDA applicant, the court decision triggering the exclusivity must be the one that finally resolves the patent infringement litigation related to the ANDA.[4] Therefore, for purposes of section 505(j)(5)(B)(iv), FDA determined that *court* means "the court that enters final judgment from which no appeal can be or has been taken" (21 CFR 314.107(e)(1) (1999)).

III. LITIGATION, CURRENT ISSUES, AND AGENCY POSITION

FDA's interpretation of the term *court* has been successfully challenged in the context of both the timing of ANDA approvals and the commencement of 180-day exclusivity. In *TorPharm v. Shalala*, the D.C. District Court found the FDA's interpretation not supported by the statute and directed FDA to approve an ANDA upon a decision of the district court finding a patent invalid, unenforceable, or not infringed. When the case became moot, FDA's appeal of that decision was withdrawn, and the district

---

[3] 54 FR 28872, 28893-95 (July 10, 1989); 59 FR 50338, 50352-54 (October 3, 1994).

[4] 54 FR 28893-95 (July 10, 1989); 59 FR 50352-54 (October 3, 1994).

GENERIC AND INNOVATOR DRUGS

court opinion was vacated. In the period since the *TorPharm* decision, FDA has continued to apply the definition of *court* set out at 314.107(e).[5]

Recently, in *Mylan Pharmaceuticals, Inc. v. Shalala.*, the D.C. District Court found FDA's interpretation of *court* as used in the 180-day exclusivity context inconsistent with the statute's plain meaning. However, the court also determined that the applicant who relied in good faith on FDA's interpretation of the 180-day exclusivity provision should not be punished by losing its exclusivity. The court therefore refused to order FDA to begin the running of 180-day exclusivity upon the decision of the district court in the patent litigation at issue.

These recent decisions add considerable uncertainty to FDA's implementation of the ANDA approval and 180-day generic drug exclusivity programs. These regulatory programs already have been disrupted by the changes in eligibility for 180-day exclusivity necessitated by *Mova Pharmaceutical Corp. v. Shalala* and *Granutec, Inc. v. Shalala*.[6] Therefore, in determining its response to the *TorPharm* and *Mylan* decisions, a primary concern for the Agency has been to identify an approach that will minimize further disruption and provide the regulated industry with reasonable guidance for making future business decisions.

The government has decided not to appeal the *Mylan* decision and will follow that court's interpretation of the statute in approving ANDAs and calculating the commencement of 180 days of exclusivity. Although the Agency believes that the statutory provisions at issue may properly be interpreted as FDA sets out in § 314.107(e), the Agency nonetheless has determined that it is in the interest of the regulated industry and the Agency to accept the interpretation of the *TorPharm* and *Mylan* courts. Therefore, the Agency will not apply the definition of the *court* found at § 314.107(e) (1) and (2) (i)-(iii).[7] The Agency intends to formally remove the relevant sections of § 314.107(e), and will incorporate the *TorPharm* and *Mylan* courts' interpretation of the statute into the final rule implementing the changes in 180-day exclusivity.[8] As described in section IV, FDA will implement the new interpretation of the term "court" prospectively, in a manner consistent with the court's approach in *Mylan*.

---

[5] Guidance for industry *180-Day Generic Drug Exclusivity Under the Hatch-Waxman Amendments to the Federal Food, Drug, and Cosmetic Act*, June 1998, p. 2, n. 3.

[6] *Mova Pharmaceutical Corp. v. Shalala*, 140 F.3d 1060 (D.C.Cir. 1998); *Granutec, Inc. v. Shalala*, 46 U.S.P.Q.2d 1398 (4th Cir. 1998).

[7] Applicants will still be required to submit a copy of the relevant order or judgment to the Office of Generic Drugs under § 314.107(e)(2)(iv).

[8] 64 FR 42873 (August 6, 1999).

3

APPENDIX 91

IV. EFFECT ON ANDA APPROVALS AND 180-DAY EXCLUSIVITY

A. New Definition of *Court*

FDA will interpret the term *court* as found in section 505(j)(5)(B)(iii)(I) and 505(j)(5)(B)(iv) to mean the first court that renders a decision finding the patent at issue invalid, unenforceable, or not infringed. When it is the district court that renders such a decision, FDA may approve the ANDA as of the date the district court enters its decision. For eligible applicants, 180-day exclusivity will also begin to run on that date, unless it has already begun with commercial marketing. If the district court finds the patent is infringed, but that decision is reversed on appeal, the Agency may approve the ANDA on the date the district court issues a judgment that the patent is invalid, unenforceable, or not infringed pursuant to a mandate issued by a court of appeals.[9]

Neither a stay nor a reversal of a district court decision finding the patent invalid, unenforceable, or not infringed will have an effect on the approval of the ANDA or on the beginning, or continued running, of exclusivity. Should the NDA holder or patent owner wish to prevent an applicant with an approved ANDA from marketing its product during the course of an appeal, it must obtain an injunction from the court. If there is an injunction barring marketing of an approved drug, the ANDA applicant and NDA holder are asked to notify FDA, and the Agency will move the drug to the discontinued section of *Approved Drug Products with Therapeutic Equivalence Evaluations* (the *Orange Book*), so as to minimize confusion in the marketplace. Once the injunction is lifted or expires and if the ANDA applicant notifies the Agency it has begun marketing its product, the drug will be moved back to the active section of the *Orange Book*. The 180-day exclusivity period will continue to run during the pendency of a stay or injunction.

B. Implementation of New Definition of *Court*

The new definition of *court* will apply to certain ANDAs submitted after the publication of this guidance. Specifically, the new definition will be used for approval and exclusivity determinations for ANDAs containing a paragraph IV certification where the ANDA cites a reference listed drug for which no other ANDA containing a paragraph IV certification has been submitted.

This new interpretation of the statute may substantially change the value of the 180-day exclusivity. As Judge Roberts recognizes in the *Mylan* opinion, applicants who have made certain business decisions in good faith reliance upon an FDA regulation should not be penalized for their actions. For example, the potential change in the value of exclusivity may have considerable effect upon an ANDA applicant's willingness to file a paragraph IV certification to a patent and to undertake the effort and expense of litigating a patent infringement suit. This may be particularly true for patent challenges that are seen as risky, but for which the possible award of a full exclusivity was an adequate incentive. Judge Roberts also noted that based upon FDA's interpretation of the statute, ANDA applicants have held products off the market even after a victory in the district court.

---

[9] This is the same process as described in current § 314.107(e)(2)(iii).

The Agency believes that an implementation plan for the new definition of *court* that recognizes the industry's reliance on the previous definition and establishes a *bright line* for ANDAs affected by the new definition will minimize the disruption to the ANDA approval and 180-day exclusivity programs. Moreover, the Agency believes that this approach will lessen the likelihood that ANDA applicants will sue the Agency alleging that they, like Geneva in the *Mylan* case, relied in good faith on the Agency's regulation and would be irreparably injured by application of the new interpretation to pending ANDAs.

5

APPENDIX 92

Food and Drug Administration, Proposed Rule on Patent Listing Requirements and 30-Month Stays on ANDAs, 67 Fed. Reg. 65448 (October 24, 2002)

Thursday,
October 24, 2002

Part III

Department of Health and Human Services

Food and Drug Administration

21 CFR Part 314
Applications for FDA Approval to Market a New Drug: Patent Listing Requirements and Application of 30-Month Stays on Approval of Abbreviated New Drug Applications Certifying That a Patent Claiming a Drug is Invalid or Will Not be Infringed; Proposed Rule

GENERIC AND INNOVATOR DRUGS

DEPARTMENT OF HEALTH AND HUMAN SERVICES

Food and Drug Administration

21 CFR Part 314

[Docket No. 02N–0417]

RIN 0910–AC48

Applications for FDA Approval to Market a New Drug: Patent Listing Requirements and Application of 30-Month Stays on Approval of Abbreviated New Drug Applications Certifying That a Patent Claiming a Drug is Invalid or Will Not be Infringed

AGENCY: Food and Drug Administration, HHS.

ACTION: Proposed rule.

SUMMARY: The Food and Drug Administration (FDA) is proposing to amend its patent listing requirements for new drug applications (NDAs). The proposal would clarify the types of patents that must and must not be listed and revise the declaration that NDA applicants must provide regarding their patents to help ensure that NDA applicants list only appropriate patents. The proposal would also revise the regulations regarding the effective date of approval for certain abbreviated new drug applications (ANDAs) and certain applications submitted under section 505(b)(2) of the Federal Food, Drug, and Cosmetic Act (the act) (505(b)(2) applications). In certain situations, Federal law bars FDA from making the approval of an ANDA or 505(b)(2) application effective for 30 months if the applicant certified that the patent claiming a drug is invalid or will not be infringed, and the patent owner or NDA holder brings suit for patent infringement. The proposal also would state that there will be only one opportunity for a 30-month stay in the approval date of each ANDA or 505(b)(2) application. The proposal is designed to make the patent listing process more efficient and to enhance the ANDA and 505(b)(2) application approval processes.

DATES: Submit written or electronic comments by December 23, 2002. Submit written comments on the information collection requirements by November 25, 2002.

ADDRESSES: Submit written comments to the Dockets Management Branch (HFA–305), Food and Drug Administration, 5630 Fishers Lane, rm. 1061, Rockville, MD 20852. Submit electronic comments to http://www.fda.gov/dockets/ecomments. Submit written comments on the information collection provisions to the Office of Information and Regulatory Affairs, Office of Management and Budget (OMB), New Executive Office Bldg., 725 17th St. NW., rm. 10235, Washington, DC 20503, Attn: Stuart Shapiro, Desk Officer for FDA.

FOR FURTHER INFORMATION CONTACT: Jarilyn Dupont, Office of Policy, Planning, and Legislation (HFW–14), Food and Drug Administration, 5600 Fishers Lane, Rockville, MD 20857, 301–827–3360.

SUPPLEMENTARY INFORMATION:

I. Background

A. What Is the Relationship Between Patent Listing, Patent Certification, and the Date of Approval for Certain Applications?

Title I of the Drug Price Competition and Patent Term Restoration Act (Public Law 98–417, 98 Stat. 1585 (1984) ("Hatch-Waxman amendments")) amended the act to authorize the approval of duplicate or "generic" versions of approved drug products. Title I also amended section 505(b)(1) of the act (21 U.S.C. 355(b)(1)) by requiring all NDA applicants to file, as part of the NDA, "the patent number and the expiration date of any patent which claims the drug for which the applicant submitted the application or which claims a method of using such drug and with respect to which a claim of patent infringement could reasonably be asserted if a person not licensed by the owner engaged in the manufacture, use, or sale of the drug." Section 505(c)(2) of the act imposes a similar patent listing obligation on persons whose NDAs we have approved when the NDA holder could not have filed the patent information with its application (either because the application was filed before the act required NDA applicants to submit patent information or because the patent issued after we had approved the NDA).

We publish patent information in our approved drug products list entitled "Approved Drug Products With Therapeutic Equivalence Evaluations." The list is known popularly as the "Orange Book" because of its orange-colored cover.

The Hatch-Waxman amendments also require persons submitting a 505(b)(2) application or ANDA to make certifications regarding the listed patents pertaining to the drug which they intend to duplicate (see sections 505(b)(2)(A)(i) through (b)(2)(A)(iv) and 505(j)(2)(A)(vii)(I) through (j)(2)(A)(vii)(IV) of the act). In brief, these certifications state that:

• Patent information has not been filed;
• The patent has expired;
• The patent will expire on a specific date; or
• The patent is invalid or will not be infringed.

If the ANDA or 505(b)(2) application applicant certifies that the patent is invalid or will not be infringed (a certification known as a "paragraph IV" certification because it is the fourth type of patent certification described in the act), the act requires the applicant to notify the patent owner and NDA holder (see sections 505(c)(3) and 505(j)(2)(B) of the act.) In general, the notice states that an abbreviated application has been submitted for the drug with respect to which the paragraph IV certification is made and also includes a "detailed statement of the factual and legal basis of the applicant's opinion that the patent is not valid or will not be infringed" (id.). If an action for patent infringement is brought within 45 days after the paragraph IV certification has been received, then we may not make the approval of an abbreviated application effective for 30 months, or such shorter or longer period as a court may order or the date of a court decision (see sections 505(c)(3)(C) and 505(j)(4)(B)(iii) of the act).

These statutory provisions reflect the Hatch-Waxman amendments' attempt to balance two competing interests: Promoting competition between "brand-name" and "generic" drugs and encouraging research and innovation. The act promotes competition by creating a process to expedite the filing and approval of ANDAs and 505(b)(2) applications and for resolving challenges to patents before marketing begins. At the same time, the act seeks to protect the patent owner's or NDA holder's interests by giving it the opportunity to list patents, to receive paragraph IV certifications, and to delay an ANDA's or 505(b)(2) application's effective date of approval during patent infringement litigation. (We will refer to the date the approval is made effective as the "approval date" throughout the remainder of this preamble.)

We published regulations pertaining to patent listing and patent certifications in the **Federal Register** on October 3, 1994 (59 FR 50338). The regulations regarding the submission of patent information are at §§ 314.50(h) and 314.53 (21 CFR 314.50(h) and 314.53), while the patent certification requirements are at §§ 314.50(i) and 314.94(a)(12) for 505(b)(2) applications and ANDAs respectively.

APPENDIX 92

Federal Register/Vol. 67, No. 206/Thursday, October 24, 2002/Proposed Rules   65449

B. What Events Led to This Proposal?

In recent years, we have seen NDA applicants list new patents shortly before other listed patents for the same drug product are scheduled to expire. Some listings, such as those for BuSpar (buspirone hydrochloride), Paxil (paroxetine hydrochloride), Tiazac (diltiazem hydrochloride), and Prilosec (omeprazole), have resulted in high profile litigation. (We discuss some of these cases in section II.A of this document.) A number of disputes over recently listed patents have addressed whether the patent meets the regulatory requirements for listing in the Orange Book and have sometimes resulted in decisions that are not entirely consistent with our regulatory policy or our interpretation of our regulations.

Additionally, on May 16, 2001, the Bureau of Competition and the Policy Planning Staff of the Federal Trade Commission (FTC) submitted a citizen petition (FDA docket number 01P–0248) (FTC Citizen Petition) that requested our guidance concerning the criteria that a patent must meet before it is listed in the Orange Book. The FTC Citizen Petition asked us to clarify several patent listing issues and indicated that FTC was conducting an extensive study of generic drug competition. FTC issued the study in July 2002, in a report entitled *Generic Drug Entry Prior to Patent Expiration: An FTC Study* (FTC Report). The FTC Report focused on the procedures used to facilitate a generic drug's entry into the market before the expiration of a patent or patents that pertain to the brand-name drug product. The FTC Report noted that FTC had submitted a citizen petition to us. FTC also recommended that the law be changed to "permit only one automatic 30-month stay per drug product per ANDA to resolve infringement disputes over patents listed in the Orange Book prior to the filing date of the generic applicant's ANDA" (see FTC Report at page ii). The FTC Report explained, "To permit only one 30-month stay per drug product per ANDA should eliminate most of the potential for improper Orange Book listings to generate unwarranted 30-month stays" (*id.* at page v (footnote omitted)). In an appendix to its report, FTC asked that we issue a regulation or guidance clarifying whether an NDA holder could list various types of patents in the Orange Book. The types of patents for which FTC sought clarification were patents that claimed metabolites, polymorphs, or intermediates, product by process patents, and double patents (see FTC Report at pages A–39–A–45).

II. Description of the Proposed Rule

Given these patent listing issues, the FTC citizen petition, and the FTC Report, we decided to issue this proposed rule to help NDA applicants and NDA holders determine whether specific patents must be submitted to us for listing and to help 505(b)(2) application applicants, ANDA application applicants, and other interested parties determine whether a patent listing is proper. This proposed rule will address:

• The types of patents that must and must not be listed;

• The patent certification statement that NDA applicants must submit as part of an NDA, an amendment to an NDA, or a supplement to an NDA; and

• The 30-month stay in effective dates of approval for a 505(b)(2) application or an ANDA.

A. Proposed § 314.53(b)—What Patents Must Be Listed in the Orange Book?

1. *What Does the Current Regulation Say?*

Our patent listing regulation, at § 314.53, applies to persons submitting an NDA, an amendment to an NDA, or a supplement to an NDA. Section 314.53(b) describes the patents for which information must be submitted and states, in part, that the applicant:

* * * shall submit information on each patent that claims the drug that is the subject of the new drug application or amendment or supplement to it and with respect to which a claim of patent infringement could reasonably be asserted if a person not licensed by the owner of the patent engaged in the manufacture, use, or sale of the drug product. For purposes of this part, such patents consist of drug substance (ingredient) patents, drug product (formulation and composition) patents, and method of use patents. Process patents are not covered by this section and information on process patents may not be submitted to FDA.

Section 314.53 reflects the statutory provision that requires NDA applicants to file the patent number and expiration date of any patent which "claims the drug for which the applicant submitted the application or which claims a method of using such drug and with respect to which a claim of patent infringement could reasonably be asserted if a person not licensed by the owner engaged in the manufacture[,] use, or sale of the drug" (see section 505(b)(1) of the act). Thus, both the act and our regulations establish two distinct criteria for a patent intended for listing in the Orange Book: (1) The patent must claim the approved drug product or a method of using the approved drug product; and (2) the patent must be one with respect to which a claim of patent infringement could reasonably be asserted if a person

not licensed by the patent owner sought to engage in the drug's manufacture, use, or sale.

2. *How Have We Interpreted the Regulation?*

As we mentioned earlier in section I.B of this preamble, the FTC Citizen Petition sought our guidance on whether an NDA holder can list a patent claiming an unapproved aspect of an approved drug. The petition maintained that the act and our regulations do not allow listing of a patent that claimed "only an unapproved component, an unapproved formulation, or an unapproved use of a drug product" (see FTC Citizen Petition at page 3).

Our longstanding interpretation is that the term "drug" in the patent listing provisions means the approved drug product. We successfully argued in *Pfizer* v. *FDA*, 753 F. Supp. 171 (D. Md. 1990), that the term "drug" as used in sections 505(b)(1) and 505(c)(2) of the act refers to the "drug product" for which the NDA was filed. Pfizer had maintained that "drug" meant both the drug substance (active ingredient) and the drug product, and thus any patent claiming any drug product which contained the active ingredient that was the subject of the approved NDA must be submitted, regardless of whether the patent claims the approved drug product itself. This case began with our refusal to list the patent in the Orange Book because Pfizer did not certify that the drug and the formulation or composition of the drug claimed by the patent were currently approved. The drug dosage form covered by Pfizer's approved NDA was a capsule, but the patent Pfizer had sought to list claimed a tablet.

The court upheld our position that: (1) An NDA approval covers a specific drug product; (2) the approved drug product becomes the approved drug; and (3) ANDA applicants must certify only to patents claiming that listed drug. The court found that "FDA's interpretation is not only reasonable but also consistent with the language of the statute, Congressional intent, prior judicial interpretations of [21 U.S.C.] § 355, and the agency's own regulations" (see 753 F. Supp. at 171–72). It also found that section 505(b)(1) of the act modifies the statutory definition of "drug" at section 201(g)(1) of the Act (21 U.S.C. 321(g)(1)) to allow listing only of patents which claim the drug "for which the applicant submitted the application." Further, the court noted that sections 505(b)(1)(B) and (C) of the act require that an NDA application contain "a full list of the articles used as components of such drug" and "a full statement of the

157

composition of such drug," and that these requirements made sense only for a drug product and not for a drug substance that was independent of the approved NDA. Because Pfizer's NDA covered a specific drug product in capsule form (as opposed to covering the drug product's active ingredient alone or covering other dosage forms that contain the active ingredient), the court held that Pfizer could not list the patent covering the tablets.

In 1994, after the *Pfizer* decision had issued, we published a final rule that codified the patent listing requirement at 21 CFR 314.53 (see 59 FR 50338 (October 3, 1994)). Although the rule repeated the statutory requirement that the patent must claim the drug that is the subject of the NDA, the final rule replaced the proposed rule's reference to patents consisting of "drug (ingredient) patents" with patents consisting of "drug *substance* (ingredient) patents" (see 59 FR 50338 at 50343) (emphasis added). We also replaced "patents that claim a drug or drug product" with "patents that claim a drug *substance* or drug *product*" (*id.*) (emphasis added). Our intent was to clarify that the rule's reference to "drug" in the phrase "drug or drug product" was intended to mean "drug substance" rather than "drug product." (The rule mentioned drug products separately.) We made this change because some patents claim the approved drug product's active ingredient rather than the entire drug product (i.e., the drug product's active and inactive ingredients). In other words, if the patent claims the drug substance that was approved in the NDA, it must be listed.

However, some courts interpreted § 314.53 differently than we had intended. In *Zenith Laboratories, Inc.* v. *Abbott Laboratories, Inc.*, 1996 WL 33344963 (D. N.J. 1996), Abbott had listed patents claiming the dihydrate form of terazosin hydrochloride (the drug substance in the NDA-approved product whose trade name was Hytrin) and also for the anhydrous form of terazosin hydrochloride that differed from Hytrin's drug substance only in its crystalline forms. (An anhydrous form of a chemical contains no water molecules, whereas a dihydrous form contains two water molecules.) Zenith had filed an ANDA to market a drug product containing a different form of terazosin hydrochloride, and claimed that the active ingredient in its product had a different crystalline structure from Hytrin, did not infringe the patent on Hytrin, and that Abbott's patents on the anhydrous form of the active ingredient did not cover the approved drug product. The court found that the patents at issue did claim the approved drug product. The court interpreted § 314.53(b) to mean that, if a patent claims the drug substance of an approved drug product, then the patent is covered by the approved drug product and may be listed in the Orange Book even if the patent claims a form of the drug substance that is different than the form in the approved drug product. Moreover, the court indicated that we may approve an ANDA for a drug product that contains the patented form of the active ingredient. The court also cited two statements from the Orange Book to support its ruling that different forms of the same active ingredient may be considered pharmaceutically equivalent if their dissolution, solubility, and absorption are the same as the listed drug. The court concluded that the patents were likely to be construed as claiming the drug substance for the NDA-approved drug product regardless of the differences in hydration.

In *Ben Venue Laboratories, Inc.* v. *Novartis Pharmaceutical Corp.*, 10 F. Supp.2d 446 (D.N.J. 1998), Novartis had listed a patent which claimed the crystalline pentahydrate form of Aredia (pamidronate disodium). The ANDA applicant argued that the appropriateness of the patent listing turned on whether Novartis' approved product contained a crystalline hydrate of pamidronate (*id.* at page 453). The parties did not dispute that the final drug product did not contain the pentahydrate form of pamidronate. Novartis admitted that its dosage form contained an anhydrous form of pamidronate, but argued that patent was properly submitted because the patent covered the "drug substance" and because § 314.53 required the listing of such patents (*id.*). The court found that it was proper to list a patent that claims a component of the approved drug product even when that component does not appear in the exact same form in the final drug product (*id.* at pages 453–457). The court distinguished the *Pfizer* opinion as depending largely on the applicant's attempt to list a patent for a new, unapproved tablet (*id.* at page 455).

The court also noted that *Pfizer* predated our 1994 final rule and stated that:

The statute governing listing of patents merely states that NDA applicants shall file "any patent which claims the drug." 21 U.S.C. § 355(b)(1). The regulations clearly indicate that the FDA interprets the ambiguous term "drug" in 21 U.S.C. § 355(b)(1) to include certain drug substances or active ingredient patents, and requires their listing in the Orange Book. The Court concludes that the FDA's construction of the statute to require listing of certain drug substance patents as well as drug product patents is a permissible reading of the statute, and the parties do not argue otherwise. See *Chevron, U.S.A., Inc.* v. *Natural Resources Defense Counsel* [sic], 467 U.S. 837 (1984).

Therefore Ben Venue's assertion that "the drug substance or active ingredient does not determine proper listing" and that "the drug product—and it alone—controls the proper listing," * * * are inaccurate. See 10 F. Supp.2d at page 455.

Although we were not a party to the litigation, we implicitly did not accept the conclusion or reasoning of the *Zenith Laboratories* and *Ben Venue Laboratories* decisions. On February 7, 2001, we wrote to Biovail Laboratories to confirm the propriety of a corrected patent listing under § 314.53(f). Biovail had changed its manufacturing process for Tiazac (diltiazem hydrochloride), but had not sought our approval before making those changes. The approved product contained diltiazem hydrochloride in time-release coated beads, whereas Biovail's changed product contained both immediate release diltiazem hydrochloride powder and time-release coated beads. Biovail asserted that the changes were within the scope of its approved NDA, yet we learned about the changes only through litigation between Biovail and another company. In our letter to Biovail, we stated that, "FDA does not list patents for drug substances, compositions, formulations and methods of use that are not approved for the listed drug" (see Letter from Ralph Lillie, Director, Office of Information Technology, Center for Drug Evaluation and Research, to Biovail Laboratories, Inc., dated March 23, 2001). We also took the position that Biovail had to submit a supplement to its NDA to cover the immediate release diltiazem component and stated that:

Patents for drug substances, composition, formulations, and methods of use that are not approved for the listed drug are not listed in the Orange Book. A patent submitted in an application or supplement that is not yet approved will be listed in the Orange Book only if, and when the drug product is approved.
(See *id.* at page 2.)

On November 21, 2000, we responded to a citizen petition (FDA docket number 00P–0499) submitted by Lord, Bissell & Brook on behalf of Apotex, Inc. The petition asserted, in part, that two patents claiming anhydrous forms of paroxetine hydrochloride did not claim the hemihydrate listed drug. (An anhydrous form of paroxetine hydrochloride has no water molecules associated with it, whereas a hemihydrate form has one water molecule associated with every two paroxetine molecules.) Relying on the NDA holder's representations that the patents claimed the approved drug product, we concluded that the patents had been correctly submitted for listing. We stated that, "Patents must be listed if they claim the drug substance, or active ingredient, of an approved drug product, or if they claim a drug substance that is the component of such a product" (Response from Janet Woodcock, M.D., Director, Center for Drug Evaluation and Research, to Hugh L. Moore et al., Lord, Bissell & Brook, dated November 21, 2000, at page 6 (footnote omitted)). In a footnote, we noted that our position was "fully consistent with *Pfizer*" because the *Pfizer* case "involved the question of the listing of patents for a drug in a dosage form other than the dosage form approved by FDA" (*id.* at page 6, note 18), whereas the paroxetine situation involved a patent which, according to the NDA holder, claimed the approved drug product. We further stated that we considered anhydrous and hemihydrous forms of drug substances to be pharmaceutical equivalents and to contain the same active ingredient (*id.* at page 6, note 16). We cited *Zenith Laboratories* and *Ben Venue Laboratories* for the proposition that courts, rather than FDA, would resolve whether the patent covered the approved drug. Our letter did not take issue with the holdings of those courts (*id.* at page 5, note 13).

Recently, in *Andrx Pharmaceuticals, Inc.* v. *Biovail Corp.*, 276 F.3d 1368 (Fed. Cir. 2002), a case involving the patent listing correspondence with Biovail Laboratories described in a preceding paragraph, the court held that "the critical question is the relationship of the patent to the drug products and drug substances covered by the NDA" (*id.* at page 1376). The issue in the *Andrx Pharmaceuticals* case was Biovail's listing of a patent that claimed an extended release formulation of diltiazem that was different from the one we had approved. In a footnote, the Court of Appeals for the Federal Circuit cited our 1994 final rule and interpreted the final rule as changing our patent listing procedures (*id.* at page 1377, note 5). The court stated that our supposed change in position was a "more liberal construction" of the statute and led to more patents being listed in the Orange Book (*id.*).

3. *Which Patents Would the Proposal Require to Be Listed or Not Listed?*

Given these court decisions which are not entirely consistent with our policies, the FTC Report, the FTC Citizen Petition, and other documents questioning patent listing requirements, we decided to clarify our regulations to describe the types of patents that must and must not be listed. Consequently, proposed § 314.53(b) would state, in relevant part, that an applicant submitting an NDA, amending an NDA, or submitting a supplement to an NDA:

* * * shall submit information on each patent that claims the drug or a method of using the drug that is the subject of the new drug application or amendment or supplement to it and with respect to which a claim of patent infringement could reasonably be asserted if a person not licensed by the owner of the patent engaged in the manufacture, use, or sale of the drug product. For purposes of this part, such patents consist of drug substance (ingredient) patents, drug product (formulation and composition) patents, *product by process patents*, and method of use patents. Process patents, *patents claiming packaging, patents claiming metabolites*, and *patents claiming intermediates* are not covered by this section, and information on these patents may not be submitted to FDA. *For patents that claim the drug substance, the applicant shall submit information only on those patents that claim the drug substance that is the subject of the pending or approved application or that claim a drug substance that is the same as the active ingredient that is the subject of the approved or pending application within the meaning of section 505(j)(2)(A)(ii) of the Act. For patents that claim a drug product, the applicant shall submit information only on those patents that claim the drug product that is the subject of a pending or approved application. For patents that claim a method of use, the applicant shall submit information only on those patents that claim indications or other conditions of use that are the subject of a pending or approved application. For approved applications, the applicant shall identify the indication or other condition of use in the approved labeling that corresponds to the listed patent and claim identified.* * * *

We have italicized the new or revised regulatory language to make it more readily identifiable for this preamble discussion. We explain the proposed changes in more detail in the following paragraph.

a. *What Patents Must Not Be Listed Under the Proposal?*

Proposed § 314.53(a) would expressly state that information on patents claiming packaging, patents claiming metabolites, and patents claiming intermediates must not be submitted. In general, we find that these patents fail to meet the two prong criteria for listing because they do not claim the approved drug product.

Patents claiming a drug product's packaging or container may not be listed. We find that, although information regarding a drug's packaging or container is part of an NDA (see 21 CFR 314.50(d)(1)(ii)(a)), we do not approve that packaging or container per se. The packaging or container is therefore distinct from the approved drug product, so a patent that claims a type of packaging or container fails to satisfy the first prong because the patent does not claim the drug. In addition, in contrast to the active ingredient, inactive ingredients, and conditions of use, the Hatch-Waxman amendments do not identify a listed drug's packaging or container as an element for us to review or consider in determining whether to approve an ANDA or 505(b)(2) application.

The failure to claim the approved product is especially apparent for patents claiming metabolites because those metabolites exist only *after* a person has taken the drug and his or her body has broken the drug down into the metabolite. While there have been no court decisions regarding the listing of patents claiming a metabolite, one court has examined whether a person can seek patent term restoration for a patent claiming a metabolite rather than the approved drug itself. In *Hoechst-Roussel Pharmaceuticals, Inc.* v. *Lehman*, 103 F.3d 756 (Fed. Cir. 1997), a court had to decide whether the Patent and Trademark Office correctly interpreted the patent term extension provisions at 35 U.S.C. 156. The patent term extension provisions were part of the Hatch-Waxman amendments (as Title II of the Hatch-Waxman amendments). The patent term extension provisions require that the patent for which an extended term is sought to "claim" the approved drug (see 35 U.S.C. 156(a) and 156(g)(1)(B) (discussing how a product must have been subject to a regulatory review period before its commercial marketing or use and defining the regulatory review period, in part, in terms of an NDA approval)). However, the patent in question claimed a metabolite rather than the approved drug itself. The court considered the meaning of the term "claim," and the term's relationship to the concept of infringement, and concluded that a patent claiming a metabolite or the use of a metabolite does not claim the approved drug product. The court's reasoning and conclusion are equally applicable to patent listings. Therefore, we conclude that a patent claiming a metabolite does not claim an approved drug and does not meet the statutory requirements for listing in the Orange Book.

The proposal would also instruct applicants not to submit patent information if the patent claims an intermediate. Intermediates are materials that are produced during the steps of the processing of active pharmaceutical ingredient, but are not

GENERIC AND INNOVATOR DRUGS

present in the final drug product themselves (see Food and Drug Administration, "Guidance for Industry: Q7A—Good Manufacturing Practice Guidance for Active Pharmaceutical Ingredients" (August 2001)). Under existing FDA regulations, intermediates are "in-process materials" rather than drug substances or even drug components (see 21 CFR 210.3(b)(9); 211.110). Thus, patents that claim intermediates do not claim the approved drug product and, for that reason, fail the first prong for listing.

We note that, as is currently the case, patents that claim methods of use that are not approved for the listed drug or are not the subject of a pending application may not be submitted.

b. *What Additional Patents Would the Proposal Require to be Listed?*
1. *Product by Process Patents*

The proposal would include "product by process patents" in the class of patents that must be listed because product by process patents are a type of product patent. In brief, a product by process patent claims a product by using or listing process steps to wholly or partially define the claimed product (see *In re Luck*, 476 F.2d 650 (C.C.P.A. 1973); *In re Brown*, 459 F.2d 531, 535 (C.C.P.A. 1972)). In a product by process patent, the claims must particularly point out and distinctly claim the product or genus of products for which patent protection is sought (see *In re Brown*, 459 F.2d at page 535). These patents, therefore, meet the two-prong criteria for patent listing because they claim the approved drug product and are of a type with respect to which a claim of patent infringement could reasonably be made by a person not licensed by the patent owner engaged in the manufacture, use, or sale of the drug; consequently, including product by process patents in the class of patents that must be listed is appropriate.

We must emphasize that product by process patents differ from process patents because, in a product by process patent, the patented invention is the product (as opposed to the process used to make the product) (see *In re Bridgeford*, 357 F.2d 679, 682 (C.C.P.A. 1966)). Section 505(b)(1) of the act does not require information on process patents, and we do not list process patents in the Orange Book (see §§ 314.50(i)(2) and 314.53(b)).

We are concerned, however, that persons unfamiliar with patent law might confuse product by process patents with process patents, and seek to list process patents with us. Therefore, we invite comment on ways to ensure that only appropriate product by process patents are listed, while maintaining the act's restriction against listing process patents.

2. *Patents Claiming a Different Form of the Drug Substance*

Section 314.53(b) currently states, "For patents that claim a drug substance or drug product, the applicant shall submit information only on those patents that claim a drug product that is the subject of a pending or approved application." The proposal would revise this sentence to read as follows:

For patents that claim the drug substance, the applicant shall submit information only on those patents that claim the drug substance that is the subject of the pending or approved application or that claim a drug substance that is the same as the active ingredient that is the subject of the approved or pending application within the meaning of section 505(j)(2)(A)(ii) of the act. For patents that claim a drug product, the applicant shall submit information only on those patents that claim a drug product that is the subject of a pending or approved application.

This would mean that an applicant would be able to submit patent information on a drug substance even when the patented drug substance was a different form than the drug substance that is the subject of the pending or approved NDA as long as the drug substances are the "same" active ingredient under section 505(j)(2)(A)(ii) of the act. Whether two different drug substances are the "same" active ingredient is a scientific determination based upon the specific characteristics of the drug substances involved. We have, for example, determined that anhydrous and hydrated entities, and different polymorphs (different crystalline forms of the same substance), may be the "same" active ingredient (see Food and Drug Administration, "Approved Drug Products With Therapeutic Equivalence Evaluations," 22nd Ed., section 1.7 at page xv (2002)). Therefore, for example, if the approved drug substance was an anhydrate, and the patent claimed a hemihydrate, proposed § 314.53(b) would allow the applicant to submit patent information for the hemihydrate *if* the anhydrate and hemihydrate are the "same" active ingredient.

In making a determination that two drug substances are the same active ingredient, the NDA holder should consider whether the drug substances can be expected to perform the same with respect to such characteristics as dissolution, solubility, and bioavailability. We invite comment on whether we should revise the codified language to require the NDA holder to submit additional information regarding the basis for the assertion that the drug substances are the same active ingredient.

We recognize that allowing NDA applicants and NDA holders to submit such patent information appears to conflict with our longstanding position that the patent must claim the approved drug product or the drug product that is the subject of the application. However, we believe this change in our patent listing policy is both reasonable and appropriate, and may even conserve agency and industry resources. Our rationale for allowing such drug substance patents to be listed depends, in large part, on our position concerning pharmaceutical and therapeutic equivalence. We consider drug products to be pharmaceutically equivalent if they have the same active ingredient(s), the same dosage form, the same route of administration, and are identical in strength or concentration. We consider drug products to be therapeutically equivalent if they are pharmaceutically equivalent and can be expected to have the same clinical effect and safety profile when administered to patients under the conditions specified in the labeling. A major premise in the ANDA approval system is that the ANDA drug is therapeutically equivalent to the brand-name or "reference listed drug." In assessing whether the active ingredients in the reference listed drug and the generic drug product are the "same," and would support a determination of therapeutic equivalence, we have concluded that, in certain instances, the generic drug's active ingredient does not have to have the exact physical form as the reference listed drug's active ingredient (see Letter from Dennis Baker, Associate Commissioner for Regulatory Affairs, FDA, to Donald O. Beers and David C. Korn, Arnold & Porter, and to William J. McNichol, Jr., Marc J. Scheineson, and Tracy Zurzolo Frisch, Reed Smith LLP, dated February 15, 2002, at pages 3–4, 7, 9–11). We have approved ANDAs when the drug substance in the generic drug product was a different polymorph than the drug substance in the listed drug. These products are therapeutically equivalent.

If a generic drug product can be the "same" as the reference listed drug, notwithstanding differences in the drug substances' physical form, then it is consistent to interpret "drug substance," for purposes of listing patent information, as including drug substances having different physical forms. We note that the Hatch-Waxman amendments contained the patent listing and ANDA provisions in the same title, so it would be logical for us to interpret these two provisions of the act in a consistent manner (see Ben

APPENDIX 92

Venue Laboratories, 10 F.Supp.2d, at page 457).

Additionally, it is conceivable that an ANDA applicant may file an ANDA for a drug product that contains a drug substance that does not share the same chemical structure as the NDA-approved drug, but is nevertheless covered by a patent. For example, assume that the NDA drug is a hydrated form of the drug substance, and the ANDA drug substance would be an anhydrate. If the patent for the NDA drug claims the hydrated drug substance, the ANDA applicant would be able to certify, correctly under current FDA regulations, that it was not infringing the patent and file a paragraph IV certification. However, if the patent owner also had a patent on the anhydrous form and the NDA holder were not allowed to submit patent information on the anhydrate because the patent does not claim the approved drug product, the ANDA applicant consulting the Orange Book would have no notice of the patent claiming the anhydrate. The missing patent information could mislead potential ANDA applicants into submitting ANDAs containing the anhydrate and unknowingly infringing the patent claiming the anhydrate. We, in turn, could expend resources on reviewing an ANDA for a drug that is covered by the unlisted patent, and the patent owner could expend resources in defending the patent. This waste in agency and industry resources could be avoided if we require NDA applicants and NDA holders to submit information on patents that claim drug substances that are the same active ingredient as that in the listed drug product.

Again, we recognize that requiring the submission of patent information on drug substances that are the same active ingredient, even when those drug substances are in a form that differs from the drug substance in the approved drug product, appears to be a change from our previous position. As discussed previously, we believe this change is justified by our position on pharmaceutical and therapeutic equivalence. We invite comment as to the potential impact of this change on the submission of ANDAs and 505(b)(2) applications.

We also acknowledge that the interaction between the act's requirements, our pre-existing regulations, and our positions in court cases and elsewhere can make it difficult to interpret the act's patent listing requirements and ANDA and 505(b)(2) application approval requirements in a simple, harmonious manner. Although patents on different forms of an active ingredient are properly listed, and a pending ANDA containing a different form of the drug substance may be considered to have the "same" active ingredient as the reference listed drug, we must emphasize that this proposed rule does not alter the requirement for NDA holders to submit a supplement before changes are made to the synthesis of the drug substance (see 21 CFR 314.70(b)(1)(iv)). If an NDA holder wishes to use an active ingredient whose form is different from the active ingredient described in the approved NDA, the NDA holder must seek our approval before it uses the different form of the active ingredient. Changes in the form of an active ingredient warrant the filing of a supplemental NDA because of the possible health consequences associated with the new form of the drug substance.

B. Proposed § 314.53(c)(2)(i)—What Does the Patent Declaration Say?

Section 314.53(c)(2)(i) requires a person submitting an NDA, an amendment to an NDA, or an NDA supplement, to submit a signed declaration as part of its submission of patent information if the patent covers the drug's formulation, composition, and/or method of use. The declaration states:

The undersigned declares that Patent No. ____ covers the formulation, composition, and/or method of use of (name of drug product). This product is (*currently approved under section 505 of the Federal Food, Drug, and Cosmetic Act*) [or] (*the subject of this application for which approval is being sought*).

(Emphases in original.) We designed this declaration to help ensure that appropriate patents are listed and to preclude any need on our part to decide patent issues because we lack the patent expertise, resources, and statutory mandate to scrutinize patent listings (see 54 FR 28872 at 28909 (July 10, 1989)).

This declaration may be insufficient in practice to prevent NDA applicants and NDA holders from attempting to list inappropriate patents. The FTC Report suggested that "many of the later-issued patents do not appear to claim the approved drug product or an approved use of the drug" (see FTC Report at 37), but recognized that we lack the expertise and resources to review or decide patents disputes (*id.* at page 41; see also *aai Pharma* v. *Thompson*, 296 F.3d 227 (4th Cir. 2002) ("the FDA has no expertise in making patent law judgments")). The courts have also concurred in our view that we lack the authority to review the "listability" of patents (see *American Biosci.* v. *Thompson*, 269 F.3d 1077, 1084 (D.C. Cir. 2001); *In re Buspirone Patent Litigation*, 185 F.Supp.2d 363, 371 (S.D.N.Y. 2002); *Watson Pharm., Inc.* v. *Henney*, Civ. No. U.S. Dist. LEXIS 2477, at 7–8 (D. Md. Jan. 17, 2001); *Mylan Pharm., Inc.* v. *Thompson*, 139 F.Supp.2d 1, 10–11 (D.D.C.) *rev'd on other grounds*, 268 F.3d 1323 (Fed. Cir. 2001)). The FTC Report also noted that ANDA applicants must certify to a listed patent even if they dispute the appropriateness of the listing (see FTC Report at 37; see also 21 CFR 314.94(a)(12)(vii)). Although we continue to lack the expertise, resources, and legal authority to examine patent issues, we can ask NDA applicants and NDA holders to provide more patent information to help ensure that only appropriate patents are listed. The proposed rule, if finalized, will prompt NDA holders and NDA applicants to make careful and well-considered representations in their patent declarations and produce greater compliance with our patent listing requirements.

The proposed rule would, therefore, revise § 314.53(c)(1) and (c)(2) by rewording the general patent declaration requirement in paragraph (c)(1) and by replacing the existing, general declaration at paragraph (c)(2)(i) with a more detailed declaration that would act as a "checklist" that would focus on patent claims and would ensure that applicants submit only appropriate patent information and stand behind the accuracy of that information. Proposed § 314.53(c)(1) and (c)(2)(i) would read as follows:

(1) *General requirements*. An applicant described in paragraph (a) of this section shall submit the declaration described in paragraph (c)(2) of this section for each claim of the patent that meets the requirements described in paragraph (b) of this section.

(2) *Patent declaration*. For each patent that claims a drug substance (active ingredient), drug product (formulation and composition), and/or method of use, the applicant shall submit the following declaration:

This is a submission of patent information for an NDA submitted under section 505 of the Federal Food, Drug, and Cosmetic Act (the Act). Time sensitive patent information pursuant to 21 CFR 314.53 for NDA #

The following is provided in accordance with section 505(b) of the Act:
Trade Name: _____
Active Ingredient(s): _____
Strength(s): _____
Dosage Form(s): _____

GENERIC AND INNOVATOR DRUGS

65454   Federal Register / Vol. 67, No. 206 / Thursday, October 24, 2002 / Proposed Rules

Approval Date (if the submission is a supplement to an approved NDA):
____
Please provide the following information for each patent submitted, and identify the relevant claim(s) by number.
A. 1. United States patent number:
____
2. Expiration date: ____
3. Name of the Patent Owner:
____
4. Agent (if patent owner or applicant does not reside or have a place of business in the United States)
____
B. For each patent identified in A, please provide the following information:
 1. The type of patent claims that apply to the drug substance or drug product that is the subject of the application:
2. Drug Substance (Active Ingredient)
 ___ Yes ___ No
 a. Claim number(s): ____
3. Drug Product (Composition/Formulation):
 ___ Yes ___ No
 a. Claim number(s): ____
4. Method of Use:
 ___ Yes ___ No
 a. Claim number(s): ____
C. For each drug substance claim identified, please provide the following information:
1. Is the claim one that claims the drug substance that is the active ingredient in the approved or pending NDA, an amendment to the NDA, or a supplement to the NDA?
 ___ Yes ___ No
If "yes," please identify the claim(s) by number.
2. Is the claim one that claims a drug substance that is the "same" active ingredient as the active ingredient in the pending or approved NDA, amendment to the NDA, or a supplement to the NDA?
 ___ Yes ___ No
If "yes," please identify the claim(s) by number.
3. If the answer to question C.1 or C.2 is "yes," do you acknowledge that an ANDA or 505(b)(2) application containing the same active ingredient that is claimed by the patent is the "same" for ANDA or 505(b)(2) approval purposes?
 ___ Yes ___ No
[If the answers to questions C.1, and C.2, or C.3 is "no," stop here. The patent may not be listed in the Orange Book as a patent that claims the drug substance.]
D. For each drug product claim identified, please provide the following information:

1. Is the claim one that claims the approved formulation or composition and/or the formulation or composition for which approval is being sought?
 ___ Yes ___ No
If "yes," please identify the claim(s) by number.
[If the answer to question D.1 is "no" in every instance, stop here. The patent may not be listed in the Orange Book as a patent that claims the drug product.]
E. For each method of use claim identified, please provide the following information:
1. Is the claim one that claims:
 (a) an approved method of use of the approved drug product? If "yes," please identify the use with reference to the approved labeling for the drug product and identify the relevant patent claim number(s);
 ___ Yes ___ No
 (b) a method of use of the approved drug product for which use approval is being sought; or
 ___ Yes ___ No
 (c) a method of use of the drug product for which approval is being sought?
 ___ Yes ___ No
If the answer to questions E.1(b) or (c) is "yes", please identify the use with reference to the proposed labeling for the drug product and identify relevant patent claim number(s).
[If the answers to questions E.1(a) through (c) are "no," stop here. The patent may not be listed in the Orange Book as a patent that claims a method of use.]
 Note that the proposed declaration would emphasize identification of the relevant patent claims by number. The number would correspond to the patent claim number in the patent itself. Precise identification of the relevant patent claims will help all parties focus on the same claim and may prevent arguments as to whether a particular claim pertained to the approved drug product or was infringed by the product described in an ANDA or 505(b)(2) application.
 We are also proposing to require NDA holders and NDA applicants to identify the specific pending or approved use claimed by a method of use patent. This information will assist parties in assessing patent infringement matters and should expedite our approval of ANDAs and 505(b)(2) applications that do not seek approval for the protected use.
 The proposal would also amend § 314.53(c)(2)(ii) to place more emphasis on patent claims rather than on the patent generally. Section 314.53(c)(2)(ii) currently instructs an NDA holder to amend its patent declaration within 30 days after approval of its application.

Current FDA regulations also address the content of the notice of certification of invalidity or noninfringement of patent that ANDA and 505(b)(2) application applicants must submit if their applications contain a paragraph IV certification (see §§ 314.95(c) and 314.52(c) respectively (21 CFR 314.95(c) and 314.53(c))). Section 505(j)(2)(A) of the act, however, states that we may "not require that an abbreviated application contain information in addition to that required by clauses (i) through (viii)." (No comparable statutory restriction exists for 505(b)(2) applications.) We invite comment on whether our current regulations regarding notice to the NDA holder and patent owner by ANDA applicants and 505(b)(2) application applicants could or should be amended.
 C. Proposed §§ 314.94(a) and 314.52(a)—How Many Times Can an Application's Approval Date Be Delayed for a 30-Month Period?
 We have consistently maintained that the Hatch-Waxman amendments create the opportunity for multiple 30-month stays to an ANDA's or 505(b)(2) application's approval date if those applicants submitted a paragraph IV certification and an action is brought for patent infringement within the statutory 45-day period. For example, assume that an ANDA applicant submitted a paragraph IV certification, provided the proper notice to the NDA holder and patent owner, and was sued for patent infringement within 45 days after providing the notice. Under section 505(j)(4)(B)(iii) of the act, we would be obliged to not approve the ANDA for a 30-month period beginning on the date of the receipt of the notice provided by the ANDA applicant to the NDA holder and patent owner, although the 30-month period could be longer or shorter depending on a court order or resolution of the litigation. If the NDA holder submitted new patent information to us, and the new patent information resulted in another paragraph IV certification and another action for patent infringement, our position has been that another 30-month stay in the effective date of ANDA approval could result.
 We recently stated our position in *Andrx Pharmaceuticals, Inc. v. Biovail Corp.*, No. 01–6194-civ-Dimitrouleas/Johnson (S.D. Fla.). We argued that the 30-month stay provided by section 505(j)(5)(B)(iii) of the act "is not rendered inapplicable to a patent newly listed in the Orange Book simply because the holder of the NDA has already received the benefit of such a stay with respect to a previously listed patent for the same drug" (see Memorandum of Federal Defendants in

Opposition to Plaintiff's Motion for Summary Judgment Declaring Additional 30-Month Stay Inapplicable or Eliminated, at page 5). Andrx had argued that a 30-month stay in the approval date applies only where an ANDA applicant provides notice in the context of an original ANDA and not in an amended ANDA. We argued that section 505(j)(5)(B)(iii) of the act provides for a stay of up to 30 months regardless of whether the paragraph IV certification was part of an original ANDA or an amended ANDA. We stated that the act's reference to section 505(j)(2)(B)(i) of the act, which itself refers to sections 505(j)(2)(B)(ii) and (B)(iii) of the act, required that section 505(j)(2)(B) be read as a whole and, as a result, requires us to make a 30-month stay available whenever a paragraph IV certification was filed and timely patent litigation ensued, thereby permitting multiple 30-month stays of a single ANDA approval.

We also maintained, in *Andrx Pharmaceuticals, Inc.*, that if the 30-month stay applied only when an original ANDA contained a paragraph IV certification, an applicant could amend an ANDA to include a paragraph IV certification, and there would be no notice to the NDA holder or patent owner and no opportunity for even a single, 30-month stay. We stated that such a result could not be reconciled with the Hatch-Waxman amendments' intent to strike a balance between generic drug approval and encouraging future innovation (*id.* at page 9, note 6).

We note, along with the FTC Report, that the number of 30-month stays per product has been increasing. The FTC Report found that, before 1998, patent infringement litigation "generated, at most, one 30-month stay per drug product per ANDA," and most cases (eight out of nine) involved alleged infringement of one or two patents (see FTC Report at page 36). However, after 1998, FTC found that, for drug products with substantial annual net sales, patent litigation was increasing, with a growing number of NDA holders or patent owners (five out of eight cases) alleging infringement of three or more patents (*id.*). The FTC Report even noted one instance where the NDA holder had listed 12 patents in the Orange Book (*id.* at page 45). The FTC Report also found that NDA holders were beginning to list later-issued patents, many of which "do not appear to claim the approved drug product or an approved use of the drug," after an ANDA had been filed, and this resulted in a delay of FDA approval by 4 to 40 months (*id.* at page 36). In some cases, a single ANDA has been subject to as many as five stays (*id.*

at page 46). The FTC Report addressed multiple stays in the context of a limited number of "blockbuster" drugs. The total number of stays in ANDA approvals is higher, and we agree with FTC that the number of stays appears to be increasing over time.

Consequently, we examined the act to assess whether requiring successive 30-month stays was the only reasonable interpretation of the act. We determined that another reasonable interpretation existed. Accordingly, through this proposed rule, we intend to adopt a different interpretation of the act. Our revised interpretation would limit the number of 30-month stays to the opportunity for only one stay per ANDA. Our reasoning is as follows:

• Section 505(j)(2)(B)(iii) of the act states that if an ANDA is amended to "include" a paragraph IV certification, then the notice to the NDA holder and to the patent owner "shall be given when the amended application is submitted."

• However, if the ANDA contained a paragraph IV certification, then any ANDA amendment containing a paragraph IV certification does not amend the ANDA to "include" a paragraph IV certification because the ANDA already contained a paragraph IV certification.

• In the circumstances described previously, the submission of a second paragraph IV certification in an ANDA amendment or supplement does not trigger the notice requirement in section 505(j)(2)(B)(ii) of the act because the ANDA is never amended or supplemented to "include" (i.e., contain) a paragraph IV certification.

• Consequently, under section 505(j)(5)(B)(iii) of the act, only one 30-month stay in the ANDA's approval date is possible, because the subsequent paragraph IV certifications will not have resulted in a second notice to the patent owner and NDA holder, and the 45-day period for filing a patent infringement suit, as described in section 505(j)(5)(B)(iii) of the act, will not have run. To put it another way, if the ANDA applicant is not obliged to submit the notice to the patent owner and NDA holder, then the pre-requisites to trigger the 30-month stay in an ANDA's approval date are not met, so the 30-month stay would not be available.

A similar argument for a single, 30-month stay per application can be made for 505(b)(2) applications that contain a paragraph IV certification.

Under this interpretation of the act, ANDA and 505(b)(2) application applicants would still be required to make paragraph IV certifications where applicable, but the addition of a second

paragraph IV certification to an ANDA or a 505(b)(2) application that had already contained at least one paragraph IV certification would not trigger an obligation to provide a second notice to the NDA holder or to the patent owner and would not result in another opportunity for a 30-month stay. Instead, as in the case of paragraph I (no patent information has been filed) or paragraph II (patent has expired) certifications, the subsequent paragraph IV certification would allow us to approve the ANDA or 505(b)(2) application immediately if the Act would otherwise permit us to do so.

The parties would, of course, be free to litigate issues regarding patent infringement, but proposed multiple, 30-month stays per ANDA or 505(b)(2) application would no longer be possible. Our interpretation would not adversely affect a patent owner's ability to protect its patent rights. If an ANDA or 505(b)(2) application applicant makes one paragraph IV certification, the patent owner and the NDA holder would always receive notice and would always have the opportunity to protect the patented invention. If the NDA holder files *another* patent later, and the ANDA or 505(b)(2) application applicant believes that the later-filed patent is invalid or will not be infringed, the patent owner and NDA holder are still able to protect the later-filed patent because: (1) The notice already alerted the patent owner and NDA holder to the existence of the ANDA or 505(b)(2) application; and (2) any defense of the later-filed patent will not depend on the existence of a subsequent notice to the patent owner or NDA holder. In other words, with respect to later-filed or subsequently filed patents, the patent owner and NDA holder still have patent infringement and judicial remedies available to them even without receiving another notice. The patent owner, for example, can still seek an injunction to protect the patent on such terms as a court deems reasonable under 35 U.S.C. 283. If a court finds that the patent is infringed, the patent owner would be entitled to damages under 35 U.S.C. 284.

We recognize that there are other arguments to support a single, 30-month stay in each ANDA or 505(b)(2) application's approval date. For example, one argument could be that the act contemplates only one 30-month stay in an ANDA's approval date because section 505(j)(5)(B)(iii) of the act refers to "the" 30-month stay. This argument presumes that the original ANDA contained a paragraph IV certification and resulted in a 30-month stay. We do not concur with this interpretation of the act because, in certain situations, it could result in no notice to the patent owner or NDA holder. For example, if the original ANDA contained a paragraph III certification (stating that the patent will expire on a specific date), and the ANDA applicant later amends the ANDA to contain a paragraph IV certification, one could argue that no notice to the patent owner or NDA holder would be necessary, and there would not be an opportunity for even a single, 30-month stay. In contrast, under our proposed interpretation of the act, the opportunity for one 30-month stay in the abbreviated application's effective date always exists, and the patent owner and NDA holder would always receive one notice from the ANDA or 505(b)(2) application applicant who challenges at least one of the listed patents. This would preserve the balance between encouraging ANDA and 505(b)(2) application approvals and encouraging innovation because: (1) The elimination of multiple 30-month stays will lead to faster ANDA or 505(b)(2) application approvals, and (2) the patent owner and NDA holder will still receive notice and will be able to take steps to defend the patented invention from alleged patent infringement. As courts have observed, "The Hatch-Waxman Act represented Congress's efforts to strike a compromise between the competing interests of pioneer pharmaceutical companies and generic manufacturers" (see *Mylan Pharmaceuticals, Inc.* v. *Thompson*, 139 F.Supp.2d 1, 4 (D.D.C. 2001); see also *Mylan Pharmaceuticals, Inc.* v. *Henney*, 94 F.Supp.2d 36, 52–53 (D.D.C. 2000) (interpretation of Hatch-Waxman must take into account the compromise nature of the statute); *Fisons Corp.* v. *Shalala*, 860 F.Supp. 859, 862 (D.D.C. 1994) ("A variety of federal courts have recognized that this Act represents a compromise, and aids both sets of drug manufacturers; see, e.g., *Tri-Bio Laboratories* v. *United States*, 836 F.2d 136, 139 (3rd Cir. 1987))." A maximum of one 30-month stay per ANDA or 505(b)(2) application represents a reasonable compromise.

Additionally, we note that interpreting the act to allow only a maximum of one 30-month stay per ANDA or 505(b)(2) application is consistent with the specific legislative history that accompanied the passage of the Hatch-Waxman amendments.[1]

---

[1] We further note that, although reliance on legislative history may have its perils, its use is more justified where, as in this case, the statute is ambiguous (see, e.g., *PanAmSat Corp.* v. *FCC*, 198 F.3d 890, 895 (D.C. Cir. 1999) (stating that a court does not resort to legislative history "to cloud a statutory text that is clear") (citation omitted).

When the 97th Congress considered patent term extension legislation, many members were concerned that the bill would not prevent brand-name companies from obtaining multiple patent term extensions for patents that claimed a drug and, by doing so, inhibit competition from generic drugs (see 128 Cong. Rec. H6916, H6919 (September 13, 1982) (remarks of Rep. Kastenmeier)). Some charged that the bill would extend the effective patent life of top-selling drugs for more than 17 years (the patent term that existed at the time) through "pyramiding" or "evergreening" of patents (*id.* at page H6922) (remarks of Rep. Gore). The House of Representatives, by a vote of 250 to 132, rejected passing the bill by suspension of the rules, and so the bill failed to be passed despite unanimous support in the Senate and strong support in the House. When the Senate revisited the legislation in the next year, the President of the Pharmaceutical Manufacturers Association (now known as the Pharmaceutical Research and Manufacturers of America) testified that, in 1982:

* * * critics of the bill sought to create the impression that innovative firms were acquiring patents in constellation, pyramiding one on top of another to extend effective protection. Among people not knowledgeable about the intricacies of patent law, this understandably occasioned alarm and suspicion.

(See Hearing on S. 1306, Senate Judiciary Cmte., 98th Cong., 1st Sess. 56–57 (testimony of Lewis A. Engman, President, Pharmaceutical Manufacturers Association)).

The statutory language creating paragraph IV certifications, provisions for giving notice of such certifications, and rules governing amended applications is identical to language in S. 2748 as introduced by Senator Hatch in 1984. The House Judiciary Committee reported essentially identical language by voice vote, and the only relevant report language states that notice is required under paragraph 505(j)(2)(B)(iii) when an ANDA "is subsequently amended so as to bring it *within* this notice requirement" (see H. Rep. 98–857, Part 2, 98th Cong., 2d Sess. 14 (1984) (emphases added)). This understanding by the House Judiciary Committee suggests that if an ANDA applicant had provided notice to the patent owner and NDA holder, and then amended the ANDA to make a patent certification regarding a newly-filed patent, then the ANDA applicant would not have to provide another notice because, by virtue of its first notice to the patent owner and NDA holder, the ANDA applicant was *already* within the notice requirement. Our proposed interpretation is thus consistent with the legislative history.

For all these reasons, we propose to amend §§ 314.95(a)(3) and 314.52(a)(3) to state that the requirement to provide a notice of invalidity or noninfringement of patent:

* * * does not apply to a use patent that claims no uses for which the applicant is seeking approval. This paragraph also does not apply if the applicant amends its application to add a certification under [§ 314.94(a)(12)(i)(A)(*4*) for an ANDA applicants or § 314.50(i)(1)(i)(A)(*4*) for 505(b)(2) application applicants] when the application already contained a certification under [§ 314.94(a)(12)(i)(A)(*4*) or § 314.50(i)(1)(i)(A)(*4*)] to another patent.

The proposed amendments to §§ 314.95(a)(3) and 314.52(a)(3), if made final, will lead to a changed interpretation of §§ 314.95(d) and 314.52(d) respectively. Sections 314.95(d) and 314.52(d) state that if an application is amended to include a paragraph IV certification, then the ANDA or 505(b)(2) application applicant shall send the notice of certification of invalidity or noninfringement of patent at the same time that it submits its amendment to us. Under the proposed rule, an ANDA or 505(b)(2) applicant who is amending its application to include a paragraph IV certification must provide notice to the patent owner and NDA holder only if the ANDA or 505(b)(2) application did not previously contain a paragraph IV certification.

III. Implementation

A. How Would the Rule Affect Notices?

Under the framework proposed in this rule, the possibility exists that if two ANDA applicants file paragraph IV certifications to a later-filed patent, and one ANDA applicant has already submitted a paragraph IV certification to a previously-filed patent, one ANDA applicant could be subject to a 30-month stay with respect to the later-filed patent while the other would not. To illustrate this problem:

1. Assume that ANDA applicant #1 files a paragraph IV certification to a patent, while ANDA applicant #2 files a paragraph III certification to the same patent. The patent owner brings a suit for patent infringement against ANDA applicant #1 and obtains a 30-month stay in the ANDA's approval date.

2. Assume that the NDA holder files another patent.

3. If ANDA applicants ## 1 and 2 both file paragraph IV certifications for the second patent, the proposed rule, if finalized, would not require ANDA applicant #1 to provide notice to the

patent owner and NDA holder, because the ANDA previously contained a paragraph IV certification. However, ANDA applicant #2 is subject to a potential 30-month stay in the ANDA approval date because it would be required to provide notice to the patent owner and NDA holder.

While this hypothetical situation appears to treat the two ANDA applicants differently, we believe that our interpretation does treat the ANDA applicants alike, because both ANDA applicants would be subject to the possibility of only one 30-month stay in the ANDA approval date.

Our proposed interpretation of the 30-month stay does not affect an ANDA applicant's eligibility for 180-day exclusivity. In brief, section 505(j)(5)(B)(iv) of the act gives the ANDA applicant who files the first paragraph IV certification for a listed patent 180 days of exclusivity (against other ANDA applicants). We interpret the 180-day exclusivity provision as providing 180-day exclusivity to the first ANDA applicant whose ANDA contains a paragraph IV certification to a patent, even if the paragraph IV certification is one that would not result in an obligation to notify the patent owner and NDA holder and would not subject the applicant to the risk of patent litigation and a 30-month stay. The FTC Report suggested that if only a single, 30-month stay per ANDA were allowed, the number of patents listed after NDA approval might decrease (see FTC Report at page v).

B. How Would the Rule Affect Pending Applications?

Assuming that we issue a final rule, we intend to apply the rule to pending applications as follows:

• For patents filed for an NDA that has not been approved by the effective date of a final rule, the rule would apply on the effective date. For example, if the final rule were to become effective 60 days after the date of publication in the **Federal Register**, and an NDA was pending on the 60th day after the final rule's publication date, the NDA applicant would have to comply with the final rule's patent listing and patent declaration requirements. ANDA and 505(b)(2) application applicants would be subject to the revised notice requirement. Each ANDA or 505(b)(2) application referencing that NDA would be subject to the possibility of only one 30-month stay per ANDA or 505(b)(2) application.

• If we have approved the NDA as of the final rule's effective date, and no ANDA has been filed before that date, then any patent listed before that date would be subject to the pre-existing regulation. For example, if the final rule were to become effective 60 days after the date of publication in the **Federal Register**, and we approved the NDA on the 59th day after the date of publication, the NDA applicant would *not* have to amend its patent listing and patent declaration to comply to the final rule. ANDA and 505(b)(2) applications submitted after the effective date would be subject to the revised notice requirement. Each ANDA or 505(b)(2) application referencing that NDA would be subject to the possibility of only one 30-month stay per ANDA or 505(b)(2) application.

• If we have approved the NDA as of the final rule's effective date, and an ANDA or 505(b)(2) application has been filed before that date, then any patent listed before that date would be subject to the pre-existing regulation, as described in the example immediately above. The ANDA or 505(b)(2) application applicant would have to provide notice to the patent owner and NDA holder if the ANDA or 505(b)(2) application contained a paragraph IV certification. Multiple 30-month stays in the approval date would be possible.

• If the NDA holder or NDA applicant files patent information after the final rule's effective date, then the NDA holder or applicant is subject to the final rule's patent listing and patent declaration requirements, and ANDA or 505(b)(2) application applicants would not have to provide notice if their applications previously contained a paragraph IV certification. Only one 30-month stay per each ANDA's or 505(b)(2) application's approval date would be possible.

This proposed rule provides sufficient notice to all interested parties, whether they are NDA holders, NDA applicants, ANDA applicants, or 505(b)(2) application applicants, to adjust their submissions and actions by the time we issue a final rule. (This assumes, of course, that we issue a final rule.) NDA holders who wish to receive the benefits of the pre-existing regulation will have enough time to decide whether to pursue additional patents and to list them. ANDA and 505(b)(2) application applicants will be able to plan their submissions more efficiently as they will know whether their applications will be subject to the possibility of one or more 30-month stays of approval if they make a paragraph IV certification. If we were to adopt an alternative implementation plan, we would risk upsetting legitimate expectations held by those who had relied on our earlier interpretation of the act. However, we invite comments on how a final rule should be implemented.

IV. Legal Authority

Our principal legal authority for the proposed rule exists at sections 505 and 701 (21 U.S.C. 371) of the act. Section 505(b) of the act describes the contents of an NDA and 505(b)(2) applications, including the patent listing and patent certification requirements. Section 505(j) of the act describes the contents of an ANDA, including patent certification requirements. Both sections 505(b) and 505(j) of the act also describe the 30-month stay of approval dates of a 505(b)(2) application or ANDA if the 505(b)(2) applicant or ANDA applicant made a paragraph IV certification and a timely action for patent infringement ensues.

The proposed rule would clarify the types of patents which NDA applicants and NDA sponsors must and must not submit to FDA for listing in the Orange Book. It would also require a more detailed patent declaration from NDA applicants and ANDA holders.

For 505(b)(2) applicants and ANDA applicants, the proposal would have the effect of reducing the number of notifications sent to patent owners and NDA holders. Sections 505(b)(2)(A) and 505(j)(2)(A)(vii) of the act, respectively, require patent certifications, while sections 505(b)(3)(A) and 505(j)(2)(B) of the act require those applicants who have made a paragraph IV certification to provide a notice to the patent owner and NDA holder. Because the proposal would not require ANDA applicants and 505(b)(2) applicants to provide notice if: (a) the original ANDA or 505(b)(2) application contained a paragraph IV certification; and (b) the applicants amend their applications to include another paragraph IV certification in response to another patent listing, fewer notifications of invalidity or noninfringement of a patent would result.

Thus, section 505 of the act, in conjunction with our general rulemaking authority in section 701(a) of the act, serves as our principal legal authority for this proposal.

V. Environmental Impact

The agency has determined under 21 CFR 25.30(h) and 25.31(a) that this action is of a type that does not individually or cumulatively have a significant effect on the human environment. Therefore, neither an environmental assessment nor an environmental impact statement is required.

GENERIC AND INNOVATOR DRUGS

VI. Executive Order 13132: Federalism

The agency has analyzed this proposed rule in accordance with the principles set forth in Executive Order 13132. We have determined that the rule does not contain policies that have substantial direct effects on the States, on the relationship between National Government and the States, or on the distribution of power and responsibilities among the various levels of government. Accordingly, we have concluded that the rule does not contain policies that have federalism implications as defined in the Executive order and, consequently, a federalism summary impact statement is not required.

VII. Paperwork Reduction Act of 1995

This proposed rule contains information collection requirements that are subject to public comment and review by the Office of Management and Budget (OMB) under the Paperwork Reduction Act of 1995 (44 U.S.C. 3501–3520). We describe these provisions below in this section of the document with an estimate of the annual reporting burden. Our estimate includes the time for reviewing instructions, searching existing data sources, gathering and maintaining the data needed, and completing and reviewing each collection of information.

We invite comments on: (1) Whether the collection of information is necessary for the proper performance of FDA's functions, including whether the information will have practical utility; (2) the accuracy of FDA's estimate of the burden of the collection of information, including the validity of the methodology and assumptions used; (3) ways to enhance the quality, utility, and clarity of the information to be collected; and (4) ways to minimize the burden of the collection of information on respondents, including through the use of automated collection techniques, when appropriate, and other forms of information technology.

Title: Applications for FDA Approval to Market a New Drug: Patent Listing Requirements and Application of 30-month Stays on Approval of Abbreviated New Drug Applications Certifying That a Patent Claiming a Drug Is Invalid or Will Not Be Infringed

Description: The proposed rule would clarify the types of patent information that must and must not be submitted to FDA as part of an NDA or as an amendment or supplement to an NDA. The proposal would also require persons submitting an NDA or amendment or supplement to such an application to make a detailed patent declaration as part of the application. The proposal would also permit the possibility of only one 30-month stay of each ANDA's or 505(b)(2) application's approval date in the event of patent infringement litigation because the proposal would not require ANDA applicants or 505(b)(2) applicants to provide a notice of certification of invalidity or noninfringement of patent if their applications already contain such a certification.

Description of Respondents: Persons submitting, amending, or submitting a supplement to an NDA, and persons submitting an ANDA or 505(b)(2) application containing a patent certification of invalidity or noninfringement of patent.

We estimate the burden of this collection of information as follows:

TABLE 1.—ESTIMATED ANNUAL REPORTING BURDEN[1]

21 CFR Section	No. of Respondents	Frequency of Responses	Total Annual Responses	Hours per Response	Total Hours
314.50(a) through (f), (h), and (k)	80	1.55	124	1,690	209,560
314.52(a)(3) and 314.95(a)(3)	37	1	37	16	592
Total					210,152

[1] There are no capital costs or operating and maintenance costs associated with this collection of information.

Our estimates are based on the following assumptions.

• According to our earlier information collection estimates for §§ 314.52 and 314.95, there are an estimated 37 respondents who provide a notice of certification of invalidity or noninfringement of patent each year, and each respondent submits an estimated 2 responses, with an estimated 16 hours per response. Because the proposed rule would allow only one 30-month stay in the effective date of approval for each 505(b)(2) application or ANDA, this would mean that these 505(b)(2) or ANDA applicants would (if the rule is finalized) file only one notice per year (unless they are filing multiple applications for different drugs and making paragraph IV certifications in more than one case). So, assuming that these applicants submit only one 505(b)(2) application or ANDA per year that contains a paragraph IV certification, the applicants would submit only one notice of certification of invalidity or noninfringement of patent each year. Thus, the information collection burden for §§ 314.52 and 314.95 would decrease to 592 hours (37 respondents x 1 response per respondent x 16 hours per response = 592 hours).

• To estimate the number of enhanced patent declarations that will be submitted annually, we referred to historical data on submissions of NDAs. In 2001 and 2002, we received 94 and 66 NDAs respectively. We therefore estimate that there will be 80 ((94 applications + 66 applications)/2 years = 80 applications/year) annual instances where an NDA applicant or NDA holder would be affected by the proposed patent listing and patent declaration requirements. According to our earlier information collection estimates for § 314.50(h) (the provision under which we covered patent listing and patent declaration matters as described in § 314.53), there are an estimated 1.55 annual responses per respondent. So, using the same 1.55 ratio, this would mean that 80 NDA applicants and NDA holders would submit 124 annual responses (80 respondents x 1.55 responses per respondent = 124 responses). However, proposed § 314.53(b) and (c) would have different impacts on the hours per response. On the one hand, proposed § 314.53(b) might decrease the reporting burden because it would specify certain patents that must not be filed in the Orange Book and thus discourage NDA applicants and NDA holders from submitting information on those patents. On the other hand, proposed § 314.53(b) would also require NDA applicants and NDA holders to submit patent information on different forms of the drug substance, and this could result in more patent information being submitted. We cannot determine whether the potential net effect will increase, decrease, or not change the overall burden associated with submitting patent information, so we

APPENDIX 92

have not assigned any change in the total reporting burden for the proposed change in patent information alone. In contrast, proposed § 314.53(c) would make the patent declaration more detailed. The change in the declaration would increase the burden hours per response in § 314.50(h) (the provision under which we covered patent declarations described in § 314.53(c)) because respondents would be required to be more precise in their declarations. Based on other rules that require respondents to compile and submit information in their possession, we estimated that the revised patent declaration will result in an additional information collection burden of 24 hours. However, the previous burden hour estimate of 1,666 hours for § 314.50 covered paragraphs (a) through (f), in addition to paragraphs (h) and (k). We are unable to determine how many of the 1,666 hours were devoted to patent declarations, so, in this table, we simply add 24 hours to the 1,666 hour estimate for § 314.50(a) through (f), (h), and (k), resulting in a burden hour estimate of 1,690 hours (1,666 hours + 24 hours) to account for a respondent's need for more time to make and verify the patent declaration. Thus, the information collection burden for § 314.50(a) through (f), (h), and (k) would increase to 209,560 hours (124 annual responses x 1,690 hours per response = 209,560 hours). We invite comment as to whether we need to adjust our estimate of 24 burden hours per response.

We have submitted the information collection requirements of this rule to OMB for review. Interested persons are requested to send comments regarding information collection to the Office of Information and Regulatory Affairs, OMB (see **ADDRESSES**).

VIII. Analysis of Impacts

FDA has examined the impacts of the proposed rule under Executive Order 12866, and the Regulatory Flexibility Act (5 U.S.C. 601–612), and under the Unfunded Mandates Reform Act (UMRA) (2 U.S.C. 1501 et seq.). Executive Order 12866 directs agencies to assess all costs and benefits of available regulatory alternatives and, when regulation is necessary, to select regulatory approaches that maximize net benefits (including potential economic, environmental, public health and safety, and other advantages, distributive impacts, and equity). Unless the agency certifies that the rule is not expected to have a significant economic impact on a substantial number of small entities, the Regulatory Flexibility Act, as amended by SBREFA, requires agencies to analyze regulatory options that would minimize any significant economic impact of a rule on small entities. Section 202 of UMRA requires that agencies prepare a written statement of anticipated costs and benefits before proposing any rule that may result in an expenditure by State, local, and tribal governments in the aggregate, or by the private sector, of $100 million in any one year (adjusted annually for inflation). We have conducted analyses of the proposed rule, and have determined that the proposed rule is consistent with the principles set forth in the Executive order and in these statutes.

The proposed rule is an economically significant regulatory action as defined by the Executive order. With respect to the Regulatory Flexibility Act, the agency certifies that this proposed rule is not expected to have a significant impact on a substantial number of small entities. The proposed rule is also a major rule under the Congressional Review Act. The discussion of costs and benefits is consistent with the requirements of the Unfunded Mandates Reform Act.

A. Objectives of the Proposed Regulation

The proposed rule has multiple objectives. We are clarifying the types of patents that must and must not be listed and revising the declaration that NDA applicants must provide regarding their patents. In addition, through this proposal, we are adopting a different interpretation of the act that will limit the number of 30-month stays to one per ANDA or 505(b)(2) application. This clarification, revision, and reinterpretation will help ensure that NDA applicants list appropriate patents in the Orange Book while preventing the NDA holders from thwarting generic entry through the use of multiple 30-month stays. Through these actions, we are preserving the balance struck in the Hatch-Waxman Amendments between encouraging innovation and encouraging the availability of generic drugs. The estimated 10-year total costs of this proposed rule are approximately $51.5 billion and the annualized cost is $4.9 billion. The estimated 10-year total benefits of this proposed rule are approximately $53.9 billion and the annualized benefit is $5.1 billion. These 10-year total benefits include consumer savings of approximately $34.8 billion from earlier access to less expensive prescription pharmaceuticals. The 10-year benefits exceed the costs by approximately $2.4 billion and the annualized benefits exceed the annualized costs by approximately $230 million.

1. The 30-Month Stay

The Hatch-Waxman Amendments benefit consumers by bringing lower priced generic versions of previously approved drugs to market, while simultaneously promoting new drug innovation through the restoration of patent life lost during regulatory proceedings. A firm wishing to market a generic version of a previously approved innovator drug can submit an ANDA. An ANDA refers to a previously approved NDA (the "listed drug") and relies upon our finding of safety and effectiveness for the listed drug.

Persons submitting an ANDA or a 505(b)(2) application must make certifications regarding the listed patents claiming the drug they wish to duplicate. The applicant must certify one of the following for each patent: (1) That no patent information on the drug product that is the subject of the ANDA has been submitted to us; (2) that such patent has expired; (3) the date on which such patent expires; or (4) that such patent is invalid or will not be infringed by the manufacture, use, or sale of the drug product for which the ANDA is submitted. These certifications are known as "paragraph I," "paragraph II," "paragraph III," and "paragraph IV" certifications, respectively.

A paragraph IV certification begins a process in which the question of whether the listed patent is valid or will be infringed by the proposed generic product may be answered by the courts prior to the expiration of the patent. The ANDA or 505(b)(2) application applicant who files a paragraph IV certification to a listed patent must notify the patent owner and the NDA holder for the listed drug that it has filed an application containing a paragraph IV certification. The notice must include a detailed statement of the factual and legal basis for the applicant's opinion that the patent is not valid or will not be infringed. If the NDA holder or patent owner files a patent infringement suit against the ANDA or 505(b)(2) application applicant within 45 days of the receipt of notice, we may not give final approval to the ANDA or 505(b)(2) application for at least 30 months from the date of the notice. This 30-month stay per ANDA or 505(b)(2) application will apply unless the court reaches a decision earlier in the patent infringement case or otherwise orders a longer or shorter period for the stay.

We recognize that, in recent years, NDA holders have been able to use multiple 30-month stays to delay

GENERIC AND INNOVATOR DRUGS

generic competition. Under current regulations, the patent certification process allows for one or more 30-month stays of an ANDA or 505(b)(2) application's approval. NDA holders can prevent FDA approval of ANDAs or 505(b)(2) applications beyond the initial 30-month stay by listing an additional patent in the Orange Book after the applicant has filed its ANDA or 505(b)(2) application. These applicants would be required to re-certify to the newly-listed patent. The NDA holder would then be given 45 days to file suit for patent infringement, and our approval of the initial ANDA or 505(b)(2) application would be delayed for an additional 30-month period from the notice date or until a court decision in the newly instituted patent litigation.

According to the FTC Report, from 1992 to 2000, NDA holders have listed patents in the Orange Book after an ANDA has been filed for a drug product on eight occasions. Six of these eight occasions have occurred since 1998. In all eight of these instances, the subsequent patent resulted in a delay to generic access to markets beyond the initial 30-month stay. We are not aware of any case in which a court has decided that the ANDA infringed upon the subsequent listed patent. According to the FTC Report, in the four instances of multiple stays in which a court has decided on the validity or infringement of a later-listed patent, the patent has been found either invalid or not infringed by the ANDA.[2]

2. The Economic Impact of Generic Competition

The generic drug industry plays an important role in the economics of the healthcare industry. According to Caves, Whinston, and Hurwitz (1991), generic drug prices can be as little as 20 percent of the brand-name price for the same product.[3] Laws encouraging doctors to prescribe generic drugs when available are a part of the current effort to hold down the cost of healthcare.[4] A report from the Congressional Budget Office (CBO) report estimated that in 1994 (when the generic drug market was smaller than its current size) consumers saved between $8 and $10 billion by substituting generic for brand-name

---

[2] FTC Report, p. iv.
[3] Caves, Richard, M. D. Whinston, and M. A. Hurwitz, 1991. "Patent Expiration, Entry, and Competition in the U.S. Pharmaceutical Industry," Brookings Papers in Economic Activity: Microeconomics, p. 36.
[4] Hellerstein, Judith K. 1994. "The Importance of the Physician in the Generic Versus Trade-Name Prescription Decision," RAND Journal of Economics: 29:1:108–136.

drugs in pharmacy sales.[5] While the first 30-month stay enhances the incentive to innovate, subsequent stays generated by later-listed patents do not seem to give rise to the same incentives in most cases. By using multiple 30-month stays, NDA holders are able to delay competition from generic drugs. Delaying generic competition harms consumers by slowing the introduction of lower priced products to the market and thwarts the intent of the Hatch-Waxman Amendments.

The agency considered potential impacts on innovation and believes any negative effect to be minimal. While the initial 30-month stay is part of the balance struck in the Hatch-Waxman amendments to reward innovation, the subsequent stays are not part of this balance. The patents that form the basis for these subsequent stays do not appear to warrant automatic protection from generic competition.

According to the FTC report, every court ruling involving a subsequent 30-month stay has found the underlying patent to be either invalid or not infringed. Also according to the FTC report, extending patents through multiple stays is a strategy that has become popular in the last few years and is not a longstanding universally-recognized source of research funding. Subsequent stays could actually hinder innovation through the replacement effect, in that they provide a disincentive for an NDA holder to improve upon its own product. Moreover, to the extent that subsequent 30-month stays might be associated with increases in spending on research, these increases do not necessarily improve social welfare.[6]

B. Costs of the Regulation

This section develops estimates of the cost to NDA holders from the proposed rule. As previously stated, this proposed rule clarifies those types of patents that must or must not be listed and eliminates the use of multiple 30-month stays per ANDA to delay generic competition. The innovator drug industry, as NDA holders, would be expected to bear the costs of the proposed rule. Generic drug companies and consumers would be expected to

---

[5] Congressional Budget Office, How Increased Competition From Generic Drugs Has Affected Prices and Returns in the Pharmaceutical Industry (July 1998). Note that the sale of drugs through pharmacies is a subset of all drug sales so total savings to consumers would be expected to be higher than the given figure.
[6] A more detailed discussion of the replacement effect and of the relationship between research and social welfare can be found in Jean Tirole, The Theory of Industrial Organization (Cambridge: MIT Press, 1988), pp. 392, 399–400.

benefit. The impact on these entities that benefit is addressed in section III.C of this preamble. We do not estimate a specific impact involving those submitting 505(b)(2) applications. We recognize these applicants, like those submitting ANDAs, must make certifications and would be affected by this proposed rule. We believe any benefits would be difficult to quantify with any precision and would be quite small, relative to the benefits to generic drug companies.

This proposed rule will be costly to NDA holders because earlier generic competition will erode innovator market share. This loss of market share to generics will result in reduced revenues to the innovator. These reduced revenues would be mitigated somewhat by a reduction in the administrative, marketing, and sales expenses.

To estimate the impact of earlier generic competition, we estimate the revenues to NDA holders and generics under a base case scenario under which multiple 30-month stays per ANDA are not allowed and a scenario in which generic entry may be delayed subject to an additional stay. The impact of the proposed rule would be the difference between the two scenarios.

1. Delaying Generic Competition

To estimate the impact of delays to generic competition, we use a modified version of the economic model from our report to Congress on the pediatric exclusivity provision to the Food and Drug Administration Modernization Act.[7] Generic entry erodes the listed drug's market share, typically over a period of several years. At the same time, the price of the typical generic drug is also falling. By tracking the decline of listed drug's market share and the fall in the price of the generic competition, the model calculates changes in sales over time for innovator and generic sectors.

In the model, we assume the reference listed drug's market share falls from 100 percent to 60 percent in the first year of generic marketing, and then to 45 and 30 percent in years two and three. The price of the average generic drug falls with time, and this is also captured by the model. The model assumes for each 6-month interval over the first 3 years of competition, the generic price as a fraction of innovator price falls from 100 percent at introduction, to 80 percent after 6 months, and finally 33.5 percent after 3 years.[8] Several studies have

---

[7] U.S. Food and Drug Administration, The Pediatric Exclusivity Provision: Status Report to Congress, January 2001, p. 43
[8] The decline over 3 years at 6-month intervals is as follows: 100 percent at introduction (0 months);

shown generic competition to have only very small effect on innovators' prices.[9] Innovator prices do frequently rise after generic entry, but we lack the data to confidently incorporate an estimate of this into this model. If innovator price increases were incorporated into this model, the magnitudes of the estimated impacts would be expected to be larger. We request comment providing data on price behavior after generic entry into the market.

The model calculates the impact on innovator and generic sectors each month for a 10-year period. Using immediate generic entry as a base case, the model calculates the relative impact of delaying entry for a certain number of months. These monthly impacts on each sector are converted to present value using a 7 percent discount rate.

According to appendix H of the FTC report, there have been 8 multiple 30-month stays, but the frequency of these stays has been increasing. Four drugs experienced multiple stays during 2000 and 2001. Based on this information, we assume that, absent this proposed rule, there would be 2 (4 drugs/2 years) situations with multiple 30-month stays each year. Thus, in calculating the annual impact of this proposed rule, we multiply the peak annual sales of the average affected drug by 2 to account for the frequency of the event. While we believe this to be a reasonable estimate, we recognize, as mentioned in the FTC Report, that a substantial sales volume of brand-name drug products will be coming off patent in the next few years. If there are more drugs affected by this rule than we estimate, this would increase both the benefits and costs of this rule.

To develop a profile of the typical drug for which there were multiple 30-month delays, we started with the instances in Appendix H and table 4–3 of the FTC Report. As two instances from the FTC report concern different dosage forms of the same drug, gabapentin, we count it only once in our analysis. Generic competition for one of the drugs, Cisplatin, was delayed because of a single 30-month stay and an alleged double patent. As we do not believe this situation is addressed by this proposed rule, we eliminated it from the analysis. The information on the six remaining drugs is contained in table 2.

TABLE 2.—DRUGS USED IN ANALYSIS

Active Ingredient	FTC Stay Period (Months)	Estimated Additional Stay Period (Months)	Estimated Peak Sales (000)
Buspirone	30[1]	4	$700
Terazosin	70[2]	46	$580
Gabapentin	37	24	$1,710
Paroxetine	65	34	$3,780
Paclitaxel	60[1]	3	$1,020
Diltiazem	60[1]	28	$380
Average	50 (+20)	+23	$1,360

[1] Potentially, but actually shorter because of a court decision.
[2] Periods not overlapping.
Sales Data Sources: Buspirone 2000 data, BMS Web site; Terazosin 1999 data, Pharmacy Times Web site; Gabapentin 2001 data, Drug Topics Web site; Paroxetine 2001 data, Scrip 2737, p. 15; Paclitaxel 2000 data, BMS Web site; Ditiazem 2001 data, Forest Form 10K. For data prior to 2001, sales were escalated to the 2001 level using CPI-U. For drugs that have not yet reached peak sales, the peak was estimated with a linear projection.

Table 2 includes the inflation adjusted peak sales and subsequent delay for each of the six drugs. As a reference, we include delay information from the FTC report. Based on the delay and sales information for the six drugs, we find the typical delayed drug to have peak annual sales of $1,360 million and subject to a 23-month delay. As we do not possess current sales figures for all the drugs involved, we invite comment on the accuracy of these estimates.

2. Impact of Delay on the Innovator Sector

The model results obtained from comparing the no delay and delay scenarios are provided in table 3. To account for the frequency of occurrence, we multiply the peak sales estimate by 2. To the extent that this proposed rule would eliminate multiple 30-month stays per ANDA after the first, the estimated impact on innovators would be an annual revenue decrease of $3,159.50 million (approximately $3.2 billion).

TABLE 3.—RESULTS OF DELAY ANALYSES

Scenario	Sales (000)	Delay (Months)	Impact (In Millions)		
			Innovator	Generic	Consumer
Base Case	$2,720[1]	23	($3,160)	$1,120	$2,040

[1] Includes 2.0 frequency factor.

80 percent (6 months); 60 percent (12 months); 52.5 percent (18 months); 45 percent (24 months); 37.5 percent (30 months); 33.5 percent (36 months). The ultimate price ratio of 33.5 percent is consistent with a market with 10 generic entrants, per Caves, Whinston, and Hurwitz (1991), p. 36, table 9.

[9] See Box 4 in Congressional Budget Office (1998), p. 30.

GENERIC AND INNOVATOR DRUGS

The cost impact on innovators is driven by the fact that a delay in generic entry extends the time the innovator collects peak sales and shortens the time the innovator collects 30 percent of peak sales. Absent discounting, the impact on innovators would be the length of the delay times 70 percent of the peak innovator drug revenues.

This impact on innovators may be mitigated to a small degree by potential decreases in the administrative, marketing, and sales costs associated with the product. A recent study of top pharmaceutical companies found that marketing, administrative, and advertising expenses averaged 27 percent of revenues.[10] Part of this figure includes certain fixed costs that would not change with a decline in revenues. Moreover, to the extent that some of these support costs are discretionary, they would most likely be focused on periods of intense marketing, such as product roll-outs. Nevertheless, with the erosion of market share, the rewards to marketing would decline and the need for administrative support would be expected to decrease.

Assuming half the 27 percent figure to be discretionary support costs, and the discretionary support costs for the product in question to be one-third of the average, then discretionary support costs would be 4.5 percent of revenues (27 percent/6). The relevant annual cost reduction would be $142.2 million ($3.160 billion x 4.5 percent). As we lack precise data on the relationship between revenues and support costs, we invite comment on the accuracy of this estimate.

3. Other Issues Related to Burdens to Innovators

The proposed rule would require NDA holders to submit a more detailed patent declaration. To estimate the number of enhanced patent declarations that will be submitted annually, we referred to historical data on submission of NDAs, excluding those for orphan drugs. In 2000 and 2002, there were 94 and 66 NDAs respectively. We therefore estimate that there will be 80 ((94 + 66) / 2) annual instances where an NDA holder or NDA applicant will face this additional declaration burden. Based on earlier information collection estimates, we assume there to be an estimated 1.55 annual responses per respondent. Using this same 1.55 ratio, this would mean that the 80 NDA applicants and NDA holders would submit 124 annual responses (80 respondents x 1.55 responses per respondent).

[10] Families USA, *Profiting From Pain: Where Prescription Dollars Go*, July 2002, p. 3.

We believe that, while the NDA holder or NDA applicant possesses the additional patent information, there will be a burden in completing the more detailed declaration. Based on other rules that require respondents to compile and submit information in their possession, we estimate the burden to be 24 hours per event. A regulatory affairs specialist could perform the tasks associated with this process. Based on the total average hourly compensation (including a 40 percent load factor for benefits) of $55.72, the cost would be $1,337 ($55.72 per hour x 24 hours) per event.[11] The burden on individual firms would depend on the number of declarations they submit. The estimated annual burden to all declarants is $165,778 ($1,337 per event x 124 annual events).

We also considered a potential impact due to the numbers of patents listed. The proposed rule would require the submission of patent information for patents that claim different forms of the drug substance, and this would appear to increase the number of patent filings. At the same time, the proposed rule would clarify the types of patents that must not be submitted, and this would appear to reduce the number of patent filings. These two countervailing effects are of uncertain magnitude. We cannot quantify an impact, if any, from a change in the number of patents listed, but we invite comment.

4. Enforcement Costs

The proposed rule, if finalized, can be enforced using existing resources.

5. Total Costs of the Regulation

The annual cost of the proposed rule includes the lost revenues to innovator firms from the erosion of market share, mitigated by the decrease in support costs, and the additional cost of completing the more detailed patent declaration. The estimated 1-year loss in revenues from erosion of market share is $3,159.50 million, the reduction in support costs would reduce this loss by $142.20 million, and the estimated annual additional cost of completing the revised declarations is approximately $166,000. Thus, the estimated 1-year cost to innovator firms is $3,017.47 million (approximately $3.0 billion).

According to projections produced by the Office of the Actuary at the Centers for Medicare and Medicaid Services, expenditures on prescription pharmaceuticals are expected to

[11] Hourly rate for "lawyer" from the Bureau of Labor Statistics 2000 National Compensation Survey is $38.70, adjusted for inflation at 2.85 percent (unadjusted CPI–U) and 40 percent for benefits.

increase dramatically in the near future. This $3.0 billion 1-year estimate does not take these increases into consideration and must be adjusted to account for them. Prescription drug expenditures for 2003, for example, are expected to be 12.8 percent greater than for 2002.[12] After using the average annual percent changes in prescription drug expenditures to adjust the annual cost, the total reduction in revenues to the innovator sector over the 10-year period 2002 through 2011 is estimated to be $51,507.55 million, or approximately $51.5 billion. Annualizing this impact over that 10-year period at a 7 percent discount rate yields an annualized cost of $4,863.76 million, or approximately $4.8 billion.

C. Benefits of the Regulation

This section develops estimates of the benefits from the proposed rule. Eliminating multiple 30-month stays per ANDA will prevent delays in generic drug competition. The 70 percent of the market lost by innovators is a gain to both generic drug companies and consumers. Generic drug companies gain through additional sales, and, to the extent that generic prices are lower than innovator prices, consumers benefit from the "price gap."

1. Gains to the Generic Drug Industry

We estimated the increase in sales to generic drug companies using the same model used to estimate losses in sales to innovators. Assuming typical drug peak sales to be $2.72 billion (including 2.0 frequency factor) and a typical delay of 23 months, the estimated increase in 1-year revenues to generic firms is $1,119 million (approximately $1.1 billion). After accounting for the baseline increases in pharmaceutical expenditures, the total increase in generic industry revenues for the period 2002 to 2011 is estimated to be $19,117.47 million or approximately $19.1 billion. The annualized cost, using a 7 percent discount rate is $1,805.23 million or approximately $1.81 billion.

While we recognize that the generic drug industry is doing more marketing than it used to do, the effort is still substantially smaller than what is done by innovator firms, and we do not make adjustments for reductions associated support costs.

[12] The annual percent increases in prescription drug expenditures for each year, 2003 through 2011, are assumed to be 12.8 (2003), 12.3 (2004), 11.7 (2005), 11.0 (2006), 10.7 (2007), 10.5 (2008), 10.3 (2009), 10.2 (2010), and 10.1 (2011). See National Health Care Expenditures Projections: 2001–2011, Centers for Medicare & Medicaid Services, Office of the Actuary, table 11.

2. Gains to Consumers

The model assumes that after generic entry, the market will eventually stabilize where the price of a generic drug will be 33.5 percent of the equivalent innovator drug. The gain to consumers would be the difference between the generic and innovator price. This price gap is equal to 66.5 percent of the innovator price. Under our assumptions, the estimated consumer impact of the proposed rule is a 1-year gain of $2,040 million (approximately $2 billion). This gain would be from the elimination of multiple 30-month stays per ANDA that delay the availability of less expensive drugs.

After increasing this 1-year estimate to account for the annual expected increases in baseline pharmaceutical expenditures, the total expected benefit to consumers for the period 2002 to 2011 is $34,822.35 or approximately $34.8 billion. The annualized benefit to consumers, using a 7 percent discount rate, would be $3,288.21 or approximately $3.3 billion.

It is difficult to determine which subgroups of consumers will benefit most from access to generic drugs. The previously cited report on Pediatric Exclusivity noted that about 21 percent of pharmaceutical spending came from public sources (Federal, State & Local, Medicare and Medicaid) and that this figure was expected to rise. The report also noted that cheaper drugs would disproportionately benefit lower income consumers in that these consumers would be less likely to have insurance.

3. Other Issues Related to Benefits

In the past, some studies have allocated a portion of the gains to generic drugs to the distribution sector (e.g., retail drug stores). These studies typically based this approach on the belief that generic drugs carried a substantially larger retail markup, in absolute dollar terms, than did innovator drugs.

This belief appears to be based on literature using limited data from the mid–1980s, a period when the generic drug industry was substantially different from its current state. For this analysis, we referred to more recent information, such as that found in the CBO report, and found no evidence of substantially larger absolute retail markup for generic drugs. While we believe recent data supports our belief that the absolute markups are approximately the same, we invite comment on this issue.

4. Total Benefits of the Regulation

The 1-year benefits of the regulation will include the increase in revenues to generic firms and the savings to consumers from the earlier availability of less expensive pharmaceuticals. The estimated total 1-year benefit is $3,159 million (approximately $3.2 billion). Adjusting this benefit to account for the expected increase in baseline pharmaceutical expenditures, the total benefit for the years 2002 through 2011 is expected to be $53,931.97 million or approximately $53.9 billion. Annualizing this stream of benefits over that 10-year period at a 7 percent discount rate yields an annualized cost of $5,093 million or approximately $5.1 billion.

TABLE 4.—BENEFITS OF THE PROPOSED RULE TO GENERICS AND CONSUMERS

Issue	One-Year Impact (Millions)
Generic Earlier Access to Market	$1,119.96
Consumer Drug Savings	$2,039.54
Total Benefits	$3,159.50

D. Comparison of Costs and Benefits

The estimated 10-year total costs of this proposed rule are $51,508 million. These costs would be borne by innovator firms in the form of reduced revenues, mitigated by a reduction in support costs, and an increased cost of completing the revised patent declaration. The estimated annualized cost is $4,864 million.

The estimated 10-year benefits of this proposed rule are $53,932 million. These benefits would accrue to the generic drug firms and consumers in the form of increased revenues and increased income from access to cheaper drugs, respectively. The estimated annualized benefit is $5,093 million. Absent the additional cost of completing the declaration and the reduction in support costs, the costs equal the benefits because the economic impact of this proposed rule is a transfer, as consumers shift consumption from the products of the innovator drug firms to those of generic drug firms. The total 10-year quantified benefits exceed the costs by $2,424 million and the annualized benefits exceed the annualized costs by $229 million. While the quantified benefits do exceed the quantified costs, this proposed rule has the additional important benefit of preserving the balance struck in the Hatch-Waxman amendments.

E. Regulatory Alternatives

In creating this proposed rule, we considered several regulatory alternatives, including not regulating. We rejected the alternative of not regulating because under the current situation, NDA holders are able to use multiple 30-month stays to delay generic entry and thwart the intent of the Hatch-Waxman amendments. We also considered using the current system of patent declarations. This alternative was also rejected because the current declaration may be insufficient to prevent NDA holders and NDA applicants from listing patents that should not be listed under the law. This is particularly important in light of the fact that we lack the resources, expertise, and authority to evaluate patents to determine whether they should be listed in the Orange Book.

F. Impact on Small Entities

Unless the agency certifies that the rule is not expected to have a significant impact on a substantial number of small entities, the Regulatory Flexibility Act, as amended by SBREFA requires agencies to analyze regulatory options that would minimize any significant economic impact of a rule on small entities. According to standards established by the Small Business Administration, a small pharmaceutical manufacturer employs fewer than 750 employees. We do not know the precise number of innovator companies expected to use multiple 30-month stays to delay generic entry. Nevertheless, we do not believe any of these innovator companies to be small. Moreover, none of the innovator companies identified in the FTC report as having used multiple 30-month stays would qualify as a small entity. Therefore, the agency certifies that this proposed rule is not expected

GENERIC AND INNOVATOR DRUGS

65464 Federal Register / Vol. 67, No. 206 / Thursday, October 24, 2002 / Proposed Rules

to have a significant impact on a substantial number of small entities.

Interested persons may submit to the Dockets Management Branch (see **ADDRESSES**) written or electronic comments regarding this proposal. Two copies of any comments are to be submitted, except that individuals may submit one copy. Comments are to be identified with the docket number found in brackets in the heading of this document. Received comments may be seen in the Dockets Management Branch between 9 a.m. and 4 p.m., Monday through Friday.

List of Subjects in 21 CFR Part 314

Administrative practice and procedure, Confidential business information, Drugs, Reporting and recordkeeping requirements.

Therefore, under the Federal Food, Drug, and Cosmetic Act and under authority delegated to the Commissioner of Food and Drugs, it is proposed that 21 CFR part 314 be amended as follows:

PART 314—APPLICATIONS FOR FDA APPROVAL TO MARKET A NEW DRUG

1. The authority citation for 21 CFR part 314 continues to read as follows:

Authority: 21 U.S.C. 321, 331, 351, 352, 353, 355, 355a, 356, 356a, 356b, 356c, 371, 374, 379e.

2. Section 314.52 is amended by redesignating paragraph (a)(3) as paragraph (a)(4) and by adding new paragraph (a)(3) to read as follows:

§ 314.52 Notice of certification of invalidity or noninfringement of a patent.

(a) * * *

(3) This paragraph does not apply to a use patent that claims no uses for which the applicant is seeking approval. This paragraph also does not apply if the applicant amends its application to add a certification under § 314.50(i)(1)(i)(A)(*4*) when the application already contained a certification under § 314.50(i)(1)(i)(A)(*3*) to another patent.

* * * * *

3. Section 314.53 is amended by revising paragraphs (b) and (c)(1) through (c)(2) to read as follows:

§ 314.53 Submission of patent information.

* * * * *

(b) *Patents for which information must be submitted.* An applicant described in paragraph (a) of this section shall submit information on each patent that claims the drug or a method of using the drug that is the subject of the new drug application or amendment or supplement to it and with respect to which a claim of patent infringement could reasonably be asserted if a person not licensed by the owner of the patent engaged in the manufacture, use, or sale of the drug product. For purposes of this part, such patents consist of patents that claim the drug substance (ingredient), patents that claim the drug product (formulation and composition), product by process patents, and patents that claim a method of use. Process patents, patents claiming packaging, patents claiming metabolites, and patents claiming intermediates are not covered by this section, and information on these patents may not be submitted to FDA. For patents that claim the drug substance, the applicant shall submit information only on those patents that claim the form of the drug substance that is the subject of the pending or approved application or that claim a drug substance that is the "same" as the active ingredient that is the subject of the approved or pending application within the meaning of section 505(j)(2)(A)(ii) of the act. For patents that claim a drug product, the applicant shall submit information only on those patents that claim a drug product that is the subject of a pending or approved application. For patents that claim a method of use, the applicant shall submit information only on those patents that claim indications or other conditions of use that are the subject of a pending or approved application. For approved applications, the applicant shall identify the indication or other condition of use in the approved labeling that corresponds to the listed patent and claim identified.

(c) * * * (1) *General requirements.* An applicant described in paragraph (a) of this section shall submit the declaration described in paragraph (c)(2) of this section for each claim of the patent that meets the requirements described in paragraph (b) of this section.

(2) *Patent declaration.* (i) For each patent that claims a drug substance (active ingredient), drug product (formulation and composition), and/or method of use, the applicant shall submit the following declaration:

This is a submission of patent information for an NDA submitted under section 505 of the Federal Food, Drug, and Cosmetic Act (the Act).

Time sensitive patent information pursuant to 21 CFR 314.53 for NDA #_____

The following is provided in accordance with section 505(b) of the Act:

Trade Name: _____
Active Ingredient(s): _____
Strength(s): _____
Dosage Form(s): _____
Approval Date (if the submission is a supplement to an approved NDA): _____

Please provide the following information for each patent submitted, and identify the relevant claim(s) by number.

A. 1. United States patent number: _____
2. Expiration date: _____
3. Name of the Patent Owner: _____
4. Agent (if patent owner or applicant does not reside or have a place of business in the United States) _____

B. For each patent identified in A, please provide the following information:

1. The type of patent claims that apply to the drug substance or drug product that is the subject of the application:

2. Drug Substance (Active Ingredient)
___ Yes ___ No
a. Claim number(s): _____

3. Drug Product (Composition/Formulation):
___ Yes ___ No
a. Claim number(s): _____

4. Method of Use:
___ Yes ___ No
a. Claim number(s): _____

C. For each drug substance claim identified, please provide the following information:

1. Is the claim one that claims the drug substance that is the active ingredient in the approved or pending NDA, or a supplement to the NDA?
___ Yes ___ No
If "yes," please identify the claim(s) by number.

2. Is the claim one that claims a drug substance that is the "same" active ingredient as the active ingredient in the pending or approved NDA, amendment to the NDA, or a supplement to the NDA?
___ Yes ___ No
If "yes," please identify the claim(s) by number.

3. If the answer to question C.1 or C.2 is "yes," do you acknowledge that an ANDA or 505(b)(2) application containing the same active ingredient that is claimed by the patent is the "same" for ANDA or 505(b)(2) approval purposes?
___ Yes ___ No

[*If the answers to questions C.1, and C.2, and C.3 is "no," stop here. The patent may not be listed in the Orange Book as a patent that claims the drug substance.*]

D. For each drug product claim identified, please provide the following information:

1. Is the claim one that claims the approved formulation or composition and/or the formulation or composition for which approval is being sought?
___ Yes ___ No
If "yes," please identify the claim(s) by number.

[*If the answer to question D.1 is "no" in every instance, stop here. The patent may not be listed in the Orange Book as a patent that claims the drug product.*]

E. For each method of use claim identified, please provide the following information:

1. Is the claim one that claims:
(a) an approved method of use of the approved drug product? If "yes," please identify the use with reference to the approved labeling for the drug product and identify the relevant patent claim number(s);
___ Yes ___ No
(b) a method of use of the approved drug product for which use approval is being sought; or

172

APPENDIX 92

___ Yes ___ No
(c) a method of use of the drug product for which approval is being sought?
___ Yes ___ No
If the answer to questions E.1(b) or (c) is "yes," please identify the use with reference to the proposed labeling for the drug product and identify relevant patent claim number(s). [*If the answers to questions E.1(a) through (c) are "no," stop here. The patent may not be listed in the Orange Book as a patent that claims a method of use.*]

(ii) Amendment of patent information upon approval. Within 30 days after the date of approval of its application, if the application contained a declaration required under paragraph (c)(2)(i) of this section, the applicant shall, by letter, amend the declaration to identify the patent claims that claim the drug substance, drug product, or method of use that has been approved.

* * * * *

4. Section 314.95 is amended by revising paragraph (a)(3) to read as follows:

§ 314.95 Notice of certification of invalidity or noninfringement of a patent.

(a) * * *

(3) This paragraph does not apply to a use patent that claims no uses for which the applicant is seeking approval. This paragraph also does not apply if the applicant amends its application to add a certification under § 314.94(a)(12)(i)(A)(*4*) when the application already contained a certification under § 314.94(a)(12)(i)(A)(*4*) to another patent.

* * * * *

Dated: September 19, 2002.

Lester M. Crawford,
Deputy Commissioner.

Tommy G. Thompson,
Secretary of Health and Human Services.
[FR Doc. 02–27082 Filed 10–14–02; 11:57 am]
BILLING CODE 4160-01-S

TABLE OF CASES

References are to sections in the supplement.

aaiPharma Inc. v. Thompson, 296 F.3d 227 (4th Cir. 2002)	2.02[C]
Alcon Laboratories, Inc., Allergan, Inc. v., 200 F. Supp. 2d 1219 (C.D. Cal. 2002)	4.03[C]
Allergan, Inc. v. Alcon Laboratories, Inc., 200 F. Supp. 2d 1219 (C.D. Cal. 2002)	4.03[C]
American Bioscience v. Thompson, 269 F.3d 1077 (D.C. Cir. 2001)	2.02[C]
American Bioscience, Inc. v. Bristol-Myers Squibb Co., 2000 WL 1278348 (Sept. 7, 2000)	2.02[C]
Amgen, Inc. v. Hoechst Marion Roussel, Inc., 3 F. Supp. 2d 104 (D. Mass. 1998)	4.05[A]
Andrx Pharm., Inc. v. Biovail Corp., 276 F.3d 1368 (Fed. Cir. 2002)	2.02[C], 4.03[A]
Andrx Pharmaceuticals, Inc. v. Friedman, Civ. No. 98-0099 (D.D.C. Mar. 30, 1998)	4.02[H]
Apotex Corp., Warner-Lambert Co. v., No. 98 C 4293, 2001 WL 1104618 (N.D. Ill. Sept. 14, 2001)	4.03[C]
Apotex, Inc. v. Shalala 53 F. Supp. 2d 454 (D.D.C. 1999), *aff'd*, 1999 WL 956686 (D.C. Cir. Oct. 8, 1999)	4.02[H]
Apotex, Inc., Glaxo Group Ltd. v., 2001 WL 1246628 (N.D. Ill. Oct. 16, 2001)	4.05[C]
Association of American Physicians and Surgeons v. USFDA, 2002 WL 31323411 (D. D.C. Oct. 17, 2002)	3.02[C]
AstraZeneca AB v. Mutual Pharmaceutical Co., 2002 WL 393119 (E.D. Pa. Mar. 12, 2002)	3.03[B][3]
Bae v. Shalala, 44 F.3d 489 (7th Cir. 1995)	8.02[B]
Baker Norton Pharmaceuticals, Inc. v. United States Food and Drug Administration, 132 F. Supp. 2d 30 (D.D.C. 2001)	4.02[K][2], 7.02
Bayer AG v. Elan Pharmaceutical Research Corp., 212 F.3d 1241 (Fed. Cir. 2000)	4.05[B]

GENERIC AND INNOVATOR DRUGS

Ben Venue Labs., Inc. v. Novartis Pharmaceutical Corp., 10 F.
Supp. 2d 446 (D.N.J. 1998) .... 2.02[C]
Biovail Corp., Andrx Pharm., Inc. v., 276 F.3d 1368
(Fed. Cir. 2002) .... 2.02[C], 4.03[A]
Boehringer Ingelheim Corp. v. Shalala, 993 F. Supp. 1
(D.D.C. 1997) .... 4.02[H]
Bristol-Myers Squibb Co., American Bioscience, Inc. v., 2000
WL 1278348 (Sept. 7, 2000) .... 2.02[C]
Bristol-Myers Squibb Co. v. Royce Laboratories, 69 F.3d 1130
(Fed. Cir. 1995), cert. denied, 516 U.S. 1067 (1996) .... 4.03[C]
Buspirone Patent Litigation, In re, 185 F. Supp. 2d 363
(S.D.N.Y. 2002) .... 2.02[C]
Danbury Pharmacal, Inc., Yamanouchi Pharmaceutical Co., Ltd.
v., 231 F.3d 1339 (Fed. Cir. 2000) .... 3.03[B][3]
DiCola v. Food and Drug Administration, 77 F.3d 504
(D.C. Cir. 1996) .... 8.02[B]
Dr. Reddy's Laboratories v. Thompson, No. 02-CV-452
(D.N.J. filed Jan. 31, 2002) .... 4.02[H]
Elan Pharmaceutical Research Corp., Bayer AG v., 212 F.3d
1241 (Fed. Cir. 2000) .... 4.05[B]
Eli Lilly and Co. v. Medtronic, Inc., 496 U.S. 661 (1990) .... 4.03[C]
Eli Lilly Co. v. Zenith Gold Line Pharmaceuticals, Inc., 2001
WL 238090, 58 U.S.P.Q.2d 1543 (S.D. Ind. Mar. 8, 2001) .... 4.03[A]
Eli Lilly and Co. v. Zenith Goldline Pharm., Inc., No. IP 99-38-
C H/K, 2001 WL 1397304 at *25-26
(S.D. Ind. Oct. 29, 2001) .... 3.03[B][3]
FDA, Merck and Co., Inc. v., 148 F. Supp. 2d 27 (D.D.C. 2001) .... 4.02[J]
FDA, Public Citizen Health Research Group v., 185 F.3d 898
(D.C. Cir. 1999) 5.01
FDA, Teva Pharmaceuticals, USA, Inc. v.,182 F.3d 1003
(D.C. Cir. 1999), on remand 1999 WL 1042743
(D.D.C. Aug. 19, 1999), aff'd, 254 F.3d 316 (D.C. Cir. 2000) .... 4.02[H]
Food and Drug Administration, DiCola v., 77 F.3d 504 (D.C.
Cir. 1996) .... 8.02[B]
Friedman, Andrx Pharmaceuticals, Inc. v., Civ. No. 98-0099
(D.D.C. Mar. 30, 1998) .... 4.02[H]
Friedman, Purepac Pharmaceutical Co. v., 162 F.3d 1201
(D.D.C. Cir. 1998) .... 4.02[H]
Glaxo, Inc. v. Heckler, 623 F. Supp. 69 (E.D.N.C. 1985) .... 4.03[A]
Glaxo Group Ltd. v. Apotex, Inc., 2001 WL 1246628
(N.D. Ill. Oct. 16, 2001) .... 4.05[C]
Glaxo, Inc. v. Torpharm, Inc., No. 95 C 4686, 1997 WL 282742
(N.D. Ill. May 18, 1997) .... 4.03[C], 4.04[A]

TABLE OF CASES

Granutec, Inc. v. Shalala, 1998 WL 153410
(4th Cir. Apr. 3, 1998) .... 4.02[H]
Henney, Mylan Pharmaceuticals, Inc. v., 94 F. Supp. 2d 36
(D.D.C. 2000), *vacated as moot sub nom. Pharmachemie B.V. v. Barr Laboratories, Inc.*, 276 F.3d 627 (D.C. Cir. 2002) .... 4.02[H]
Henney, National Pharmaceutical Alliance v., 47 F. Supp. 2d 37
(D.D.C. 1999) .... 4.02[J]
Henney, Watson Pharmaceuticals, Inc. v., 194 F. Supp. 2d 442
(D. Md. 2001) .... 2.02[C]
Heckler, Glaxo, Inc. v., 623 F. Supp. 69 (E.D.N.C. 1985) .... 4.03[A]
Hoechst Marion Roussel, Inc., Amgen, Inc. v., 3 F. Supp. 2d 104
(D. Mass. 1998) .... 4.05[A]
Hoechst Marion Roussel, Inc. v. Par Pharm. Inc., 1996 WL
468593 (D.N.J. 1996) .... 4.05[C]
In re Omeprazole Patent Litigation., _____ F. Supp. _____ ,
2002 WL 31319475 (S.D.N.Y. Oct. 16, 2002) .... 4.02[H]
Inwood Laboratories, Inc. v. Young, 723 F. Supp. 1523
(D.D.C. 1989), *appeal dismissed*, 43 F.3d 712
(D.C. Cir. 1989) .... 4.02[H]
Kessler, Upjohn Co. v., 938 F. Supp. 439
(W.D. Mich. 1996) .... 4.02[G][4], 4.02[K][2]
Landgraf v. USI Film Products, 511 U.S. 244 (1994) .... 8.02[B]
Medtronic, Inc., Eli Lilly and Co. v., 496 U.S. 661 (1990) .... 4.03[A]
Merck and Co., Inc. v. FDA, 148 F. Supp. 2d 27 (D.D.C. 2001) .... 4.02[J]
Mova Pharmaceutical Corp. v. Shalala, 955 F. Supp. 128
(D.D.C. 1997), *aff'd*, 140 F.3d 1060 (D.C. Cir. 1998). .... 4.02[H]
Mutual Pharmaceutical Co., AstraZeneca AB v., 2002 WL
393119 (E.D. Pa. Mar. 12, 2002) .... 3.03[B][3]
Mylan Pharmaceutical, Inc., Zeneca LTD. v., 173 F.3d 829
(Fed. Cir. 1999) .... 4.05[B]
Mylan Pharmaceuticals, Inc. v. Henney, 94 F. Supp. 2d 36
(D.D.C. 2000), *vacated as moot sub nom.*
Pharmachemie B.V. v. Barr Laboratories, Inc., 276 F.3d 627
(D.C. Cir. 2002) .... 4.02[H]
Mylan Pharmaceuticals, Inc. v. Sullivan, No. 89-0036-C (K)
(N.D. W. Va. May 5, 1989) .... 4.02[H]
Mylan Pharmaceuticals, Inc. v. Thompson, 2001 WL 1654781
(N.D. W. Va. Apr. 18, 2001) .... 2.02[C], 4.02[H], 4.02[K][2]
National Pharmaceutical Alliance v. Henney, 47 F. Supp. 2d 37
(D.D.C. 1999) .... 4.02[J]
Novartis Pharmaceutical Corp., Ben Venue Labs., Inc. v., 10 F.
Supp. 2d 446 (D.N.J. 1998) .... 2.02[C]

Novopharm Ltd., Pfizer Inc. v., 2001 WL 477163 (N.D. Ill.
May 3, 2001) .... 4.05[C]
Par Pharm. Inc., Hoechst Marion Roussel, Inc. v., 1996 WL
468593 (D.N.J. 1996) .... 4.05[C]
Pfizer Inc. v. Novopharm Ltd., 2001 WL 477163
(N.D. Ill. May 3, 2001) .... 4.05[C]
Pfizer, Inc. v. Shalala, 1 F. Supp. 2d 38 (D.D.C. 1998), *aff'd in
part, rev. in part, Pfizer, Inc. v. Shalala*, 182 F.3d 975
(D.C. Cir. 1999) .... 3.02[C][1]
Pharmachemie B.V., Zeneca Limited v., 16 F. Supp. 2d 112
(D. Mass. 1998) .... 4.03[A]
Philip Morris, Inc. v. Reilly, Nos. 00-2425, 00-2449, 2001 WL
1215365 (1st Cir. Oct. 16, 2001) 6
Public Citizen Health Research Group v. FDA, 185 F.3d 898
(D.C. Cir. 1999) 5.01
Purepac Pharm. Co., Warner-Lambert Co. v., 2001 WL 883232
(D.N.J. Mar. 30, 2001) .... 4.05[C]
Purepac Pharmaceutical Co. v. Friedman, 162 F.3d 1201
(D.D.C. Cir. 1998) .... 4.02[H]
Reilly, Philip Morris, Inc. v., Nos. 00-2425, 00-2449, 2001 WL
1215365 (1st Cir. Oct. 16, 2001) 6
Royce Laboratories, Bristol-Myers Squibb Co. v., 69 F.3d 1130
(Fed. Cir. 1995), *cert. denied*, 516 U.S. 1067 (1996) .... 4.03[C]
Sage Pharmaceuticals, Inc., United States v., 210 F.3d 475
(4th Cir. 2000) .... 1.06[A]
Schwetz, Sigma-Tau Pharmaceuticals, Inc. v., 288 F.3d 141
(4th Cir. 2002) 7.02
Serono Laboratories, Inc. v. Shalala, 974 F. Supp. 29
(D.D.C. 1997), *rev'd* 158 F.3d 1313, 1326
(D.C. Cir. 1998) .... 3.03[D]
Shalala, Apotex, Inc. v., 53 F. Supp. 2d 454 (D.D.C. 1999), *aff'd*,
1999 WL 956686 (D.C. Cir. Oct. 8, 1999) .... 4.02[H]
Shalala, Bae v., 44 F.3d 489 (7th Cir. 1995) .... 8.02[B]
Shalala, Boehringer Ingelheim Corp. v., 993 F. Supp. 1
(D.D.C. 1997) .... 4.02[H]
Shalala, Granutec, Inc. v., 1998 WL 153410
(4th Cir. Apr. 3, 1998) .... 4.02[H]
Shalala, Mova Pharmaceutical Corp. v. 955 F. Supp. 128
(D.D.C. 1997), *aff'd*, 140 F.3d 1060 (D.C. Cir. 1998). .... 4.02[H]
Shalala, Pfizer, Inc. v., 1 F. Supp. 2d 38 (D.D.C. 1998), *aff'd in
part, rev. in part, Pfizer, Inc. v. Shalala*, 182 F.3d 975
(D.C. Cir. 1999) .... 3.02[C]

TABLE OF CASES

Shalala, Serono Laboratories, Inc. v., 974 F. Supp. 29
(D.D.C. 1997), *rev'd* 158 F.3d 1313, 1326
(D.C. Cir. 1998)..3.03[D]
Shalala, TorPharm Inc. v., Civ. No. 97-1925(JR), 1997 U.S.
Dist. LEXIS 21983 (D.D.C. Sept. 15, 1997), *remanded*,
1998 U.S. App. LEXIS 4681 (D.D.C. Cir. Feb. 5, 1998),
vacated on remand (D.D.C. Apr. 9, 1998) ....4.02[H], 4.03[A]
Sigma-Tau Pharmaceuticals, Inc. v. Schwetz, 288 F.3d 141 (4th
Cir. 2002)..7.02
Sullivan, Mylan Pharmaceuticals, Inc. v., No. 89-0036-C (K)
(N.D. W. Va. May 5, 1989)...4.02[H]
Tegal Corp. v. Tokyo Electron America Inc., 257 F.3d 1331
(Fed. Cir. 2001) ....4.05[C]
Teva Pharmaceuticals, USA, Inc. v. FDA, 182 F.3d 1003 (D.C.
Cir. 1999), *on remand* 1999 WL 1042743 (D.D.C.
Aug. 19, 1999), *aff'd*, 254 F.3d 316 (D.C. Cir. 2000)....................4.02[H]
Thompson, aaiPharma Inc. v., ___ F.3d ___, 2002 WL 1473429
(4th Cir. July 10, 2002)...2.02[C]
Thompson, American Bioscience v., 269 F.3d 1077
(D.C. Cir. 2001)...2.02[C]
Thompson, Dr. Reddy's Laboratories v., No. 02-CV-452 (D.N.J.
filed Jan. 31, 2002)..4.02[H]
Thompson, Mylan Pharmaceuticals, Inc. v., 2001 WL 1654781
(N.D. W. Va. Apr. 18, 2001) ....2.02[C], 4.02[H], 4.02[K][2]
Tokyo Electron America Inc., Tegal Corp. v., 257 F.3d 1331
(Fed. Cir. 2001) ....4.05[C]
TorPharm Inc. v. Shalala, Civ. No. 97-1925(JR), 1997 U.S. Dist.
LEXIS 21983 (D.D.C. Sept. 15, 1997), *remanded*, 1998 U.S. App.
LEXIS 4681 (D.D.C. Cir. Feb. 5, 1998), *vacated on remand* (D.D.C.
Apr. 9, 1998)...4.02[H], 4.03[A]
Torpharm, Inc., Glaxo, Inc. v., No. 95 C 4686, 1997 WL 282742
(N.D. Ill. May 18, 1997) ....4.03[C], 4.04[A]
*United States Food and Drug Administration, Baker Norton
Pharmaceuticals, Inc. v.*, 132 F. Supp. 2d 30
(D.D.C. 2001) ....4.02[K][2], 7.02
Upjohn Co. v. Kessler, 938 F. Supp. 439
(W.D. Mich. 1996)..4.02[G][4], 4.02[K][2]
USI Film Products, Landgraf v., 511 U.S. 244 (1994).........................8.02[B]
Warner-Lambert Co. v. Apotex Corp., No. 98 C 4293, 2001 WL
1104618 (N.D. Ill. Sept. 14, 2001)..4.03[C]
Warner-Lambert Co. v. Purepac Pharm. Co., 2001 WL 883232
(D.N.J. Mar. 30, 2001)...4.05[C]

Watson Pharmaceuticals, Inc. v. Henney, 194 F. Supp. 2d 442
(D. Md. 2001) .... 2.02[C]
*Yamanouchi Pharmaceutical Co., Ltd. v. Danbury Pharmacal,
Inc.*, 231 F.3d 1339 (Fed. Cir. 2000) .... 3.03[B][3]
Young, Inwood Laboratories, Inc. v., 723 F. Supp. 1523 (D.D.C.
1989), *appeal dismissed*, 43 F.3d 712 (D.C. Cir. 1989) .... 4.02[H]
Zeneca Ltd. v. Pharmachemie B.V., 16 F. Supp. 2d 112
(D. Mass. 1998) .... 4.03[A]
Zeneca Ltd. v. Mylan Pharmaceutical, Inc., 173 F.3d 829
(Fed. Cir. 1999) .... 4.05[B]
Zenith Gold Line Pharmaceuticals, Inc., Eli Lilly Co. v., 2001
WL 238090, 58 U.S.P.Q.2d 1543 (S.D. Ind. Mar. 8, 2001) .... 4.03[A]

TABLE OF STATUTES

References are to sections in the supplement.

Food, Drug, and Cosmetic Act (FDCA)

201(cc), 21 U.S.C. 321(cc)	8.02[D][4]
201(dd), 21 U.S.C. 321(dd)	8.02[B]
201bb, 21 U.S.C. 321(bb)	8.04[A]
306-308, 21 U.S.C. 335a-335c	8.02[A]
306(b)(2)(A)(i)(II), 21 U.S.C. 335a(b)(2)(A)(i)(II)	8.02[B]
306(b)(2)(B)(iii), 21 U.S.C. 335a(b)(2)(B)(iii)	8.02[D], 8.02[D][2], 8.02[H]
306(d)(4)(C), 21 U.S.C. 335a(d)(4)(C)	8.02[G][2]
306(i), 21 U.S.C. 335a(i)	8.02[F]
308(a)(1), 21 U.S.C. 335c(a)(1)	3.04[C][3], 9.02
308(a)(2), 21 U.S.C. 335c(a)(2)	3.04[C][3]
308(b), 21 U.S.C. 355c(b)	3.04[C][3]
308(c), 21 U.S.C. 335c(c)	3.04[C][3]
308(d), 21 U.S.C. 335c(d)	3.04[C][3]
503A(b)(1)(C), 21 U.S.C. 353a(b)(1)(C)	3.02[B][2]
505(b)(2), 21 U.S.C. 355(b)(2)	4.01
505(c)(1)(B), 21 U.S.C. 355(c)(1)(B)	2.03[C][1]
505(c)(3)(B), 21 U.S.C. 355(c)(3)(B)	4.04[F][2][a]
505(c)(3)(C)(i), 21 U.S.C. 355(c)(3)(C)(i)	4.02[H], 4.03[A]
505(c)(3)(C), 21 U.S.C. 355(c)(3)(C)	4.03[B]
505(c)(3)(D)(ii)-(iv), 21 U.S.C. 355(c)(3)(D)(ii)-(iv)	2.02[C]
505(c)(3)(D)(v), 21 U.S.C. 355(c)(3)(D)(v)	4.02[A]
505(i), 21 U.S.C. 355(i)	13.02
505(j), 21 U.S.C. 355(j)	8.02[A]
505(j)(4)(J), (K), 21 U.S.C. 355(j)(4)(J), (K)	4.04[F][2][a]
505(j)(5)(D)(ii)-(iv), 21 U.S.C. 355(j)(5)(D)(ii)-(iv)	2.02[C]
505(j)(5)(A), 21 U.S.C. 355(j)(5)(A)	3.04[A]
505(j)(5)(B)(ii), 21 U.S.C. (j)(5)(B)(ii)	4.04[F][2][a]
505(j)(5)(B)(iii)(I), 21 U.S.C. 355(j)(5)(B)(iii)(I)	4.02[H]
505(j)(5)(B), 21 U.S.C. 355(j)(5)(B)	4.03[B]
505(j)(5)(D)(v), 21 U.S.C. 355(j)(5)(D)(v)	4.02[A]
505(j)(7)(A)(i)(III), 21 U.S.C 355(j)(7)(A)(i)(III)	3.03[A][4]

GENERIC AND INNOVATOR DRUGS

505(j)(8)(B)(ii), 21 U.S.C. 355(j)(8)(B)(ii) .... 3.03[A][1]
505A(b), 21 U.S.C. 355a(b) .... 4.02[J]
505A(c), 21 U.S.C. 355a(c) .... 4.02[J]
505A(d)(4)(A), 21 U.S.C. 355a(d)(4)(A) .... 4.02[J]
505A(d)(4)(B), 21 U.S.C. 355a(d)(4)(B) .... 4.02[J]
505A(d)(4)(F), 21 U.S.C. 355a(d)(4)(F) .... 4.02[J]
505A(d)(4), 21 U.S.C. 355a(d)(4) .... 4.02[J]
505A(g), 21 U.S.C. 355a(g) .... 4.02[J]
505A(k), 21 U.S.C. 355a(k) .... 4.02[H]
505A(n), 21 U.S.C. 355a(m) .... 4.02[J]
505A(n), 21 U.S.C. 355a(n) .... 4.02[J]
510(j)(2), 21 U.S.C. 360(j)(2) .... 12.02[B]
512(c)(2)(D), 21 U.S.C. 360b(c)(2)(D) .... 4.03[B]
512(E)(1)(D), 21 U.S.C. 360b(d)(1)(G) .... 2.02[C]
520(g), 21 U.S.C. 360j(g) 13.02
526(a)(1), 21 U.S.C. 360bb(a)(1) .... 12.02[A][1]
526(c), 21 U.S.C. 360bb(c) 7.01
735(1), 21 U.S.C. 379g(1) .... 12.02[A][1]
735(8), 21 U.S.C. 379g(8) 12.05
736(a)(1)(E), 21 U.S.C. 379h(a)(1)(E) .... 12.02[A][1]
736(a)(1)(F), 21 U.S.C. 379h(a)(1)(F) .... 12.02[A][1]
736(b), 21 U.S.C. 379h(b) .... 12.02[A][2]
736(c)(1), 21 U.S.C. 379h(c)(1) .... 12.02[A][2]
736(c)(2), 21 U.S.C. 379h(c)(2) .... 12.02[A][2]
736(c)(3), 21 U.S.C. 379h(c)(3) .... 12.02[A][2]
736(c)(4), 21 U.S.C. 379h(c)(4) .... 12.02[A][1], 12.02[A][2]
736(b), (c), 21 U.S.C. 379h(b), (c) .... 12.02[C]
736(a)(1)(D), (F), 21 U.S.C. 379h(a)(1)(D), (F) 12.03
736(f)(1), 21 U.S.C. 379h(f)(1) 12.05
736(c)(5), 21 U.S.C. 379h(c)(5) 12.05
735(6)(F), 21 U.S.C. 379(g)(6)(F) 12.05
801(a)(1), 21 U.S.C. 381(a)(1) .... 11.02[D]
804, 21 U.S.C. 384 .... 11.01, 11.03[A]
804(l), 21 U.S.C. 384(l) .... 11.03[A]

Freedom of Information Act (FOIA)

5 U.S.C. 552(b)(4) 5.01

Medicine Equity and Drug Safety Act

106-387 (2000)
    Section 745 .... 11.03[A]

TABLE OF STATUTES

Public Health Service Act

42 U.S.C. 262(a)(1)(A)	13.02
42 U.S.C. 262(a)(2)(B)(i)(I)	13.02
42 U.S.C. 262(h)	11.02[D]
42 U.S.C. 262(i)	13.01
42 U.S.C. 262(j)	13.02
42 U.S.C. 284m(c)	4.02[J]

Public Laws

102-282 (1992)	8.02[A]
102-571 (1992)	12.01
105-115 (1997)	4.02[F], 12.01
Section 123(d)	13.01
Section 124(b)	4.01
105-277 (1998)	
Section 101(a)	4.01
106-113 (1999)	
Section 4732(b)(11)	4.01, 4.04[D][2]
106-387	
Section 745	11.01
107-109 (2002)	4.02[H], 4.02[J]
Section 5	12.02[A][1]
107-188 (2002)	
Section 122(a)	10.03[A]
Section 122(c)	10.01
Section 123	2.02[A]
Section 504(d)(1)(B), (C)	12.03
Section 508	12.01

TABLE OF AUTHORITIES

References are to sections in the supplement.

Code of Federal Regulations

21 C.F.R. 1.101(b)	11.02[B][3]
21 C.F.R. 1.101(b)(2)	11.02[B][3]
21 C.F.R. 1.101(c)	11.02[D]
21 C.F.R. 1.101(e)	11.02[C]
21 C.F.R. 1.101(d)(iv)	11.02[B][1]
21 C.F.R. 3.7	13.01
21 C.F.R. 201.23(d)	2.04
21 C.F.R. 201.23	4.02[J]
21 C.F.R. 216.24	3.02[B][2]
21 C.F.R. 312.110	11.02[C]
21 C.F.R. 312.110(b)(2)	11.02[C]
21 C.F.R. 312.110(b)(4)	11.02[C]
21 C.F.R. 314.50	13.02
21 C.F.R. 314.50(l)	2.03[B]
21 C.F.R. 314.53(b)	2.02[C]
21 C.F.R. 314.55	4.02[J]
21 C.F.R. 314.55(a)	3.02[C]
21 C.F.R. 314.55(b)(2)	3.05[A][1]
21 C.F.R. 314.94(a)(12)(i)(A)(4)	3.03[B][3]
21 C.F.R. 314.94(a)(12)(ii)	3.03[B]
21 C.F.R. 314.94(a)(12)(viii)(A)	4.02[H]
21 C.F.R. 314.94(a)(12)(viii)(C)(1)	4.04[F][2][a]
21 C.F.R. 314.95(e)	3.03[B][3]
21 C.F.R. 314.107(b)(3)(i)(A)	4.03[A]
21 C.F.R. 314.107(c)(1)	4.02[H]
21 C.F.R. 314.107(e)(1)	4.02[H], 4.03[A]
21 C.F.R. 314.107(e)(2)(ii)	4.04[F][2][a]
21 C.F.R. 314.110	2.03[B]
21 C.F.R. 314.120	2.03[B]
21 C.F.R. 314.126	13.02
21 C.F.R. 314.430(f)(6)	5.01

21 C.F.R. 314.510 .... 10.03[A][2]
21 C.F.R. 314.600-314.650 .... 2.02[A]
21 C.F.R. 316.3(b)(3) 7.02
21 C.F.R. 600.3(h)(5) 13.01
21 C.F.R. 601.2 .... 13.02
21 C.F.R. 601.12(e) 13.03
21 C.F.R. 601.25 .... 13.02
21 C.F.R. 601.25(d)(2) 13.02
21 C.F.R. 601.27 .... 4.02[J]
21 C.F.R. 601.41 .... 10.03[A][2]
21 C.F.R. 601.51(e)(1) 5.01
21 C.F.R. 601.90-601.95 .... 2.02[A]
37 C.F.R. 1.740(b) .... 4.04[D]
37 C.F.R. 1.778(d)(1)(i) .... 4.04[D]
37 C.F.R. 1.778(d)(2) .... 4.04[D]
37 C.F.R. 1.779(d)(1)(i) .... 4.04[D]
37 C.F.R. 1.779(d)(2) .... 4.04[D]
37 C.F.R. 1.790 .... 4.04[D]
37 C.F.R. 1.790(a) .... 4.04[D][3]
37 C.F.R. 1.791 .... 4.04[D]

Federal Register

39 Fed. Reg. 44602 (Dec. 24, 1974) 13.03
39 Fed. Reg. 44641 (Dec. 24, 1974) 13.03
49 Fed. Reg. 50878 (Dec. 31, 1984) .... 3.03[A][2]
51 Fed. Reg. 23309 (June 26, 1986) .... 3.03[A][2]
51 Fed. Reg. 23312 (June 26, 1986) .... 3.03[A][2]
56 Fed. Reg. 46191 (Sept. 10, 1991) 9.03
56 Fed. Reg. 46200 (Sept. 10, 1991) 9.03
57 Fed. Reg. 58947 (Dec. 11, 1992) .... 10.03[A][2]
59 Fed. Reg. 50352 (Oct. 3, 1994) .... 4.02[H]
59 Fed. Reg. 50353 (Oct. 3, 1994) .... 4.02[H]
59 Fed. Reg. 55671 (Dec. 5, 1994) .... 8.02[B]
59 Fed. Reg. 55672 (Dec. 5, 1994) .... 8.02[B]
59 Fed. Reg. 62399 (Dec. 5, 1994) .... 8.02[B]
59 Fed. Reg. 62401 (Dec. 5, 1994) .... 8.02[B]
62 Fed. Reg. 13650 (Mar. 21, 1997) .... 2.02[A]
62 Fed. Reg. 43535 (Aug. 14, 1997) .... 1.05[C]
63 Fed. Reg. 11174 (Mar. 6, 1998) .... 3.03[B][3]
63 Fed. Reg. 27093 (May 15, 1998) .... 2.02[A]
63 Fed. Reg. 27733 (May 20, 1998) .... 4.02[J]
63 Fed. Reg. 32219 (June 12, 1998) .... 11.02[B][4]
63 Fed. Reg. 32222 (June 12, 1998) .... 11.02[B][4]

TABLE OF AUTHORITIES

63 Fed. Reg. 37890 (July 14, 1998) .... 4.02[H]
63 Fed. Reg. 59710 (Nov. 5, 1998) .... 4.02[H]
63 Fed. Reg. 59712 (Nov. 5, 1998) .... 4.02[H]
63 Fed. Reg. 66632 (Dec. 2, 1998) .... 2.04, 4.02[J]
64 Fed. Reg. 42873 (Aug. 6, 1999) .... 4.02[H]
64 Fed. Reg. 49496 (Sept. 13, 1999) .... 2.02[A]
65 Fed. Reg. 12154 (Mar. 8, 2000) .... 3.03[B][3]
65 Fed. Reg. 16922 (Mar. 30, 2000) .... 4.02[H], 4.03[A]
65 Fed. Reg. 43233 (July 13, 2000) .... 4.02[H], 4.03[A]
66 Fed. Reg. 65429 (Dec. 19, 2001) .... 11.02[A], 11.02[C], 11.02[D]
66 Fed. Reg. 65432 (Dec. 19, 2001) .... 11.02[A]
66 Fed. Reg. 65437 (Dec. 19, 2001) .... 11.02[A]
66 Fed. Reg. 65441 (Dec. 19, 2001) .... 11.02[B][1], 11.02[D]
66 Fed. Reg. 65442 (Dec. 19, 2001) .... 11.02[B][1]
66 Fed. Reg. 65448 (Dec. 19, 2001) .... 11.02[B][1], 11.02[C]
67 Fed. Reg. 33040 (May 13, 2002) .... 4.02[H]
67 Fed. Reg. 33045 (May 13, 2002) .... 4.02[H]
67 Fed. Reg. 37988 (May 13, 2002) .... 2.02[A]
67 Fed. Reg. 41642 (June 19, 2002) .... 11.02[C]
67 Fed. Reg. 41643 (June 19, 2002) .... 11.02[C]
67 Fed. Reg. 41644 (June 19, 2002) .... 11.02[C]
67 Fed. Reg. 41648 (June 19, 2002) .... 11.02[C]
67 Fed. Reg. 50448 (Aug. 2, 2002) .... 12.02[A][2], 12.02[B], 12.02[C]
67 Fed. Reg. 50450 (Aug. 2, 2002) .... 12.02[B], 12.02[C]
67 Fed. Reg. 65448 (Oct. 24, 2002) .... 2.02[C], 3.03[B], 4.03[A], 4.03[C]
67 Fed. Reg. 66593 (Nov. 1, 2002) .... 4.02[H]

SUBJECT INDEX

References are to sections in the supplement.

Biologics
    approval requirements 13.02
    defined 13.01
    generic 13.03